THE GREAT
CHALLENGE

Also by
Hélène Carrère d'Encausse

*The Russian Syndrome: One Thousand Years of
Political Murder*

Big Brother: The Soviet Union and Soviet Europe

*Decline of an Empire: The Soviet Socialist
Republic in Revolt*

A History of the Soviet Union, 1917–1953

THE GREAT CHALLENGE

Nationalities
and the
Bolshevik State
1917–1930

Hélène Carrère d'Encausse

Translated by Nancy Festinger

Foreword by Richard Pipes

HM

HOLMES & MEIER

New York   London

Published in the United States of America 1992 by
    Holmes & Meier Publishers, Inc.
    30 Irving Place
    New York, NY 10003

Originally published under the title *Le Grand Défi: Bolcheviks et
nations, 1917–1930*, copyright © 1987, Flammarion.

This book was published with the assistance of the Ministère de la culture et de
la communication.

BOOK DESIGN BY DALE COTTON

Library of Congress Cataloging-in-Publication Data

Carrère d'Encausse, Hélène.
    [Grand défi.   English]
    The great challenge : nationalities and the Bolshevik state,
1917–1930 / Hélène Carrère d'Encausse ; translated by Nancy
Festinger ; foreword by Richard Pipes.
        p.   cm.
    Translation of: Le grand défi.
    Includes bibliographical references and index.
    ISBN 0-8419-1285-8 (acid-free paper)
    1. Soviet Union—Ethnic relations.   2. Nationalism—Soviet
Union.   3. Minorities—Soviet Union.   4. Soviet Union—
Politics and government—1917–1936.   I. Title.
DK33.C3713   1992
305.8′00947—dc20   91–11293
                                                                     CIP

MANUFACTURED IN THE UNITED STATES OF AMERICA

To the memory of Jean Touchard

Contents

Foreword

Richard Pipes

Ethnic strife in the Soviet Union has caught the unsuspecting world by surprise. The violence in the Caucasus, Central Asia, and Moldavia, the clamor for sovereignty of the Baltic peoples and the Georgians, and, most unexpected of all, the separatism of Great Russians were events for which, apart from a small body of experts, no one had been prepared. Why this was the case it is difficult to say because the evidence of latent ethnic tension in the USSR was not invisible. Perhaps it was due to the successes of Communist propaganda in depicting the USSR as a country in which national animosities had been neutralized and the diverse peoples learned to live in peace. The power of Russian culture blinded many to the existence of non-Russian peoples under Soviet rule. Whatever the reason, five years ago, when Gorbachev assumed office, the cohesion and stability of the Union were taken for granted not only by the public at large but by the chanceries of the Western world. It has been the experience of the author of these lines that all efforts to have the United States strike a more positive attitude toward the non-Russian peoples of the USSR, if only by acknowledging their right to self-determination as guaranteed in the Soviet constitution, fell on deaf ears.

Now the situation has changed but the old attitudes continue to prevail. Although they no longer can ignore the effects of centrifugal forces, which at the time of writing have virtually shattered the cohesion of the USSR, the leaders of the great powers prefer to act as if the Kremlin still spoke for the fifteen republics. The prospect of new sovereign states arising in Eastern Europe, the Middle East, and East Asia frightens them with the specter of destabilization. They further fear that the nuclear arsenal of the Red Army may fall into irresponsible hands. The support extended to Gorbachev by the Western states is motivated by the desire to have him continue his program of internal reforms and foreign accommodation, undisturbed by ethnic separatism and the passions it tends to arouse.

But facts are stubborn things and it should be obvious to anyone able to separate realities from wishes that in 1990 the Soviet Union exists largely on paper, effective power having devolved to the governments of the constituent republics and, in the case of the Russian Republic, further down, to the cities and regions. The disestablishment of the Communist Party has been a major factor in the disruption of the Union because the Party with its instruments, the army and the security police, had been the force that held it together. Gorbachev declared the national question to be the most urgent of his problems.

Anyone familiar with the studies of Hélène Carrère d'Encausse on the subject would have been prepared for these developments. She has demonstrated with great knowledge and subtlety the complexity of the national question in the USSR and the impossibility of "solving" it with the means traditionally used by the Communist regime, namely meaningless pseudo-cultural concessions accompanied by brutal repression of genuine national aspirations. The rise of ethnic conflict in what had been the Russian empire began before the Revolution as a by-product of spreading literacy, economic development, and the penetration of democratic and socialist ideas. Peoples who had lived in relative isolation, whose culture had centered on religious institutions and practices, did not manifest national sentiments. These were born once they were exposed to education that compelled them to assume an ethnic identity, and once secular ideas began to displace religious commitments. The limited democratic opportunities available in the final years of the old regime, such as elections to the State Duma, also fostered ethnic sentiments by making it possible to vote for national candidates. In 1917, when the empire collapsed and Russia was thrown into chaos, ethnicity provided the natural rallying point for peoples confronted with anarchy and civil conflicts.

The party that came to power in October 1917 had little appreciation of the elements that produced nationalism. Lenin himself was culturally an uprooted man, a Russian politician by necessity rather than choice, for whom nationalism was a tool employed by the bourgeoisie to divert the working class from its true mission. But he was enough of a realist to develop a tactical program to exploit the burgeoning nationalist aspirations of Russia's minorities. His program, formulated in 1913, was strictly short term. Every nationality inhabiting the empire was to be given the choice of assimilation or separation: there were to be no half-measures in the form of federalism or cultural autonomy since their effect was to deepen ethnic divisions. Lenin expected the right of self-determination to be impeded by economic forces making for unity and therefore never exercised. If, nevertheless, some of Russia's subject nations chose to separate themselves, the right of "proletarian" self-determination would be invoked to bring them back into the fold.

It so happened that in 1917–18 most of the nationalities did separate from Russia, in large measure to escape the Civil War. And between 1918 and 1921 Lenin reconquered most of them and incorporated them into the newly formed Soviet Union. The Union was given a pseudo-federal structure and its "republics" received extensive rights to cultural autonomy—the very things Lenin had wanted to avoid. Their subservience was assured by the Communist Party, which was kept unitary and controlled from Moscow. In the 1930s Stalin eliminated the last vestiges of federalism and cultural autonomy. National sentiments were driven underground.

The seeming unity was maintained by sheer force. As soon as Gorbachev introduced moderate reforms, allowing freer speech and greater popular participation in government, the nationalities began to make themselves heard. The more rapidly the process of decentralization proceeded, the louder was their clamor. The breakdown of the economy accelerated the process because survival dictated that each region—Russian as well as non-Russian—hold on to its resources and products to use for barter. Soon voices were raised demanding sovereign status for each republic and, in some cases, for the autonomous regions within them. In an attempt to stem the tide, Gorbachev promised a new Union treaty which would transform the

pseudo-federation of 1922 into a genuine federation or even confeder-
ation. But he delayed releasing such a treaty with the result that the
centrifugal movement gained momentum. In November 1990 when
a draft was finally issued, it was dismissed as coming too late and
offering too little. The artificial unity created by Lenin and cemented
by Stalin has for all purposes fallen apart: nothing short of military
force could restore it, and as the events of August 1991 have demonstrated, military force is also impotent to reverse the course of events.

Madame d'Encausse's book is a reliable guide to the events that
led to the present predicament. She traces with superb command of
the facts the diverse devices which the communists employed in the
futile attempt to neutralize the forces of ethnicity and mold their subject peoples into a submissive mass. It is a particular virtue of her
book to show how despite their internationalism, the communists
were driven to use methods that resulted in forced Russification. One
can only concur with her conclusion that contrary to the expectations
of many socialists and sociologists, modernization intensifies national consciousness. Her sophisticated survey of the antecedents of
the present crisis of the Soviet state amply demonstrates its validity.

September 1991

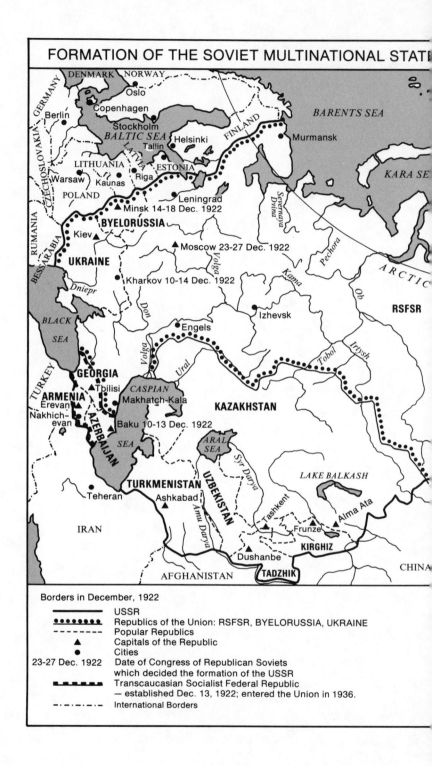

FORMATION OF THE SOVIET MULTINATIONAL STAT[E]

Borders in December, 1922

▬▬▬▬	USSR
●●●●●●●	Republics of the Union: RSFSR, BYELORUSSIA, UKRAINE
-------	Popular Republics
▲	Capitals of the Republic
●	Cities
23-27 Dec. 1922	Date of Congress of Republican Soviets which decided the formation of the USSR
▬ ▬ ▬ ▬	Transcaucasian Socialist Federal Republic — established Dec. 13, 1922; entered the Union in 1936.
─·─·─·─·─	International Borders

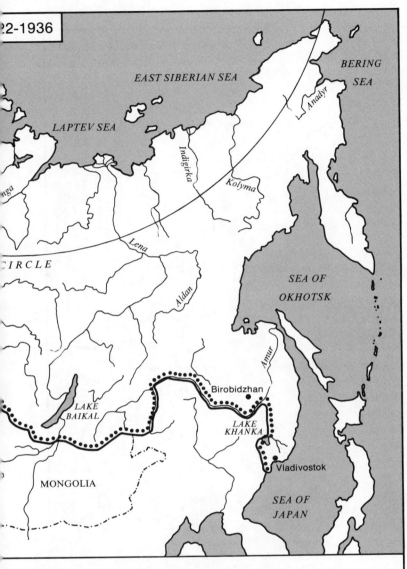

2-1936

EAST SIBERIAN SEA

BERING SEA

LAPTEV SEA

nga

Indigirka

Kolyma

Anadyr

CIRCLE

Lena

Aldan

SEA OF OKHOTSK

Amur

LAKE BAIKAL

Birobidzhan

LAKE KHANKA

Vladivostok

MONGOLIA

SEA OF JAPAN

Republics of the Union Constituted between 1924 and 1936:

UZBEK SSR — Oct. 27, 1924
TURKMEN SSR — Oct. 22, 1924
TADZHIK SSR — Oct. 16, 1929 (previously ASSR)
KAZAKH SSR — Dec. 5, 1935 (previously ASSR)
KIRGHIZ SSR — Dec. 5, 1936 (previously ASSR)

0   500   1000 Km

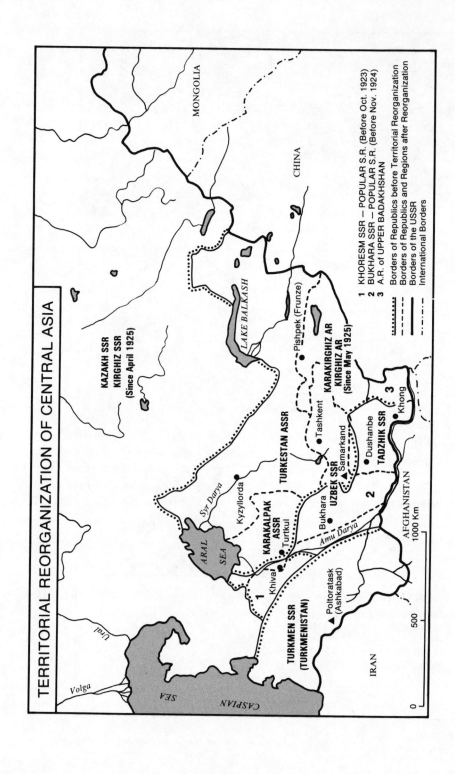

TERRITORIAL REORGANIZATION OF CENTRAL ASIA

MONGOLIA

CHINA

KAZAKH SSR
KIRGHIZ SSR
(Since April 1925)

LAKE BALKASH

Pishpek (Frunze)

KARAKIRGHIZ AR
KIRGHIZ AR
(Since May 1925)

Tashkent

Samarkand

Dushanbe

TADZHIK SSR

Khong

3

TURKESTAN ASSR

UZBEK SSR

2

Syr Darya

Kyzyllorda

KARAKALPAK
ASSR

Turtkul

Bukhara

Amu Darya

AFGHANISTAN

ARAL
SEA

Khiva

1

▲ Poltoratask
(Ashkabad)

TURKMEN SSR
(TURKMENISTAN)

IRAN

Ural

Volga

CASPIAN
SEA

1 KHORESM SSR – POPULAR S.R. (Before Oct. 1923)
2 BUKHARA SSR – POPULAR S.R. (Before Nov. 1924)
3 A.R. of UPPER BADAKHSHAN

········ Borders of Republics before Territorial Reorganization
- - - - - Borders of Republics and Regions after Reorganization
━━━━━ Borders of the USSR
─·─·─·─ International Borders

0   500   1000 Km

Introduction

1917 to 1987: three generations have passed since the collapse of the powerful Russian Empire, the beginning of the revolution, and the birth of the Soviet state. By the time Lenin's successors were celebrating the seventieth anniversary of these events, the Soviet system had produced three generations of citizens who knew nothing of the world prior to 1917; their worldview, principles, and way of life were those ushered in by the October Revolution.

As the USSR prepared to mark this solemn occasion, Mikhail Gorbachev, Lenin's sixth successor, took stock of Soviet accomplishments. Far from the radiant universe envisioned by his predecessors, the picture he painted for his compatriots was a somber one. The two key words of his discourse, *perestroika* (restructuring) and *glasnost'* (openness), were borrowed from Lenin. Like Lenin before him, Gorbachev asserted that the country had a right to know the truth in the difficult times ahead on the road to reconstruction. In saying this, he seemed to suggest that the previous seventy years had been nothing but a long series of errors.[1]

Gorbachev recognized that in the dark chapter of disappointed dreams and lost illusions, a new page had to be written, one devoted

1

to the relations among the different nationality groups of the USSR. It had been believed that the revolution would do away with minority differences and give birth, in a new world, to a new human community strengthened by ties of class solidarity. Internationalism was to replace the nationalist aspirations of the past and, under its banner, to unite individuals and diverse groups in true brotherhood. However, at the threshold of the twenty-first century, Gorbachev was well aware that the USSR was experiencing not the envisioned internationalism, but a resurgence of nationalism. In Alma Ata, Kazakh crowds protested because their Communist party leader was a Russian; in the Ukraine and Georgia, in Estonia and many other national republics, intellectuals belonging to a generation schooled in internationalism voiced their opposition to a system that in their view openly favored Russians; they now proclaimed their desire to revive local languages and minority cultures; in Central Asia and in the Caucasus, Khomeini's fundamentalism was spreading and finding an audience because he spoke to the distinctiveness of Moslem identity. Gorbachev was confronted by vehement minority peoples who in the name of *glasnost* demanded their right to freedom of speech, and who accused the Soviet establishment of attempting to "Russify" them in the guise of internationalism.

The Russians themselves were not immune to nationalist yearnings. The authorities respected intellectuals who were partial to the culture and history of ancient Russia over that of the Soviet period, when everything definably Russian had yielded to the symbols of internationalism. The authorities themselves contributed to this reevaluation of the Russian past by authorizing publication of the great historians Karamzin, Kliuchevskii, and Soloviev, whose works, long forbidden, glorified the Russian people to the exclusion of the empire's conquered nationalities.[2]

In 1922 a dying Lenin, in a solemn appeal to his successors, had warned that no single issue was more decisive for the future destiny of the revolutionary state than a national policy leading to the transcending of all nationalism, that is, of nationalist feeling on the part of the Russians as well as on the part of previously dominated peoples.

Seventy years later, as if time had passed in vain, the tenor of Gorbachev's statements conveyed the same idea. The newly educated generations maintain that doing away with national differences has proved to be a task infinitely more complex than Lenin had believed. The question then arises: Was it Marxist philosophy, which guided

Lenin's actions and those of his successors, that was to blame? Or was it the reality that Lenin's followers confronted? Or the empirical solutions they adopted?

Before discussing the operative ideas of the revolutionary period and the possible alternatives to them, we must take a closer look at the problem itself: the intriguing mosaic of the empire's minority peoples. Clearly, neither the regime that disappeared in 1917 nor the Bolsheviks understood the diversity of these nationalities and the complexity of their problems. This reality, poorly grasped, gave rise to unforeseen developments for which the old regime and the current Soviet system have paid the price.

The Russian Empire was formed between the sixteenth and the nineteenth centuries. The fall of Kazan in 1552 broke the Tatar yoke on a dominated and endangered Muscovite Russia, which in turn became a conqueror. The Volga was conquered when its tributary (Astrakhan) was seized from the Tatars. In the next century the empire expanded to Siberia and to the left bank of the Dnieper. In the eighteenth century the march toward Europe began. With the Nystad treaty (1721), Peter the Great took over Sweden, incorporated Livonia, Estonia, and Ingria as "eternal possessions," as well as part of Karelia with Vyborg, which—in addition to the semi-protectorates in Courland and Mecklenburg—transformed continental Russia into a naval power. In 1772, Catherine II, along with Prussia and Austria, partitioned Poland; she also extended her dominion, in war with the Turks, to the banks of the Black Sea in Crimea. The nineteenth century brought Georgia into the empire (1801), then Finland (1809), central Poland (1815), the Caucasus, and Turkestan. This epoch ended in 1895 with the stabilization of the border with Afghanistan.

A population census in 1897 informed the tsar of greater Russia as to the number and characteristics of his subjects. Of 126,368,000 inhabitants, 55 percent were not Russians but *inorodtsy*, or non-natives. These peoples were diverse in number, history, and way of life. In the west, a sizable group of Christians, mostly Slavs, were divided over religious, linguistic, or political differences, and over the relations between the conquered and the conquerors. Russian Orthodoxy, the religion of the empire, was practiced by Russians, the majority of Ukrainians, and some Byelorussians. A conflict between the Ukrainians and the Russians had been ignited in 1876 when the tsarist government banned the Ukrainian language. Polish Catholics rallied around the church to protest their territorial division and to commemorate repressed uprisings. The Baltic peoples, primarily divided between Catholicism and Protestantism, turned their backs on the Slavs and looked to Germanic culture, with which they identified.

Another group, to the east and south, was composed of Turkish-speaking peoples settled in Central Asia, along the Volga, and in the Caucasus, who shared a common culture and a glorious past. They had powerful ties to Islam, which linked them to Persian-speaking peoples and the mountain-dwellers of the Caucasus. The Caucasus, a combination of peoples and civilizations, also cradled the ancient cultures of the Georgians and Armenians, who were among the early Christians and who spoke languages unlike any other.

The diversity of religions, languages, and alphabets was further complicated by disparate ways of life. From one end of the empire to the other, human interactions, beliefs, and customs were so dissimilar that the empire appeared to be a veritable inventory of human civilizations. Geographical diversity gave rise to different ways of life. The Russian peasantry struggled with the forests to carve out their living space; the sedentary peoples of Central Asia struggled for an increasingly precious water supply; the nomadic peoples fought to maintain their migration areas. Their habitats reflected their surroundings: the wooden hut, or *izba*, belonged to a civilization created in forested regions and cold temperatures, the yurt to a mobile civilization.

In the midst of such diversity the only unifying force was the political system. The structure of the tsarist empire was rather paradoxical. On the one hand, the state was centralized, hierarchical, and autocratic; the authority of the sovereign—master of peoples and territories—was absolute. The Mongols' doctrine of state control had left an indelible mark on the political ideas of the Russian leaders.

Yet once the state became an empire, the new structures lost all traces of the organizing principles that had prevailed from the fifteenth century on. Three centuries of expansion won a vast, unbroken territory for the conquerors, but these areas were organized piecemeal, without a clear or consistent overall concept of empire. In the late nineteenth century, when the empire assumed its final form, several systems of authority coexisted. The relationships between the center and the periphery ran the gamut from outright integration into Russia to broad rights of autonomy.

The empire's nationalities policy was the first to suffer the consequences of the political crises that began with Alexander II's assassination in 1881 and continued through the revolution of 1905. The previously supple system that had tolerated different types of control and fostered its subjects' allegiance by asserting centralized authority and granting concessions, as needed, began to require greater uniformity and a burgeoning centralism. Although this development led to the creation of a more cohesive political and adminstrative system on the eve of revolution, it had a negative impact on the relations between Russia and its conquered peoples. The crises brewing in the peripheral territories multiplied; dominated peoples, previously divided by cultural and statutory differences, began to express their solidarity. The empire, originally a conglomeration of dispersed peoples, was divided along the lines of group identity: the dominant Russian group and the *inorodtsy*, the dominated peoples.

From 1880 on, communications were to play an important role in the developing relationship between the capital, the center of decision making, and the dominated periphery. Until then, the fragility of the communications infrastructure in Russia had isolated distant territories and added to the difficulty of controlling them. "European" Russia, where virtually all of the railroads were concentrated, had 23,000 kilometers of tracks, as compared to the 150,000 kilometers in the United States.

Beginning in 1880, the government, under continuing pressure from the governor-generals who administered the distant possessions, started to construct a railway line from Krasnovodsk to Tashkent, crossing Central Asia; in the Caucasus, Baku and Batumi were linked by rail. Ten years later, plans got under way for a Trans-Siberian railroad, which would run from Tashkent to Russia via Orenburg. By the eve of war, the empire's railroad network had grown to nearly five times its former size. Most of the connections were in "European" Russia, which had 81,000 kilometers of railway lines; Siberia and Central Asia, representing three-quarters of the empire's territory, had only 16,000 kilometers of tracks.

Russia's waterways have always played an important role in its development; however, because of variable climate conditions—rivers underused in Siberia, the Asian steppes more or less bereft of water, rivers such as Amu-Darya swallowed by sand—the railway builders did not plan to use railway lines in conjunction with waterways (where they existed). Moreover, their network of roads was not extensive, and road conditions were deplorable. Thus, in the prewar years, the empire's conquered territories were not easily supervised, for lack of means of transportation. Yet, in spite of all this, the relative improvement in communications enabled many of the Russian colonists who emigrated to central Asia and Siberia at the turn of the century to establish a sizable Russian presence in the border areas.

However, an administrative system, even one coupled with colonization, did not suffice to integrate the conquered territories. Beyond the empire's western region where urban life had developed, the native population was essentially rural. Far removed from colonized areas as well as from the colonial administrative apparatus in the cities, they were isolated from human contact. This discrete and dispersed population could only be reached through a kind of cultural control, by which all large empires have disseminated their own culture to their possessions and thus altered the cultures of the peoples under their command.

Early on, the Russian Empire recognized the importance of cultural control. In 1870, the minister of public education, D. A. Tolstoi, developed a program for the education of non-natives. He defined his doctrine in these terms: "The final objective of education to be provided to the non-natives living in the far reaches of the empire is undoubtedly their Russification [obrusenie] and their fusion with the Russian people."[3] Although this Russification program was put into practice irregularly and applied differently over time throughout the territories, it continued in place until the war. However, the program yielded uneven results. Without a doubt, it proved more damaging to the empire's cohesiveness than to the peoples in question. Russian-language education and the Orthodox religion affected only a small part of the population of each minority group, thus creating a "Russified" elite that, together with the Russians, played a role in public life. But the deep-rooted reaction of the dominated minorities was one of indifference, as long as the Russification program did not affect them personally. Some were impervious to it because of their cultural level, others because of a popular outcry against Russification. All in all, the national movement in the tsarist empire began to accelerate at exactly the same time as the implementation of the Russification plan.

In 1914 the conflict on which the empire was to founder was ignited, and the empire was obliged to pay a high price for its gargantuan, diverse, and poorly controlled possessions. Power and precariousness in the Russian Empire were two sides of the same coin. The revolution was to have no difficulty in rallying frustrated national minorities to the cause, thus precipitating the empire's collapse. On the ruins of an unenlightened empire that had not responded to the challenge of its nationalities the Soviet state was built; and it, in turn, with the means at its disposal, had to face the same challenge.

Part One

The Terms of
The Debate

CHAPTER 1

Nation, Culture,
and Revolution

The national question weighed heavily and unremittingly on the state that Lenin founded and became the subject of protracted disputes, which to some extent impeded the Bolsheviks' ability to act. The debates revolved around the character of the nation, the future of the nationalities comprising the Russian Empire, and revolutionary strategy vis-à-vis the national question.

The founding fathers of Marxism had pondered the nationalities question. But although their successors used Marxist ideas as a reference point, these ideas did not really provide them with a firm basis for action. The works of Marx and Engels on the national problem are well known and need not be described here;[1] but it bears noting that although they made every effort to understand the concrete historical problems posed by nationality groups, they did not develop any consistent theory with regard to them. On the basis of an exceedingly careful analysis of the realities of their time, they bequeathed to their heirs two certainties and one article of faith. They were certain, first, of the importance of the nationalities in a capitalist era and, second, of the alienation experienced by national minorities that did not belong to the ruling classes.[2] Their article of faith was that the triumph of the proletariat would for all practical purposes automatically resolve the national problem because victory would bring in its wake the decay and transcending of nations. Thus the founders of Marxism saw the nationalities as essentially a temporary phenomenon, one of secondary importance, linked to a period of capitalist ascendancy and class struggle. According to Marxist analysis, class alone determined the historical process, and class alone could resolve the contradictions of that process.

The Second International, responding to the growing tension and rise of nationalist feeling toward the end of the nineteenth century, set forth its position on this point at the London Congress (July-August 1896) by supporting the right of national minorities to decide their own destiny.[3] But in the same resolution the congress emphasized its view that the international solidarity of the proletariat transcended and would finally eliminate all differences among nationalities. Thus, though the Second International followed in the footsteps of Marx and Engels, it recognized the nationalities' developing strength and also held fast to the belief that class was the fundamental historical force and that nationalist conflict, born of a given period in the history of class struggle, was subordinate to it.

The praiseworthy unanimity in evidence at the Second International Congress began to come undone at the turn of the century, when the existence of two tendencies became abundantly clear. The "Western Marxists" remained obstinately attached to the exclusive importance of the class struggle; the "Eastern Marxists" recognized the growing significance and potential of nationalist aspirations. This second group included both Marxists from the Austro-Hungarian Empire and the Bolsheviks. Bolshevik thinking was influenced by the Austro-Marxist movement because the latter introduced new and specific responses to the nationalities problem. Bolshevism also had to reckon with the ongoing debate in Russia, where as much as a century earlier the Russian liberal intelligentsia had pondered the future of national minorities. In the late nineteenth and early twentieth centuries it was the minority-group intellectuals, regardless of whether they considered themselves traditional Marxists, who again took up the issue.

Three great currents of thought dominated the debate, which was centered in Eastern Europe and which concerned its various national minorities. The debate raged there because for them it was not merely a theoretical question, but one of vision, of how peoples belonging to different communities, all integrated into the same empire, saw their identities, their destinies.

The notion of nationalities, which was more or less foreign to Marx and Engels,[4] was debated by their disciples and successors because they lived in an empire made up of multiple national groups. Time and again, national minorities commanded attention and clamored to be recognized. Outside Russia, Karl Kautsky, Otto Bauer, and Karl Renner were the first to grapple with the issue, the first to define in exact terms the relationship between the nationalities question and the dynamic of the revolutionary process. Their ideas certainly enriched Marxist theory and helped to clarify the positions and plans of action outlined by Russian nationalist movements, but they also caused the relations between Bolsheviks and the empire's minority-group socialists to become strained.

Nations and National Culture

Karl Kautsky was born into a Czech family and later became an Austrian citizen. Although he lived in Germany, he did not distance himself from his minority background: he had a keen personal interest in the national question. He was to become the Second International's major theoretician on the issue, and was the first Marxist to discuss and define nationality in a book—significantly titled *Modern Nationality*.[5] Any given nationality, the product of social development, also has a cultural existence; Kautsky believed that the most decisive factor contributing to the formation of nationality was language, the language that came to exist as a commonality among peoples sharing a state.[6] The future of national language was tied to economic development. Market growth, a characteristic feature of capitalism, led to one of two things: linguistic unification based on the most widely spoken languages, or the development of a universal language.

Kautsky considered the ideas of Marx and Engels to be outdated and inapplicable, and he maintained that the workers' movement had to have a national agenda. Most early twentieth-century Marxists, including Lenin, invoked Kautsky, but it was Renner and Bauer who first published an exhaustive work on the nationalities problem in the two multi-ethnic empires, addressing the issue of the disparity among coexisting nationalities. These empires contained within their borders peoples belonging to clearly defined nationalities established in specific areas; but they also contained widely dispersed nationalities and groups that were numerically small. An organizing principle was needed that would satisfy the nationalist aspirations of each group and at the same time allow for the creation of a viable state. The dilemma was how to combine equity and efficiency: equity meant giving the nationalities their due, efficiency valued the needs of the state.

Karl Renner, a jurist, was interested in the latter. He assigned the state an important role in fulfilling nationalist aspirations and balancing them with the state's needs. His efforts were directed at defining a viable state that would be composed of multiple nationalities. In a series of works that appeared at the turn of the century under a variety of pseudonyms (Synopticus, Springer), he developed in greater detail the relationship between nationality and culture that Kautsky had posited.[7] Discussing the organization of the state, he concluded, "With the entry of the proletariat into Austrian politics, the nationalities problem ceases to be a question of power and becomes a question of culture."[8] Renner, in studying the complex problems of relations among minority groups in a nation-state, believed that belonging to a particular nationality was a personal matter: "It is the principle of personality, not of territoriality, that must serve as the basis for regulation."[9] Yet, at the same time, Renner assigned the state a regulatory function and gave the state the burden of choosing from among the different possibilities, where these existed, for territorial organization. In *The Austrian Nationalities' Struggle for the State*,[10] he outlined the major characteristics of a state in which two types of autonomy and two levels of institutions would be combined: one for each nationality and one for each community. But even more than Renner, who searched for legal and institutional solutions, it was Otto Bauer's sociological approach that significantly advanced thinking with regard to nationalities and their future. His ideas had the deepest and most enduring influence on those thinkers in multi-ethnic states that were searching at the time for a way to reconcile their yearning for nationality emancipation and for revolutionary transformation. In many respects Bauer rejected the internationalist or overly pragmatic approach favored by Marx.

In *The Nationalities Question and Social Democracy*,[11] Bauer examined the Austro-Hungarian Empire and the Czech-German conflict, on which the empire's future and, even more seriously, the future of the workers' movement, depended. Previously, Otto Bauer had been concerned with economic problems, not with the nationalities question.[12] But he could not sit passively by while the workers' movement split into factions over the nationalities issue, and he reacted to the current events of his day. He saw unequivocally that class consciousness in this instance took second place to frustrated nationalist aspirations. He brought his analysis into clearer focus not for the purpose of bolstering the nationalities' position, but in order to get the workers' movement to move forward beyond the nationalities issue, which was marring its judgment and preventing action.

As is generally known, Otto Bauer defined nation as "an aggregate of people bound into a community of character by a community of fate."[13] More explicitly, the common destiny is above all a common history, and the community of common character is first and foremost a language community.[14]

Thus, in Otto Bauer's view, a nation is not a temporary construct linked to a given period in the history of class struggle or economic development; it is rather a permanent phenomenon that predates capitalism and endures despite economic transformations, and in all probability it will survive. Thus the role of socialism as he saw it was not to ignore the nationalities or to eliminate them, but precisely the opposite— to render unto each worker his nation. It was from this perspective that Bauer reinterpreted the sentence in the Communist Manifesto that reads "The worker has no country."

Revolution, the proletariat's first conquest, would give back to every man what capitalism and the bourgeoisie had taken away—his country. Here Bauer parted company with the Marxist utopia according to which socialist countries would no longer experience national differences. Bauer's insight was to associate the diversity of nationalities with intellectual progress, which in the socialist framework would cease to be the privilege of the few and become instead the birthright of all. Intellectual progress at all levels of society would therefore result in more pronounced nationality traits, a stronger feeling of belonging to different national communities, and this in turn would weaken the international solidarity of the oppressed classes. In the view of Renner and Bauer, socialism, by virtue of the cultural progress it introduced, would integrate the masses into the country at large just as capitalism had done for its elite.

Consequently, it was believed that in paving the way for a worker's victory, any socialist program had to deal with the national problem so that the workers could conquer their birthright in an atmosphere of peace, among a multitude of nationalities, not in a climate of international antagonism.[15] Thus Bauer saw proletarian internationalism as promoting the harmonious coexistence of nationalities.

After the Brünn Congress of 1899, which favored dividing Austria into a federation of nations, Austro-Marxists developed a more specific program of extraterritorial cultural autonomy.[16] This program structured the traditional system of territorial autonomy on a new principle, that of personal cultural autonomy.

But putting personal self-determination into practice was another matter altogether. Theory did not easily translate into practice in the Austro-Hungarian Empire, where nationalities with diverse cultures were closely intermingled in the same territory. In response to this problem, Renner and Bauer differentiated between two levels of political organization, the state level and the cultural level. Federal jurisdiction would be limited to narrowly defined matters of general interest, and the principle of extraterritorial, personal self-determination would apply to cultural matters. Divided into nationality groups, the population would have separate representational rights to organize schools and legal institutions, and to participate in shared political institutions.

The theses put forward by Bauer and Renner aimed to resolve the problems plaguing both the workers' movement and the empire, where, they believed, reforms would be possible if new conditions prevailed. Bauer cast the future tasks of the empire in a socialist mold: "The integration of all peoples into the nation's cultural community, the achievement of complete self-determination for nationalities, the spiritual differentiation of nationalities—this is the direction of socialism."[17]

These thinkers all associated culture with the notion of nationality. Otto Bauer, increasingly concerned with the problems of the state, underscored internationalism, as Kautsky had done, and held unreservedly that national culture was a permanent force and a key component of the dynamics of history. By placing the nationalities in an international context, he advocated integrating the international culture of the proletariat, if such a thing came into existence, and national minority culture.[18] The affiliation between national minority culture and proletarian culture, and the idea of trying to balance them in a cohesive whole with outward signs of the existence of minority cultures, was later taken up by Stalin, Otto Bauer's great detractor, who would define in his own terms how to synthesize the two cultural presences in Russia.

Nations and the Federalist State

The Austro-Hungarian Empire was not the only hotbed of debate on the future of national minorities. In the Russian workers' movement, thinking was developing along the same lines but under very dissimilar conditions. Whereas the Austro-Hungarian Empire was divided and weakened by nationalist movements that flared up sporadically, the tsarist empire throughout the nineteenth century was continuing to expand, and many diverse minority groups were coming under its control. While minority peoples fighting openly for their independence were challenging Vienna's authority, the tsarist empire presented to the rest of the would an image of power and stability.

However, even as the mighty empire was gaining territory, the future of the nationalities inhabiting it was being debated. Even before the emergence of socialism, Russians were discussing the question; later it was taken up by the elites of the ethnic communities under the empire's domination. The Bolsheviks came belatedly to the national issue, which for them initially was a problem of the Russian political system—the problem of domination, by a great state, of peoples who were unable to protect their independence.

The national problem was debated in Russia in the early nineteenth century—in the wake of the French Revolution and the Napoleonic wars—by the liberal aristocracy, which formed secret societies and on 14 December 1825 attempted to overthrow the autocratic regime. The Decembrists were the first to propose that the empire be reorganized on a federalist foundation. Within the context of the struggle against autocracy, they defended the nationalities' right to attain a more equitable status. The liberation of nationalities was thus considered an integral part of the democratic reorganization of Russia.

Inspired by the example of the United States, the Decembrists were convinced that a federalist organization of the empire was desirable. Actually, their aspirations confused regional decentralization and autonomous nationalities, as the two projects conceived by Dmitri Dmitriev-Mamonov and Nikita Murayev will testify. Mamonov's idea of dividing the empire into autonomous states placed the previously rival major regions of Russia (he contemplated re-creating Kiev, Novgorod, Vladimir, et cetera, as states) in roughly the same category as the national states (Courland, Finland, Georgia, Poland). The Decembrists wanted above all to do away with Russian state centralism, to defy the autocrat's personal authority, and to protect the individual through local and regional structures. The Decembrists' anticentralist bent is most evident in the two projects by Murayev, in which he delineated the function of federalist institutions. He hoped thus to reconcile individual freedom, which presumed a restraint of government power, with minority-group freedom, which for him was possible only when protected by powerful political structures. The Decembrists did not unanimously support federalism, however. Pestel opposed it, believing that the diversity of nationalities in Russia would cause the decentralization effort to degenerate into separatism.[19]

This debate was extraordinarily important not only because it foreshadowed later discussions concerning the organization of a socialist state, but also because it identified the problems that such a state would have to confront. The confusion between administrative decentralization and autonomous nationalities; the dilemma of nationalities' or regional-group interests versus state interest; the coexistence of a federal state and national states—these were all questions that confounded the Bolsheviks when they first held the reins of power. Three-quarters of a century after the establishment of the state, these issues are still at the heart of constitutional debates.

Despite the repression of the Decembrists in 1825, their objectives were not forgotten. After them, Herzen and Baukunin, who disagreed with Marx over his support of pan-Slavism, attempted to define what they called *anarchist federalism*. Like the Decembrists, their primary concern was to protect individual freedoms. Their aim was to create a structural framework that suited the individual, and, like the Decembrists, they wanted this organizational framework to include all Slavic peoples. They sought to organize the Slavs in a way that would both preserve their identity and nationality and protect their rights as a group along with their individual rights.[20]

But unlike the Decembrists, who envisioned a rather traditionalist federalist state, Bakunin advocated replacing the state by a federation—to be Slavic at first and later universal—although he left the state's regulatory functions ill-defined. However, anarchist federalism, either in its pan-Slavic version or its universal one, did not attract the interest of national minorities and did not address the question of inequalities among them. Bakunin saw the state itself, in whatever guise it assumed, as the oppressor. The oppression of nationalities was just a corollary of the fundamental oppression that the state symbolized: therefore, he believed, a revolution that would do away with the conventional state would also eliminate the oppressive nature of its policies.[21] Anarchist federalism denied or underestimated the importance of the nationalities question, which explains why, though it found adherents among the Russian intelligentsia, it did not attract an eager following among the intelligentsia of the minority peoples.

At the periphery of the empire, Ukrainians, Georgians, and Armenians also debated the problem that directly affected their destiny. Their approach, although wiped from memory for a time by the tumultuous events of 1917, nonetheless influenced the manner in which the empire's nationalities reacted to the Bolsheviks in 1917. Their ideas will help us understand the national issue as well as the relations among the USSR's nationalities in the final years of the twentieth century.

The movement that developed in the part of the Ukraine that was incorporated into the Russian Empire owed a great debt to romanticism. The ideas of romanticism moved the elites in the first decades of the nineteenth century to reexamine their history, their cultural heritage, and their folklore. In urban centers such as Kharkov and Kiev, Ukrainian intellectuals awakened to their own culture, which had been stifled under the empire's centralized system. Their awareness of these limitations led them to formulate the Ukrainian problem in political terms.

The creation in 1846 of the Society of Cyril and Methodius is a case in point[22]: this secret society, established in Kiev by young intellectuals, combined in its program nationalist aspirations and a desire for general political transformation.[23] The measures proposed to achieve the latter aim were those favored by intellectuals throughout the empire—abolition of serfdom, social equality, freedom of thought, freedom of speech, introduction of an electoral system, and so on. But the Ukrainian national party went one step further in its platform: it called for the independence of the Slavic states within a larger state, to be organized federally with a general assembly composed of representatives from all sister republics. What was remarkable was the Ukrainian national party's insistence on each nationality's language, and the associative link between nationality, state, and regional language. Also noteworthy was the Ukrainian-centrist vision of Slavic federalism, given that the capital of the federation was to be Kiev.[24]

The federalist ideas developed in the Society of Cyril and Methodius were to a large degree the work of the great Ukrainian historian Mykola Kostomarov, who was wrongly accused by the tsarist police of preaching separatism.[25] In fact, Kostomarov advocated a return to the political tradition of Rus', for he traced the federalist tradition back to the political origins of Russia. The relations between medieval principalities had been contractual, he pointed out, and the organizational structure that had emerged from these agreements had been so viable that political harmony and cultural growth had resulted. This harmony was broken by Mongol influence on the Muscovite princes, who adopted the centralist, hierarchical principles of the Mongol state in order to consolidate power. The "gathering together of Russian lands" was a radical change from the historical tradition of pre-Mongol Russia, but was nothing more than the adoption of the invaders' centralist state model. While Kostomarov endorsed the idea of Kiev as the capital of Russia, he was fully cognizant of the fact that medieval dispersion of peoples could not be taken as a model for this era—contrary to the analysis proffered by Kliuchevskii and Karamzin.[26] In favoring Kiev as the future capital, he gave his federalist program a national component and, at the same time, remained prudent on the question of the nationalities' relations with Russia: "What we desire . . . is that the government, rather than prevent us Ukrainians from developing our language, help us toward this end. . . . For ourselves exclusively we ask nothing else. Our desires are the same as those of all Russia."[27]

Kostomarov's positions, like those of the Society of Cyril and Methodius, to which his name is inextricably linked, were weakened by a certain ambiguity. What was the objective: cultural autonomy, or pan-Slavism? Undoubtedly, a combination of the two, but they were unclear about how to achieve these aims.

The federalist program that Dragomanov developed in the 1880s had the virtue of addressing the Ukrainian problem as a whole; it included the Ukrainians who belonged to both empires, and examined their relation to Russia as well as to the other Eastern European nations. A refugee living in exile in Geneva, Dragomanov was in a position to evaluate his country's problems from afar, and this allowed him to develop his vision and express his thoughts with greater freedom. Opposed to the tenets of both centralism and separatism, he believed that the emancipation of all nationalities, not only the Ukrainian or Slavic peoples, presupposed decentralized power and a high degree of local autonomy.[28]

Dragomanov was troubled by two problems. First, he had to define the political structures most conducive to the development of the nationalities—and it was this conundrum that led him, along with his predecessors, to opt for federalism. But his thinking was also indebted to Bakunin and Otto Bauer for, wary of nationalist extremism, he worked toward providing nationalities with the means to reconcile their differences in order to attain true internationalism. It was this last concern that earned Dragomanov a special place in the long line of proponents of federalism in Russia. He was interested more in the harmony and brotherhood that ought to reign among nationalities than in the immediate future of oppressed minority peoples. Slavic unification was only one stage in a process, and he conceived his federation in geographic terms, not in exclusively cultural or ethnic terms. He sought to promote internationalism by implanting a federalist system across Eastern Europe—half the continent—because he knew that the virulent struggle among nationalities there was deeply rooted and well founded.

Dragomanov's final goal was the federalization of Eastern Europe in its entirety, including both Slavs and non-Slavic peoples. The solutions he offered for the future of Russia and the Ukraine left little room for interpretation. Democratic Rus' would be reorganized as a free union of twenty regions, of which four would comprise the Ukraine. The structure was to be based on the fundamental unit of the commune (hromada), along with districts (volost'), and regions. The aggregate would make up the state, which Dragomanov recognized as a necessity; and each level of the structure would have its institutions and jurisdiction. Dragomanov's vision of state institutions reflected his concern with both the national issue and internationalism: a bicameral legislature, with one house representing the overall national population and another representing the federated nationalities; and an executive, chosen from the federated nationalities to be answerable to both houses. This dual power at the head of the state was the cornerstone of Dragomanov's federalism. Although he considered ethnic and cultural elements to be significant, he refused to let them encroach on the state's functioning. One of his sayings unequivocally sums up his thinking in this regard: "A free union must be cosmopolitan in its goals and essence . . . national in form and means."[29]

Dragomanov's influence on his compatriots and contemporaries was undeniable, as can be seen in his disciples Pavlik and Franko.[30] He contributed to the growing politicization of the Ukrainian cultural movement, and his work became known both in Russia and in émigré milieux. Although Lenin makes no specific reference to him, Russian and Polish historians were quick to perceive that Lenin was influenced by Ukrainian political thought.[31]

It is noteworthy that Dragomanov's program of federalist organization and his definition of "free union" strangely foreshadow the organization of a multinational Soviet state and Stalin's definition of
cultural compromise. Dragomanov's plan, however, was originally
conceived to give priority to nationalities and their aspirations; in the
Soviet variant, nationalities were made to submit to the authority of
the federated state.

In the tsarist empire of the late nineteenth century, the federalist
idea was very much in vogue, and its principal outgrowth was the
development of pan-Slavism. But no one at the time pointed to the
contradiction between the intentions of pan-Slavism and the
federalism desired by the dominated peoples.

According to the pan-Slavic idea, federalism would lead neither to
the disintegration of Russia nor to decentralization; it would rather
organize an as-yet scattered Slavic world around Russia. In contrast,
the federalism discussed by the dominated nationalities, especially
by the Ukrainians, was centrifugal, aiming, in the name of the right
of national minorities to their own destiny, to break up Russian centralism and Russian dominance in the existing political structure.
Despite the different perspectives of the two federalist currents, both
viewed nationalities as entities with a common past, a language, a
culture, and a feeling of belonging to a definable group. As we have
seen, federalist currents were at odds with Marxism, which did not
assign a historic role to nationalities, yet these currents, influenced
the political orientation of both Marxist and non-Marxist minority
groups in the tsarist empire, lending them a federalist hue.

Federalism or Socialism?

The political agitation that shook the empire at the turn of the century caused the national minorities to react cautiously in deciding
which of their demands were most pressing. They had to decide
whether their emancipation necessarily entailed participating in the
widespread and growing revolutionary movement, or whether each
national minority would do better to seek its own emancipation,
focusing first and foremost on fighting for its own rights.

The confusion between nationalist aspirations and class interests,
which Otto Bauer had identified so clearly in the context of the Austro-Hungarian Empire, was just as great in Russia. The national elites
who advocated socialism generally remained indecisive in the face of

a multitude of tasks: wholesale separation from Russia, the preparation of national statutes within the framework of a democratic federalist state, the adoption of measures to ensure both the emancipation of national minorities and social progress.

Whereas Ukrainian intellectuals were federalists, in Poland there existed a conflict between two opposing views. The failure of the 1863 insurrection had, for a time, discouraged Polish dreams of independence. Polish socialism, which was beginning to emerge in 1892, hardly envisaged a reconstituted Polish state, but was divided over the issue of Polish-Russian relations. Rosa Luxemburg and the Social-Democratic Workers' Party of the Kingdoms of Poland and Lithuania, which had been founded in 1900, spoke out for the solidarity of the working classes of the three great empires. The Polish workers wanted the SKDPL to take part in economic development and in the social struggles in Prussia, Austria, and Russia.[32] The socialists organized by Kulcziski were opposed to the Polish centralist tendency and in favor of a federalist program, in the belief that workers' solidarity should have as its aim not only the emancipation of nationalities but social emancipation as well. This, they supposed, would require the appropriate framework, a federalist democratic state to which all nationalities would freely belong, on the basis of real equality.[33]

The early years of the twentieth century also witnessed a national debate in Georgia. Initially, Marxism had made rapid inroads, and Georgian socialism had been dominated by the Mensheviks. Noah Jordania, the party leader of the Georgian socialists, argued that a national agenda was consistent with the social struggle, for nationalist demands could not be addressed in isolation. The democratic transformation of the Russian Empire would change the predicament of the dominated peoples. And within this new political framework, the relations among nations would automatically be resolved.[34]

However, this extremely orthodox Marxist position was quickly shaken, first from within the Social Democratic Party, which split over the national question. Those who were convinced that the national question should take precedence over other issues left the party to form a new group, *Sakartvelo*, which some years later became the Socialist-Federalist Party and which sought Georgian autonomy within a Russian federalist state.[35]

The social democrats could not continue to keep the nationalities question out of the debate on the future of Georgia. The existence of the socialist-federalist group forced them to redefine their position. Furthermore, relations were frequently strained between Noah Jordania and nationalist leaders of the various social-democratic organizations. Thus, Georgian Mensheviks, impelled by their experiences, by developments in the Austrian social-democratic parties, and by the fear of losing followers to the socialist-federalist camp, progressively modified their initial position and adopted the Austro-Marxist theses of extraterritorial cultural autonomy.[36] By about 1910, Bauer's works, circulating in the Causcasus in a Russian translation, were being passionately discussed, and his ideas were gaining great acceptance in Georgia.[37]

Socialist Armenians also debated the desirability of political autonomy in a federalist state versus simple cultural autonomy. The Dashnak[38] party, which dominated Armenian politics at the time, advocated first one then the other alternative, depending on the circumstances.

In the Caucasus, where the nationalities lived in clearly defined territories, they favored forming a democratic republic that would voluntarily join a Russian federalist state. Administrative and cultural autonomy in a Transcaucasian republic would assure all minority peoples of entirely equal rights.

In sum, in the prewar years the socialist parties of the empire's national minorities defined and consolidated their positions. No socialist seriously expected the empire to collapse and independence suddenly to flourish. The empire's evolution after 1907 in a conservative direction with emphasis on "Russification" strengthened the argument of those who thought that political revolution in Russia was a prerequisite to new relations among national entities. But—and here is where almost all the socialist parties of the national minorities differentiated themselves from the social-democratic parties—the former wanted all the nationalities they represented to be assured of an autonomous existence. This is why the federalist idea found fertile ground in the programs of national-minority parties whose members were prepared to fight for the revolution alongside the Russian social democrats, even if the two groups disagreed on what structures would be created after the revolution.

The acceptance of Otto Bauer's theses by national-minority parties led the political elites, after a period of debate over the best way of guaranteeing the rights of each ethnic group, to reach a compromise whereby it was agreed that socialism was the surest way to arrive at a federalist state. Although this was an important change from previous divergent positions, the distance separating national-minority socialists from Russian socialists remained great.

Romantic ideas prevailing in the nineteenth century—respect for history and tradition, the belief that each national minority had its particular personality and was worthy of being preserved—divided the elites of the dominated peoples into two groups. For one group, the interests of the national minority came first; for the other, social progress was most important: it alone would be the liberator of nationalities and of humanity. Thus the national-minority movements and the socialist movements pursued different paths toward different destinations. In the prerevolutionary years, complex ideas came to replace an earlier, simplistic vision, but these ideas were open to interpretation, and their ambiguity was to have serious future consequences.

Socialist parties in territories with national minorities generally deviated from the classic Marxist position—hostility toward federalism and cultural autonomy, in the name of the shared, transnational interests of the working class—and in time embraced the federalist idea, with the understanding that the first attainment of the social revolution was to be the restoration of minority rights. This position took hold gradually, especially as the parties' efforts to consolidate a federalist platform had for a long time diverted attention from the decisive and growing importance of the nationalities issue. More and more people on the periphery saw socialism, which in Marx's view presupposed the disappearance of national differences, as the surest way to achieve the restoration of minority rights. On this point, national-minority socialists drew an imperceptible line between themselves and the Russian Social Democratic Labor Party. In a less direct way they distanced themselves from Otto Bauer, who wanted to unburden the social struggle of the national issue so that national interests would not be substituted for class interests. Beyond social revolution, which in 1914 was the program advocated by most national-minority socialist groups, the idea of federalism undoubtedly reconciled minority and socialist aspirations. But it reversed the end and the means through which they would be realized: the federalist program thus became the means through which the nation would recover its rights and command recognition.

CHAPTER 2

Lenin: Organization
and Strategy

To a greater extent than Austro-Marxism, social democracy in Russia was compelled from its inception to take a stand on the national question. The Bolsheviks saw the national question in terms of the profound differences separating the Russian working class from the non-Russian masses. "In the political domain," wrote Lenin, "the difference lies in the fact that the workers of the dominant nations are in a more privileged position than the workers in a dominated nation. . . . In the ideological or spiritual domain, the difference is that the workers of the dominant nations have always learned in school and in daily life to scorn and ignore the workers of the oppressed nations."[1]

The Jewish Proletariat between
Assimilation and Particularism

Quite possibly, it was the perception of the inequality between workers in the dominant and dominated nations that led Plekhanov to introduce into the program of the Liberation of Labor group a paragraph, drafted in 1880, that demanded "total equality for all citizens without regard for religion or national origin."[2] More likely, however, Plekhanov was invoking the egalitarian ideology that since 1784 had inspired all revolutionary movements. Equating religious and national discrimination, he was opposed to all that separated men, rather than to any specific condition or quality distinguishing one nation from another. In this sense Plekhanov was loyal to Marxism, which rejected any form of oppression or inequality that drew distinctions between men. However, Plekhanov's clause was absent from the program put forward in 1898 by the Russian Social Democratic Labor Party (RSDLP), which made no mention of national equality.

At its Second Congress the national question was included in the RSDLP program, a change that came about under pressure from the Bund (the General Union of Jewish Workers in Lithuania, Poland, and Russia, which had been formed in 1897). The Bund's relentless pressure forced Lenin to take a position on the relations among the various nationalities, not only for the sake of the party's organization but also for the benefit of future projects. The Bund's decisive role can be attributed to the seniority of the Jewish Workers' Party—it was the most powerful labor organization in the empire in the early twentieth century—and to its social and cultural character. The Jewish community in Russia was divided at the time between pro-Zionists and pro-assimilationists. The pro-integrationists, responding to those who saw no solution other than a return to Palestine, held that socialism, based as it was on the solidarity of the working class, would enable Jews to escape the oppression that they associated with the Russian political regime. Thus, political change and the integration of the Jews into Russian society were indissolubly linked; and the Jewish socialist movement developed initially from an assimilationist perspective. Its growth was due to the Jewish community's essentially urban way of life[3] and its concentration in the western part of the empire, where the pace of industrialization was most rapid.[4] The Jewish proletariat in these regions was characterized by a high level of intellectual development and by broad participation in industries of secondary importance that were less subject to police control.[5]

Starting in 1895, the Jewish workers' movement thoroughly reviewed its options. Previously it had worked toward integration with the Russian working class, aiming to draw Russian and Jewish workers closer together and to eliminate the obstacles between them. For purely practical reasons, Yiddish was spoken within the Jewish workers' organizations in order to reach the working class in its entirety. Martov (Yuli Osipovich

Tsederbaum), a young assimilated Jew, was the first intellectual to speak in public about the problems inherent in the assimilationist view and about the need for separate organizations. Addressing the Jews of Vilna, he declared that the interests of the Jewish and the Russian workers were not identical; that Jews could not depend on Russian workers to defend them; that they must act with two aims in mind—class struggle and the struggle for national emancipation—or all their efforts would be in vain; and that to arrive at their goals, Jewish organizations had to be created.[6] His admonition did not fall on deaf ears, for anti-Semitism was becoming a daily, menacing reality.

It was in the trying times of 1897 that the Bund was founded, and its original objective was to overcome the differences between the Jewish and Russian working classes. Arkady Kremer, one of its founders, conceived of national equality as a means of ensuring working-class unity, not as the final goal of the movement,[7] and the Bund's early steps were taken from his internationalist standpoint.

In its Third Congress of 1899, the Bund discussed the need to include in its program the demand for equality among individuals as well as a clause concerning equality among nations; in the end, however, the proposal was rejected. The Bund, like the RSDLP, was afraid that the recognition of particular interests would weaken the solidarity of the working class.[8] However, the debate raged on. The leaders of the Bund saw in Austro-Marxism a solution to the Jewish problem in the Russian Empire. To their way of thinking, extraterritorial cultural autonomy was suited to a dispersed community bereft of any territory to call its own and yet unified by language, culture, and traditions of a moral and material nature. The Bund believed that the Jewish people ought to be considered a nationality, and that Russia, where a multitude of nationalities coexisted, ought to become a federation of nationalities, all of which would be granted total autonomy, irrespective of their geographic concentration.[9] In the years that followed, the Bund, eager to gain support for its position, translated the principal Austrian works on the national question into Russian and widely disseminated them throughout the empire. Medem and Kossovsky,[10] the Bund's major theoreticians, published influential essays on the national question. The Bund adapted to its own needs the Austrian theses on the organization of a political party that would gather under its umbrella a diverse array of nationalities; it claimed to represent the Jewish proletariat and advocated a federalist reorganization of the RSDLP, in which it was interested in participating as an autonomous organization.

At this juncture, the RSDLP faced serious problems. Russian socialists, despite what some saw as the extreme positions adopted by Lenin—whose perspective was shaped by the particular political conditions in Russia and by the discipline that clandestine activism implies—unanimously favored a centralized organization. In their view, transplanting the Austrian model to Russia might result in the weakening or disappearance of an organization still in its infancy. The leaders of the RSDLP reacted to the Bund's proposals with either scorn or anger; but both reactions were evidence of their concern. In the eyes of the Russian socialists, the Bundists were merely believers in "non-Marxist chauvinism." Plekhanov expressed the sentiment of most when he proposed the exclusion of the Jewish organization from the RSDLP.[11] Although thus shunted aside, the Bund continued to press its demands and make its presence felt, with the result that at the Second Congress the RSDLP tried to satisfy the Bundists on the question of national rights, although its position remained intractable on issues related to party organization. Three clauses were added to the RSDLP program:

• self-government for regions whose inhabitants by their composition and way of life have a specific character (Clause 3);

• the equality of native languages with the official language in educational and local governmental institutions (Clause 8);

• the right of nations to self-determination (Clause 9).

These three clauses were anything but a wholesale adoption of Bundist demands, yet even so they were not unanimously accepted.[12] The first two, which recognized cultural autonomy (within certain limits), were supported by the Mensheviks; the third, which did not spell out how self-determination was to be exercised, got the votes of Lenin and his followers.

The debate set off in 1899 by the Bund engendered two conflicts: one between the Bund and the RSDLP, the other within the RSDLP itself, which revealed the ideological splits within the party.

Mensheviks and Bolsheviks: A Progressive Antagonism

In theory, up to the weeks before the war both Bolsheviks and Mensheviks were hostile to the two basic aims of Austro-Marxism, federalism and extraterritorial cultural autonomy. However, the Mensheviks gradually departed from the rigid position adopted by the socialists in the early years of the twentieth century. While maintaining their distance from the federalist idea,[13] the Mensheviks nevertheless accepted certain practical proposals that were rather close in spirit to extraterritorial cultural autonomy. At the RSDLP's Second Congress in 1903, no major divergences developed within the party when the national question was debated, but a split became readily apparent during discussions about the party itself and about Lenin's conception of its organization. It was already clear that the group later to become the Mensheviks had strong backing in some peripheral regions. When Noah Jordania explained the split to his compatriots in Georgia, local socialist committees applauded his support of the Menshevik group and refused to recognize the representation of the Unified Committee (*Soiuznyi Komitet*), around which the Bolsheviks earnestly attempted to organize a cluster group of Georgian socialists.[14] This episode and the Mensheviks' gradual alliance with the right wing of the Second International illustrates how they developed as a separate faction. Even Plekhanov, who for a long time had maintained that Marxists should refrain from going beyond "the framework of systematic criticism of nationalist arguments,"[15] went so far as to say, in response to a Bundist delegate at the Stockholm Congress who questioned him about self-determination, "The right to self-determination of nations also implies the right to secession, that is, the creation of a separate state if the majority of the people favor such a solution."[16]

However, in 1903 the Mensheviks were still a long way from endorsing the idea of self-determination and cultural autonomy. Between 1894 and 1903 Lenin was developing his ideas on the national question; uninterested in the theoretical debate in socialist circles or even among Austro-Marxists, he directed his attention to the concrete problems of the Bund's demands and the nationalities' discontent in the empire. In 1894, with "Who Are the Friends of the People?" he envisaged that the "laborers of Russia" would be able to throw off absolutism by an "uprising of all the democratic forces,"[17] with an alliance among the democratic forces as a precondition for the bourgeois revolution.

Three years later, Lenin specified what he meant by democratic forces: "In the democratic, political struggle . . . the Russian working class cannot remain isolated. Alongside the proletariat stand all the oppositionist elements of the bourgeoisie, the nationalities, the religions or sects that are persecuted by an absolutist government." Lenin accepted such an alliance because he believed that historical evolution was unpredictable: "Only those who are doctrinaire can declare that the appearance of one or another aspect of the national question on the political scene is impossible."[18] But he identified the limitations of this approach: "It boils down to support against a specific enemy; the social-democrats welcome this alliance to hasten the fall of the common enemy, but they expect nothing for themselves from these temporary allies and concede nothing."[19] To make such an alliance useful, a program had to be proposed to the nationalities movement. This became the right of nations to self-determination as defined by Lenin.

Social democrats conceived of self-determination as consistent with the basic principles of socialism, which were formulated in terms of the interests of the proletariat, on which it depended: "Social democracy's fundamental task and principle is to help not peoples or nations but the proletariat of every nationality to achieve self-determination. We must always wage an unconditional struggle for the closest unity of the proletariat of all nationalities, and only in individual exceptional cases can we advance and actively support demands for the creation of a new class state, or the replacement of the political unity of that state by looser federalist ties."[20] Thus, in 1903, self-determination was a way to forge an alliance among those forces that were capable of causing the collapse of the tsarist empire, one all the more necessary given the weakness of the working class. But no blueprint of the future was drawn up for the nationalities.

While he recognized the right to self-determination, Lenin was vague about its substance. Like all socialists, he believed that national oppression would disappear once the proletariat triumphed. Subject peoples liberated from their oppressors and their frustrations would have no further reason to exist as nationalities. Self-determination, a necessary stage in the struggle for a bourgeois democratic revolution, also offered a way to reject the Austro-Marxist alternative of federalism. In 1903 Lenin recognized the existence and strength of national groups, as did Renner and Bauer; unlike them, however, he rejected the federalist idea. He was opposed to it for the state as well as for the party of the revolution, for which unity was paramount. It was Lenin's position on this critical point, adopted by the RSDLP, that caused the break with the Bund. His primary concern was the party as the vehicle for the revolutionary struggle.

Given existing conditions in Russia, the party could only be centralized and hierarchical in structure. The introduction of national principles to the party program would undermine its efficiency and— even more critical—adversely affect its identity in a state of mixed national composition where it would be the only symbol of working-class unity. Lenin always refused to see diversity of any kind as a priority; the cornerstone of his philosophy was that the unity of the working class, as the moving force of history in an era of the collapse of capitalism, was supreme.

In his analysis of the conflicting positions of the time, Uratadze, a Georgian social democrat, noted, "In this debate what distinguishes the Bolsheviks from the Mensheviks is that the former are primarily concerned with building a solid organization while the latter are concerned more with the development of fair tactics."[21] In the fray of these major differences, the Bund's interests were to some extent passed over. Displeased that their concerns were not being taken into account, the Bund for a time withdrew from the RSDLP[22] and broke all ties. It rejoined at the Stockholm Congress in 1906, when party unity was reinforced. However, the Bund's renewed membership in the RSDLP was ambiguous at best. The major divergences that had caused the rupture among the socialists in 1903 were left unresolved. The Bund reaffirmed its adherence to the principle of extraterritorial cultural autonomy at its fourth conference, in 1905; the RSDLP, on the other hand, steadfastly maintained the position it had set forth in 1903, deeming it unnecessary to reopen the subject for further discussion.

Lenin analyzed in great detail the pitfalls of cultural autonomy, especially "educational separation granted to the interested parties," which he judged to be unacceptable.[23] He was opposed to the officially sanctioned study of national differences on the theory that schools should impart an internationalist education, and he warned that if schools served as a sounding board for national-minority cultures, they would run the danger of perpetuating cultural differences in daily life. It was doubtful that workers brought up in different milieux would suddenly be able to make the transition from a limited, national perspective to an international outlook: on the contrary, they would tend to recreate in their work environments the cultural divisions taught in school. Consequently, instead of promoting proletarian internationalism, with workers of all nationalities on one side and the ruling class as a uniform group that was uniformly oppressive on the other, separate education would cause workers and the dominant classes—having in common the national consciousness acquired at school—to unite in national solidarity. For Lenin, then, cultural autonomy was antagonistic to the interests of the proletariat because it would lead to the splintering of proletarian solidarity. Lenin's firm stance on this issue did not dissuade the partisans of Austro-Marxist theses, who made

every effort to propagate their ideas by demanding that the state be autonomous and that nationality differences be reflected in the organization of the party.

When it rejoined the RSDLP, the Bund won implicit recognition of its
separate identity. Bundist leaders fought to get the party to accept some
kind of decentralized organization and a program of cultural autonomy, but Lenin, whose opposition was implacable, rejected every
demand and every argument. His unrelenting opposition to the Bund
can be understood not only in light of their political differences but
also, and above all, because the Bund had begun to emerge from its isolation as its ideas gained acceptance by other national groups. Ukrainians in particular, haunted by the decline of Ukrainian national culture,
were seduced by the idea of cultural autonomy.[24] Much more so than
was the case with the Bund's demands, the demands of the Ukrainian
socialists put Lenin in a difficult position. Indeed, Lenin could not respond to the Ukrainians by telling them that their nation did not exist,
nor could he extol the merits of assimilation.[25] But he accused their
spokesman, Lev Yurkevich, of acting like a "narrow-minded, obtuse
bourgeois."[26]

The Ukrainians formulated the problem in terms of attaining an autonomous cultural life; the social democrats of the Caucasus cast it in
terms of party organization and the redefinition of a social-democratic
national program. In his memoirs, Uratadze emphasizes that works by
Renner and Bauer were extremely popular in the Caucasus.[27] Chau-
mian conveyed to Lenin in no uncertain terms that the Bolsheviks' defense of a monolingual state was drawing fierce opposition from his
compatriots in the Caucasus.[28] But at the London Congress (1907), the
controversial issue between the Bolsheviks and the social democrats of
the Caucasus was the party itself, and this issue caused the greatest rift
on the national question since the 1903 events that had resulted in the
Bund's withdrawal from the party. In 1907 the conflict was between the
Armenian social democrats, who demanded unconditionally that they,
like the Bund, be permitted to form their own organization within the
RSDLP, and the "internationalists" from the Caucasus under the
leadership of Noah Jordania. The tug of war between Lenin's rigid theses and the RSDLP Organizing Committee was resolved by acceding to
Armenians' demands—which in the end was not seen as a total defeat
for Lenin, as he did not participate in the debates, perhaps on account
of the complexity of the rivalries among different Caucasian factions.

From the early growth of Russian socialism until 1912, pressing organizational concerns impeded the development of a more clearly de-

fined strategy on the national question, which was effectively held in check. But in 1912 a change occurred. The renewed hope born of the 1905 revolution was followed by a period of torpor and disappointment, but a few years later, political life displayed a new, vital activism. The national question emerged once again as the main topic of debates and discussions. In 1905 the nationalities had played a decisive role in political change in Russia, a fact that later lent strength to their demands. All political parties, and especially the socialists, realized that they needed the support of the national minorities, and eventually all parties drafted national programs of one kind or another.

The Socialist Revolutionaries (SRs) showed an early interest in the national question. Beginning in 1905 they included in their program a demand for equal civil rights and broad-based autonomy founded on the desire to best apply federalist principles.[29] Although cognizant of the scope of the nationalities problem, the SR party, despite its official federalism, was divided over the concrete solutions to be applied. Their program affirmed the right of nations to self-determination, but many believed such a right could never be exercised, given the economic importance of the regions in question. Granting nations the right of self-determination might seriously compromise the chances for a radical social transformation in Russia. In 1910, the SERP, a Jewish organization affiliated with the SR party, involved the party in a great debate on the national question.[30] Viktor Chernov reserved judgment on the possibility of arriving at a general solution and, deeming local solutions to be far more realistic, lent his support to the idea of extraterritorial cultural autonomy, which he considered particularly applicable to regions where diverse national groups were intermingled.[31] Thus the SRs defined their position in 1912: they were for a federalist state and cultural autonomy.

Attentive to the aspirations of the national organizations among their members who rejected federalism and favored extraterritorial cultural autonomy, the Mensheviks followed a similar route. In August 1912 a conference, held in Vienna, brought together the right wing of the Menshevik party, in which Martov, Axelrod, and Trotsky, the party's most brilliant leaders, participated side by side with the leaders of non-Russian organizations (the Bund and Latvian and Caucasian social-democratic parties, as well as representatives of the Polish Socialist Party and the Lithuanian social-democratic party). At this meeting, a commission headed by Martov, Trotsky, and Berg (of the Bund), dubbed "the Liquidators," endeavored to draft a national program.[32] Despite Plekhanov's opposition to self-determination, the idea of cultural autonomy was gaining acceptance among the Mensheviks. During this period, the Georgian Menshevik deputy to the Duma, Akaki Chenkeli, deliberately ignoring the principle of party discipline and thus exasperating Lenin, demanded on 10 December 1912, the creation of "institutions necessary for the development of each nation." In Krakow, in January 1913, Lenin demanded that the party officially reprimand Chenkeli and lay to rest once and for all the controversial demands put forward by the Bundist and Caucasian social democrats. To the extent that the entire party was involved in this polemic it became necessary—indeed urgent—to deal a decisive blow to all those who sympathized with Bundist ideas.[33]

The "Marvelous Georgian"

Lenin's response was to mobilize Stalin against Otto Bauer and his followers. Why did he choose this path? What results did he expect to achieve? In 1912 Lenin carefully studied the writings of the Austro-Marxists and read many works devoted to the national question, the minorities in the Russian Empire, and the Jews and Ukrainians in particular. His reading notes testify to the close attention he paid to these problems.[34] But he preferred to leave the controversy in the hands of a Bolshevik directly involved in nationalities' problems. Why did he not call on Shaumian, who had already written works on the national question,[35] and who had debated with Lenin himself? One reason is that in early 1913 Shaumian was in the Caucasus and Stalin was in Krakow; moreover, Stalin was vigorously defending Bolshevik positions against Georgian Mensheviks.[36] Lenin assigned Stalin the task of going through all existing material with a fine-tooth comb (for which Stalin, who knew no German, had to depend on help from Bukharin and Troyanovsky in Vienna). In a letter to Gorky, Lenin wrote, "Here we have a marvelous Georgian who is busy working on a long article 'illuminating' the proletarian solution to the national question."[37]

The article entrusted to Stalin had a definite purpose: it was to be a polemical work designed to restore order in the house of Russian Social Democracy and to accelerate the processes of polarization on a firm base. In 1912 Lenin could not simply exclude any adversary he disliked, for he had to maintain cordial relations with the International, to whom internal quarrels among the Russian socialists were profoundly disturbing.[38] The method he consistently used was to show the error in his adversaries' way of thinking. Stalin, unschooled in ideological debates and unfamiliar with Lenin's tactics, conceived of his task as more than a digest of Lenin's reading notes, more than a mere settling of accounts with the Bund and its sympathizers—hence the nature of the work he prepared, which became a fundamental contribution to Marxist thought.

Stalin's article, "Marxism and the National Question,"[39] is divided into three distinct parts. The first is a general discussion of the concept of nation, the second a critical review of Austro-Marxist positions, and the third an examination of the problem of cultural autonomy from the standpoint of the socialist movement in Russia. In this article Stalin condemned the Austro-Marxist definition of a nation, "an aggregate of peoples linked together by a community of destiny and a community of common character" (Bauer) for being independent of the land (Renner [Springer]). The Austro-Marxists, he wrote, have confused the *tribe*—"ethnic unity"—with *nation*, "a community constituted historically, independently of ethnic particulars."[40] "A nation," he continued, "is a historically evolved stable community of language, territory, economic life, and psychological makeup manifested in a community of culture."[41]

In Stalin's view all of the above criteria had to be present to constitute a nation; if one was missing, the group was by definition not a nation. Thus Switzerland, a trinational state, was not a nation; similarly, the Jews—and here was Lenin's point—did not possess all the attributes of a nation; their destiny was to be assimilated by the nations among whom they lived.[42] Discussing the concept of nation in general, Stalin posited a historical concept, in contrast to the "quasi-mystical" notion of the Austro-Marxists. A nation, he said, was an aggregate formulation linked to the era of ascendant capitalism and thus not a permanent construct.

Given that "nation" was a historic phenomenon, what attitude should the workers' movement adopt toward it? Loyal to Lenin and opposed to Otto Bauer's thesis, Stalin's response was dialectical. The national question was not a single issue, but rather had two aspects: national democratic rights, which the workers' movement should properly defend, that is, the right to self-determination, and class interests, which had to be considered preeminent. The right to self-determination had to be seen in the light of working-class interests.[43] The socialist platform on nationalities regarded the right to self-determination as comprising civic equality, regional authority, and the protection of minority languages and their particular educational systems.[44]

Stalin opposed the Austro-Marxist position on both fronts. By defending the preservation of states of mixed national composition, he said, the Austro-Marxists rule out the right of peoples to self-determination and reduce political rights to merely cultural rights. On the other hand, by conceiving of the nation as a permanent construct, Austro-Marxism perpetuated national prejudices and the division of the world into nationalities instead of promoting the internationalist, unifying tendency of the proletariat.[45] Stalin denounced the concrete effects of Austro-Marxism on the Russian Empire, where its influence on the Bund and on the social democrats of the Caucasus had led to a weakening of the party and a splintering of the proletariat along national lines.

Significantly, in his article Stalin endorsed Lenin's criticism of Austro-Marxism and accepted the principle of self-determination; however, his critical discussion contained certain striking errors that cannot be traced to Lenin's reading notes. The errors were evidently Stalin's alone. Nor was the program he proposed identical in every respect to Lenin's. He underscored self-determination but never entered into specifics, whereas Lenin had already developed his thought on this point.

In his attack on the Austrian theses Stalin did not contribute in a new way to the ongoing debate. However, some of his errors, though minor, were novel: describing Switzerland as a trinational state, stating that in the early nineteenth century North America was known as New England; and some were more serious, for example, his analysis of Austro-Marxist positions. In blaming Bauer for having confused nation and tribe, and in accusing him of glossing over the historical framework of a nation's development, Stalin was guilty either of bad faith or of too hasty a reading of Bauer. Bauer had always stressed the need to consider a nation in terms of its historical development. Furthermore, he had stated that "national character" was not an isolated factor, for economic factors and the historical circumstances under which the nation developed always had to be taken into account.

When he turned his attention to the Austro-Marxist program, Stalin compounded errors with gaps. In a significant lapse, he maintained that the Brünn Congress had endorsed the idea of extraterritorial cultural autonomy,[46] when in fact it had gone no further than to back a territorialist position. Lenin adopted the rest of Stalin's argument to use against Russians who advocated Austro-Marxism, but stressed that at Brünn the idea of extraterritoriality[47] had not even been retained.[48] Determined to mislead the Bundists and their compatriots, Stalin declared that it was impossible to introduce the idea of extraterritorial cultural autonomy in Russia because the empire's authoritarian regime would deprive any such designed institutions of their ability to function. In saying this he deliberately ignored the fact that the Renner-Bauer plan had been drawn up on a democratic foundation and that Renner had gone so far as to envision the creation of a regional administrative system designed to prevent excessive interference from a central authority. Moreover, the proponents of Renner's thesis in the Russian Empire did not propose it as a way to reform the empire but as a program for the fundamental transformation of the Russian political system.

The "personal" aspects of Stalin's article are much more important than his errors. The Stalinist definition of a nation was foreign to Lenin's philosophy: Stalin spoke of the nation as a *stable* community; Lenin always described the nation as transitory. Although he tried to deny it, Stalin drew attention to the stability and permanence of nationalities. Some of his criteria for defining a nation have endured even though history has recoiled and transformed them: *national culture, national psychology,* and *community of psychic life.* Bauer's *community of common character* and Stalin's *community of psychic life* are similar in nature. Both phrases describe nationalities as possessing an identity that has evolved over centuries, not one exclusively linked to the stage of ascendant capitalism. Lenin, on his part, always condemned the idea of *national culture* as a "bourgeois concept."

Stalin's views on self-determination were different from Lenin's, for whom self-determination was the cornerstone of a new system. In "Marxism and the National Question" Stalin did not argue for self-determination, but he did discuss the topic in another text dated the same year, in which he wrote that the application of self-determination implied possibilities such as autonomy and federalism, solutions that Lenin decried shortly thereafter.

A close reading of Stalin's text also reveals variations in the classic Marxist position and in the view of the national problem then in vogue in social-democratic circles. Stalin was the first in the RSDLP to recognize the seriousness and permanence of the national problem.

It becomes apparent that where Stalin's ideas depart from Lenin—in his formulations of the nature of nations and in his conviction that they have the capacity to endure—Stalin's debt to Renner and Bauer was great. The same could be said of his proposed solutions: autonomy and federation, words from the vocabulary of Renner and Bauer, fitting squarely into their system of ideas. Having been instructed to refute Austro-Marxist positions, Stalin in fact refashioned their ideas. Just as similar movements had impressed the Austro-Marxists, Stalin was impressed by the development of a strictly national liberation movement in the Caucasus, where, as in the Austro-Hungarian Empire, complex entanglements on a national level reinforced national conflicts. It was surely for this reason that he saw a dimension in the nationalities' predicament that Lenin, who was otherwise highly attentive to facts, refused to recognize.[49]

Lenin and the Left: Tactical Disagreements

Not only did Austro-Marxism represent concrete problems for the RSDLP, but it also rejected the theoreticians who, despite the peculiarities of the Russian predicament, tended to follow the strictest Marxist interpretation. This tendency haunted the debates on the Polish question and bitterly divided the Polish socialists.

In the early twentieth century, Rosa Luxemburg, in discussing the economic development of Poland, remarked that the struggle for independence had lost its meaning and would have adverse consequences. To her way of thinking, the economic development of the states that had absorbed Poland was a positive historical factor and should not be undermined by futile nationalist struggles. Besides, she noted, Russian absolutism, which had justified Marx's support for Polish independence, was, practically speaking, a thing of the past. Russia had essentially passed beyond the stage of absolutism; it had a constitution, limited and ill-enforced though it was, that planted the seeds for uninterrupted change. The workers' movement was spreading throughout the empire; thus, she argued, as long as the state was developing democratically, socialists should not support a nationalities movement—a bourgeois goal. Rosa Luxemburg believed that the interests of a limited group of Poles was outweighed by the interests of millions of workers.

Lenin responded with polemics and accusations against Rosa Luxemburg and her friends, whose views he essentially shared. Indeed, he had always been and always would be of the same mind as the left wing of the party, for which the role of the proletariat was to transcend, via class solidarity, all national disagreements. But after 1905 he became convinced that the Russian working class needed allies in its struggle to overthrow power, and that nationalist aspirations could have one of two effects: it could either contribute to the struggle, enabling a numerically small working class in a country that still contained a peasant majority to impose its hegemony, or, alternatively, promote any political movement that supported nationalist aims, thus holding back the working class. Fundamentally in agreement with Rosa Luxemburg, Lenin considered her strategy to be mistaken. The axis of the program he painstakingly defined had two hubs: to keep the concept of "nation" out of working-class ideology, and to create a temporary alliance of national movements and the working class.

Lenin criticized both the left and Austro-Marxism, but each in a different way. In the program he was to develop in the two years before the war, his predominant concern was consistently to separate the *ends* (unity of the working class, which would erase national diversity) from the *means* (making temporary use of such diversity). In order to achieve his ends he did not address the national issue in general but the nationalities questions as they existed in the particular conditions of the Russian Empire. He did not develop an overall theory of nationality—far from it—but rather worked to define a national program that would preserve the hegemony of the proletariat. Lenin's concessions to the nation were temporary, limited, and conditional.

The Right of Nations to Self-Determination

Prior to 1914 Lenin was developing and fine-tuning his ideas on the self-determination of nations, for only in this way could he win the national movements' support for revolution in Russia. Although he did not delve any deeper than before into the national issue, his efforts at the time were devoted—and this was new—to defining a principle he had always defended.

The right to self-determination "is the right to secede and form an independent state,"[50] he wrote in 1913, going far beyond the stance taken by the Second International, which had considered secession merely one variation of self-determination. Lenin answered his adversaries, who accused him of focusing the attention of the oppressed nationalities on the national question and thus distracting them from the true task of the proletariat, in a key text, "The Right of Nations to Self-Determination."[51] In this and other articles on the national question written during the same period, Lenin rejected the idea that the struggle for self-determination distracted the masses from the main struggle, that of the proletariat; he did so by following Marx's reasoning on the question of Irish independence and referring to the concrete situation of the Russian proletariat. In Lenin's view, one could not relegate the struggle for national emancipation to the bourgeoisie or claim that it was of no concern to the proletariat. Quite the contrary, the proletariat had to fight for national emancipation as one of its specific demands, because the proletariat was against all forms of oppression. Here Lenin underscored the role played by recognition of the principle of self-determination in the revolution and the development of internationalism. Contrary to what his adversaries on the left maintained, he associated internationalism with the recognition of nationalist aspirations. His position rested on three arguments:

1. Recognition of the principle of self-determination would resolve the problems of a multinational state by improving relations among the diverse proletarian elements of national groups, hence relations within the party; and it would rid the party of national-group resentment and put the party in a better position to represent all the working-class elements of a multinational state.[52]

2. During the prerevolutionary period, this program would assure the working class and its party of help from the nonproletarian national movements, thus strengthening the party and accelerating the course of the revolution.

3. Finally, this program would fight nationalism and educate the proletariat in an internationalist spirit. The corollary of self-determination was national equality, which had never entered proletarian consciousness, regardless of whether the proletariat belonged to an oppressive or to an oppressed power.

Lenin thus assigned a pedagogical value to the principle of self-determination. The dominant, i.e., Great Russian, proletariat must support the rights of the lesser nations to self-determination. And, conversely, the masses of smaller nations should see in this support for their cause the premises for a truly internationalist perspective, which would help to resolve the problems of a multinational state after the takeover of power. Clearly, Lenin's unswerving support for the principle of self-determination was strategic, but it was based on an internationalist outlook. Lenin was keenly aware of dominant-nation chauvinism and he feared its effects.

Lenin's theses appear to be close to Otto Bauer's, yet in fact he did not accept the existence of nationalities in the way that Bauer did. He certainly did not endorse the underpinning for Bauer's ideas, that is to say, his concept of *national culture*. He always denounced the concept as a weapon of the bourgeoisie, for, he said, national culture was necessarily the culture of the ruling classes. Only one type of culture was acceptable to Lenin, "the international culture of the world working-class movement."[53] He undoubtedly recognized, in a reference to the Bundist Liebman, that any international culture must have particular national traits. Lenin stated: "The *elements* of democratic and socialist culture are present . . . in *every* national culture, since in every nation there are toiling and exploited masses whose conditions of life inevitably give rise to the ideology of democracy and socialism. But *every* nation also possesses a bourgeois culture (and most nations a reactionary and clerical culture as well) in the form not merely of 'elements,' but of the dominant culture. . . . In advancing the slogan of 'the international culture of democracy and of the world working-class movement,' we take *from each* national culture *only* its democratic and socialist elements."[54] "Our task is . . . not to preach or tolerate the slogan of national culture," he concluded.[55]

Lenin was rather vague about the form and content of the international culture of the working class. He recognized that culture does not exist independently of national forms, nor, certainly, independently of language, and that culture is necessarily expressed through national cultures. However he did not develop his thought on this point and, unlike Stalin, paid scant attention to cultural problems in his analysis of self-determination. In examining the relationship among nations he looked to economic and ideological factors, not to cultural ones. If Lenin discussed, or rather condemned, national cultures at all, it was because this approach allowed him to arrive logically at the repudiation of national cultural autonomy. Here we see further proof of his unwillingness to consider the concept and special characteristics of "nation." His desire to confine "nation" to a narrow and temporary framework, and to neutralize the political concept with the idea of international culture, everywhere permeates his theses on the self-determination of nations.

Why did Lenin support secession, the extreme solution? What form would self-determination assume for those nations who chose not to secede? Lenin's central concern was to maintain the unity of working-class movement prior to the revolution, and to maintain the unity of the proletarian state once the revolution was accomplished. He led the battle against Austro-Marxism to preserve party unity. The internationalist education of workers with regard to self-determination could only be carried out by a centralized party that combated tendencies to diversity. From 1903 on, Lenin tirelessly proclaimed that the party was the vehicle for the idea of a unified proletariat, and that the party could not be organized around national criteria such as language without being fundamentally distorted.[56] The party's unity, centralism, and proletarian essence guaranteed that its alliance with the national movement would in the end serve the cause of the working class, and no other.[57] It was for this reason, too, that Lenin posited only two possibilities for national self-determination— either outright secession or membership in a unified proletarian state—and rejected the intermediary solutions of federalism or autonomy.

He accepted secession in the capitalist era and in the course of the socialist revolution, but only reluctantly, as "an exception to the general principle of democratic centralism, a necessary exception due to Russia's situation."[58] "Generally, separation does not enter into our program,"[59] he wrote. He reiterated this idea on many occasions, understanding the advantages of appealing to nationalist sentiments before the revolution in order to strengthen the proletariat and disrupt the imperial state. He knew that secession was a weapon to be brandished during the revolution, to honor the promises made to the national movements and to neutralize them. But he always emphasized that despite the requirements of revolutionary combat and notwithstanding past promises, secession was not a desirable solution: the right to secede was acceptable and viable only because it coexisted with its opposite, the freedom to join. Because the proletariat of the ruling power would defend the right of dominated nations to secede, the latter would in the course of the revolution adopt the alternative solution, the freedom to choose union, an option previously imposed by force. Lenin's response to those who charged that his program would effectively perpetuate national quarrels was that it was designed rather to eliminate national quarrels by offering each nation the option of pursuing its own path. Fully empowered to exercise their choice and realizing that they were free to decide, the dominated nations would no longer wish to exercise their right to secede; thus the victory of the working class would coincide with the transcendence of nationality. Such events would not occur spontaneously, by exclusive virtue of the revolution; rather, they would occur as the result of evolution, grounded in a mutual trust that the strategy of self-determination would have permitted to flourish.

Part Two

Nationalism:
The Stakes

CHAPTER 3

The Nations "Manipulated"

Lenin had always firmly believed that war would lead to the collapse of the Russian Empire and that, in the debris of its ruins, revolution would surge forward, spurred on by national conflicts. On the other hand, he did not foresee that the powers who participated in weakening Russia might also seek to profit from minority-group antagonism toward the empire and, equally likely, toward any political system that replaced it.

Until 1914 the national question in Russia was a domestic conundrum. But once the war began, cards were shuffled on the table of international politics, and first the Central Powers, then the Allies after the revolution, tried to play the hand to their advantage. This development, which caught the Bolsheviks by surprise, sowed the seeds of ever-deepening doubts and disagreements, and affected not only the relations among national groups, but also the nature of power that would emerge from the revolution.

The war presented the nationalities with the new problem of deciding the degree of their loyalty to the Russian state. Flung far from the battlefield, those groups with no cultural or historic ties to Russia's enemies—for example, the peoples of the Caucasus—did not have a multitude of choices. Loyalty for them meant temporarily setting aside their dissensions and demands in order to participate in the defense effort. Conflicting loyalties were much more acute, however, for the peoples who had ties to the belligerent nations (the German minority group, for example, which at one time the imperial government had contemplated removing to the interior regions), for those living in a strategically vulnerable area (the Baltic peoples), and for those whose territory was being fought over by two or more belligerents (as occurred in Poland); for them, loyalty to the ruling nation meant taking up arms against brothers who were members of the enemy empire.

Policy in the East:
Revolution, or the Dismantling of Russia?

In August 1914 national groups seemed to respond with a resounding display of loyalty. Throughout the empire there was an apparent upsurge in patriotism and solidarity. In a special session of the Duma on 8 August, when war credits were approved,[1] all the deputies of the different nationality groups proclaimed their loyalty to the empire. This declaration of unanimity, however, occurred in the Duma, where the representation of nationalities had been greatly reduced.[2] Indeed, the leaders of some national groups who were not members of the Duma minced no words in manifesting their interest in Russia's defeat.[3]

All belligerent nations turned their attention to Poland because it was a divided nation from the outset, and the first battlefield to cross. Poland's future hung in the balance from the very beginning of the war. Grand Duke Nicholas, commander-in-chief of the Russian armed forces, promised the Poles autonomy.[4] At the same time, Austria, whose troops were advancing across the Russian part of Poland, declared that its conquests were not subject to negotiation. Meanwhile, the German rulers were watching to see what attitude the Poles who belonged to the Russian Empire were going to adopt toward the central power.

There were diverse reactions from the national parties in Poland. Dmowski's National Democrats[5] welcomed the commitment of Grand Duke Nicholas. Pilsudski, in the name of the Polish Socialist Party, took the opposite view and backed the Central Powers. On 6 August he dispatched the Polish Legion to Kielce, in Russian territory, and decreed that independent Poland began there. Then he created a pro-Austrian National Committee in Krakow, with active foreign offices. Its representatives in Switzerland collected funds and recruited volunteers for the Polish Legion.[6] In January 1915, with the approval of G. Motta, president of Switzerland, a Committee for Polish War Victims[7] was created in Vevey. It had 174 sections, 117 of them in the United States. Supported by prestigious men such as the pianist Paderewski and the writer Sienkiewicz, the Committee, whose base was strong in émigré Polish intellectual circles, raised sizable sums, especially in the United States, where Paderewski served as itinerant ambassador.

Yet these activities were simple measures that left the crucial problem unaddressed. A definition of policy toward the belligerent nations was sorely needed. Which definition of Poland was to be accepted? What was the future of this entity? The Committee's directors believed that none of the parties to the war could resolve the issue, and that the Polish question had to be internationalized.

In Lausanne, Jan Kucharzewski, founder of the group "Poland and the War," declared that Poland should become an independent buffer-state between the great powers. Although relations among the various Polish organizations were labyrinthine and marked by distrust, their efforts were complementary. The Austrophiles predicted the collapse of Russia and believed that for Poland to remain well off, the Poles had to support Austria. The Russophiles and supporters of the Allies hoped their loyalty would be rewarded in the event of a victory by the Allied powers. Significantly, only Austria and Russia figured directly in Polish calculations and played a part in the contacts initiated in 1915; Prussia was out of the picture. The Polish nationalist parties, despite their apparent cross-purposes, took up the debate on Poland's future. Their activism compelled the social democrats to participate in the discussions and propose solutions for the country's future. The latter were generally against independence but were divided over the issue.

Emigré Ukrainians, under Austrian influence, also entered the arena. An émigré group of varied political stripes, that had the financial backing of the Central Powers and claimed to represent all Ukrainian parties, founded the Alliance for the Liberation of the Ukraine in Vienna in August 1914. Its program called both for a national revolution that would lead to a democratic Ukraine and for agrarian reform. But the Alliance dissolved after only one month and was replaced by the Ukrainian Social-Revolutionary Party. Despite their in-fighting, the Ukrainians continued to receive aid from the Central Powers until 1915. They also attempted to establish contact with the other national groups that were organized in Switzerland. But their initiatives were not well received—Georgian social democrats in Geneva published a letter of re-

jection.[8] The Ukrainians' relations with the Russians were more ambiguous. On the one side, Trotsky and Manuilsky were violently opposed to the Ukrainian Alliance[9]; on the other, the Alliance could boast
positive contacts with Lenin, who at the time was interested in the
Ukraine. Still, in early 1915 Lenin broke with the director of the Alliance, the socialist Marian Bassok-Melenevsky.[10]

Austria, meanwhile, was quick to desert the Ukrainian cause when
its Ukrainian policy produced friction with Polish Austrophiles, who
were hostile to the Ukrainians. In the summer of 1915, when the Central Powers' armies were marching across Poland, the Austrians decided to play their Polish card to win the support of the population in a
stretch of territory that they fully intended to keep. From that time on,
the Ukrainians were perceived as a nuisance. After losing their supporters in Vienna, the leaders of the Ukrainian Alliance moved to
Constantinople.

Until then, Austria had been the only country to heed the national aspirations of minorities in the Russian Empire. Prussia continued to ignore the problem, seeing it in one-dimensional terms, as a border
issue. On 9 September 1914 the German chancellor declared, "Russia
should be pushed back as far as possible from German borders and its
domination over non-Russian peoples must come to an end."[11] At the
outbreak of war, such a statement was nothing but a pious wish. The
unity of the Russian Empire, given the war's momentum in 1914,
seemed quite intact.

The German offensive in 1915 changed everything. The fall of Lvov in
June heralded a string of Austro-German victories. On 31 July the Austrians seized Lublin; simultaneously, their allies occupied Windaw and
Mitaw. In August the German advance accelerated and was secured by
the capture of Warsaw on 5 August, Kovno on the 18th, Brest-Litovsk
on the 25th, Grodno on 2 September, and, finally, on 19 September,
Vilna, where the offensive halted. In a matter of weeks, Prussia and Austria had conquered Poland, Lithuania, and part of the Ukraine.

Russia's territorial losses were significant, and now the Prussian and
Austrian governments were confronted with many questions. Did the
nationalities of the Russian Empire have a role to play in the war? Could
they contribute to a victory of the Central Powers? Should they be included in the political strategies of the General Staff? What was to be
done with the conquered nations in the future? What solution would
best serve the interests and preserve the might of the Central Powers?

The military events of the summer of 1915 transformed German more
than Austrian strategy. Austria, for its part, had long been studying the

possibilities represented by the dominated peoples on Russia's western borders. German calculations were oriented in a different direction, but when the Germans realized that Russia would never sign a separate peace treaty, the Germans pinned their hopes on the disintegration of the empire, which was surely about to undergo a revolution. Still, German advances in Polish territory opened up new horizons. Might not Poland be the powder keg to make the entire empire explode? Germany did not modify its policy immediately or heedlessly. Change came about due to the attitude of the Russian government and the unresolved debates in Poland.

In Russia, military setbacks precipitated government action to ensure Polish loyalty. On 1 August 1915 Prime Minister Goremykin announced in the Duma that since Poland was so closely integrated into the empire, it was to have a new statute of political autonomy.[12] Germany and Austria understood the possible consequences of this declaration. The autonomy promised might turn the allegiance of Poles in the occupied territories toward Petrograd and might also seriously compromise Poles in areas belonging to the Central Powers. These concerns spurred them to open a serious debate on the future of Poland. But Russian promises did not move the Poles who belonged to the empire— they were convinced that Russia had lost the war and that promises of reform would not be honored.[13] The Polish National Democrats, led by Dmowski, distrusted the promise of autonomy within Russia and tried to discern the intentions of the Central Powers. They were aware that if the Central Powers were victorious they would not give up the conquered territories, and that their proposed changes would only affect the Russian part of Poland—that is, so long as Poland remained under Russian control. Having no faith in either the Austro-Germans or the Russians, the National Democrats concluded that Polish national rights could be respected only with outside help from the Allied powers. Dmowski's followers judged that the full restoration of Polish rights, rather than partial solutions, could come only from an Allied victory. They believed that the Polish question could be satisfactorily resolved only if it was taken out of the hands of the interested parties and made an international issue, to be decided in the territorial reorganization of the postwar period. The Polish socialists undoubtedly refused to accept that the destiny of Poland was linked to the military victory of the Allied powers.[14] But National-Democratic ideas spread widely enough to be troubling to the Central Powers, which had to come up with a plan not only to use the Poles against the Russians but also to derail pro-Allied tendencies.

Austria and Germany were not in identical positions and could not take the same route. Austria realized that a policy designed to manipulate nationalities in the Russian Empire might have formidable repercussions in the Austro-Hungarian Empire, and for this reason the Austrians stopped short of following German initiatives. However, by the summer of 1915, in the strength of unity, Germany put into action a carefully devised policy of national agitation, on the theory that minority interests, together with continued combat, would hasten Russia's collapse. Three national groups seemed particularly ripe for the aims of this strategy, the Poles, the Finns, and the Ukrainians, and German politicians did not hesitate to make use of bitter wrangling.

The Emigré Plots

Switzerland, where all the émigrés flocked, became the target of the German plan. The Poles there numbered 2,047, nearly half the number of Russian émigrés, and were very active.[15] But the Germans regarded the Poles with trepidation and directed their efforts instead to other national groups. German distrust was probably due to the desire of the Polish National Democrats for independence and their determination to hoist the Polish debate onto the international stage. The Germans felt that the Polish problem could only be properly managed as a domestic affair. In another respect, considerable Polish representation in the Bolshevik party may also have given Germany reason to pause. Revolutionary fervor could not be permitted to spread to the Central Powers. If the Poles—whatever their political orientation—received substantial support, the risk was great that Bolshevik ideas, with the help of growing Polish solidarity, would circulate abroad, beyond Russia.

German support for Ukrainian and Baltic groups was less problematical, or at least so reasoned G. von Romberg, German minister in Berne, who put the policy into effect.[16] Romberg was at the outset very hostile toward socialists and toward Lenin in particular. He was worried by Lenin's attempts to reconcile Russian and German socialists, and was instinctively extremely wary of the Poles. Even before the German successes in the summer of 1915, Romberg had established a network of agents from various national minority groups to work as infiltrators. Three men figured prominently in this scheme: Stefanowsky, a Ukrainian; Kesküla, an Estonian; and Gabrys, a Lithuanian. Kesküla had first established contact with Romberg in September 1914 to inquire about German intentions vis-à-vis the nationalities, especially toward the Estonians, in the event of victory by the Central Powers. Despite the inconsistency of German policy at the time, Kesküla obtained subsidies to foment a national revolution within the empire, or, in any event, he was charged with this task. His relations with Romberg were ambiguous. Kesküla, who had taken part with the Bolsheviks in the 1905 revolution, insisted on maintaining ties with them and with Lenin. Romberg perhaps saw Kesküla's potential as an informer on Lenin's activities.[17] A mediocre informer, Kesküla nevertheless devised a plan for a general uprising by the empire's nationalities, one that hinged on the Ukrainians. The resulting confusion was curious. While in Vienna the Austrians abandoned the Ukrainian cause in favor of that of the Poles, the Germans, uninterested in Poland, backed the Ukrainians. The Ukrainian Alliance, recently relocated to Constantinople, received encouragement from Berlin at the same time that, back in Switzerland, Romberg introduced Stefanowsky, a Ukrainian, to the small group of émigrés working with him and reporting to Kesküla.[18]

Stefanowsky, like Kesküla, had his own ideas. He wanted to create a moderately oriented Ukrainian National Committee. Romberg supported him, all the more so because his conservatism was a needed counterbalance to the Ukrainian Alliance, which favored social revolution. The minister of foreign affairs in Berlin reacted unenthusiastically, but after the summer of 1915 he gave Romberg, the only one to propose a practical policy, great freedom of action. Switzerland then became the true center of Germany's nationalities policy. Back in 1914, Kesküla had been eager to create an organization representing all the empire's nationalities. There had been no lack of obstacles, given the proliferation of ideological clashes among different national groups, but now Kesküla's idea appealed to the Germans, as it would provide a solid base for their policy. In August 1915, when Gabrys, a Lithuanian, joined Romberg's circle of agents, the new group was well on its way.

Gabrys,[19] who had founded the Union of Nationalities in Paris soon after the war broke out, gradually—as German advances in Lithuania proceeded apace—adopted a more favorable attitude toward Germany.[20] His hostility toward Russia was so acute that he saw Lithuania's incorporation into Germany as a possible solution. In 1915 he settled in Switzerland to maintain closer contacts with the Germans and to be in a better position to influence the other national movements in exile. In September he called a meeting of all representatives of the Latvian and Lithuanian national movements and proposed that they band together to form a Lithuanian-Latvian federation.[21]

The uniting of all national movements around a common goal to hasten the breakup of the Russian Empire was not the only plan Germany considered. There was also the Parvus plan,[22] which was directed at the empire's socialist organizations. In the wake of the 1905 revolution, Parvus had settled in Turkey, where he became familiar with the Ukrainian Alliance and the disagreements that divided nationalities in Russia; his idea was to fuse the national movement and the social revolution. The plan he unveiled in Berlin on 9 March 1915 had two closely related premises: social revolution in Russia and the division of the empire into small independent states. The immediate steps he suggested to spur the national movements to action were (1) the organization of a conference calling for émigré leaders to debate the national question; (2) the creation of a unified Russian social democratic party to include Jewish, Ukrainian, Finnish, and Latvian Social Democrats; and (3) German commitment to national independence for the Ukraine and, should it be necessary, for Finland and the nationality groups of the Caucasus as well. Many social democrats greeted these proposals with animosity. Trotsky violently denounced the excesses of Parvus's Germanophilia, and Alexinsky branded him "the paid agent of the Central Powers."[23] Parvus's relations with Lenin were stormy. The two met in Berne in 1915, whereupon Lenin quickly broke with Parvus and made it impossible for Bukharin to work with him. But Parvus continued to maintain regular relations with J. Furstenberg Hanecky of the Social Democratic Party of the Kingdoms of Poland and Lithuania, who at the time was very close to Lenin.

Parvus's plan found some supporters in Berlin, as evidenced by the money put at his disposal. Romberg, however, was extremely hostile to his ideas. He refused to associate the Bolsheviks with the nationalities revolution in Russia because he was convinced that only the nationalist struggle could hold at bay the danger of social revolution, which would have unforeseeable international repercussions.

The Urge for Independence:
Organizations and Programs

In the fall of 1915 the Union of Nationalities planned to draw up a map of all the nationalities in Europe, intended to illustrate the unequal status of the dominated or oppressed nations on a European scale, and to be widely disseminated (a first printing of ten thousand copies was projected). The Germans, who did not want Alsace-Lorraine to begin to clamor for independence, reacted immediately. The proposed map also represented a danger to the Austro-Hungarian Empire, for in their haste to break up the Russian Empire, the Central Powers could possibly undermine their own power base and hence the chances for a military victory. Stefanowsky[24] emphasized the fact that the Union was working in the interests of all empires and all oppressed peoples. A compromise solution was reached: the map would be released in stages, beginning with the map of the Russian Empire.[25] The conflict of interests gave the Germans to understand that the Union of Nationalities was too large a framework to accommodate their plans. Henceforth, the Germans adopted Kesküla's plan for an organization devoted exclusively to the problems of the Russian Empire.

In April 1916 the German government officially announced that none of the conquered territories would revert to Russian domination.[26] From that time forward, the future status of the territories was at issue. At the same time, Miliukov led a Russian parliamentary delegation to England, France, and Italy. The delegation included three non-Russian deputies whose sole concern was to draw as much attention as possible to the uncertain future of the empire's nationalities.[27]

When the main purpose of the trip was diverted from the relations between Russia and its allies to Russia's relations with the dominated national groups, Miliukov had to clarify his position. He declared that while Poland was part of Russia, it was desirable to grant it autonomy, by means of a statute more or less similar to that of Ireland.[28] Although he accepted the principle of autonomy, Miliukov stressed that Poland's status was a matter of Russian sovereignty, to be resolved by Russia and on no account to be the object of international negotiation. This view provoked frenzied discussion among Poles and several of their supporters among the Allies.[29]

From the Russian point of view, the Russian parliamentary delegation's trip to Europe was a failure. Russia's political leaders found that the émigrés, who back in 1914 had wanted autonomy, now embraced the idea of independence; moreover, Western leaders were warming to the idea that in some cases Russia could not and should not single-handedly resolve its nationality problems. German leaders drew their own conclusions: in the face of international weakness and internal divisions within Russia, they were encouraged to press their advantage and to offer solutions in the circles that had long since ceased to heed Russia's call.

In the spring of 1916, Berlin informed Romberg that the government was interested in exploiting the national divisions in the Russian Empire and was prepared to consider an organizational plan that would give voice to autonomous aspirations. Two projects were suggested: Gabrys proposed to Romberg that he create in Switzerland a "League of the Smaller Russian Nations" to represent minority groups and publicize their plight, and in Germany Baron von der Ropp, a Balt himself, proposed that a worldwide campaign be waged to make the public aware of "tsarist atrocities toward non-native peoples." Berlin did not hesitate to approve the creation of the League of Non-Native Peoples and provide it with ample financial resources. But from its founding the League was in an uncomfortable position. Emigrés, especially Lithuanians, were loath to depend on German goodwill and on Germany's military success. They preferred to receive bilateral support, which exasperated the German General Staff and Ludendorff in particular. In Berlin it was believed that after the war it would be Germany's job alone to decide the destiny of the Russian minorities. Rivalries among different émigré groups, each of which expressed its enmity in Berlin, only increased the General Staff's hostility toward them and helped paralyze the League.

The League's one (and probably only) success was the Lausanne Conference, over which it presided with aplomb. The conference, held in June 1916, escaped the notice of world opinion and was misunderstood by government authorities. Yet it was a landmark at a crucial stage in the history of the national movement in the empire and represented the culmination of Germany's—as well as Romberg's—policy. The Lausanne Conference was organized by the Union of Nationalities, which had held two previous conferences in Paris, in 1912 and in 1915. After the latter, the Union of Nationalities called for all the oppressed nationalities of Europe to band together to discuss their problems.[30] At the time, the Union appeared to be an impartial vehicle for national aspirations, the possible effects of which posed a danger to all multinational states.

The Lausanne Conference was the first world forum for dominated nations, and it caused early consternation in both camps. The leaders of the Russian Empire, aware of the gathering momentum of movements within its borders, feared being publicly accused, and the Central Powers were no less unsettled by the novelty of such an assembly. For Prussia, the possibility that Alsace-Lorraine would be discussed and that the Prussian conquests of 1870 would be considered ripe for emancipation was simply unacceptable. The Austro-Hungarian Empire feared that all the minorities might make demands and enhance their legitimacy. Only France and England did not see themselves as possible victims of the debate; they hoped that the Central Powers stood to lose more than their Russian allies. Such an attitude betrayed their gross ignorance of the manipulation of nationality groups by German agents in Switzerland and the German desire to use the forum to their advantage. At the conclusion of the stormy discussions—during which the represented minority groups did not merely attack their oppressors but denounced one another over confused proposals—the usefulness of the German groundwork and Germany's great ability to turn national discontent to its own account was everywhere in evidence. The Central Powers emerged unscathed from a forum whose dominant tone had been anti-Russian, with secondary hostility reserved for French and British colonialism. The various demands pressed by the delegations representing minorities of the Russian Empire ranged from equality for all peoples in the empire to outright independence; they concurred only in denouncing Russia as a "slave state" guilty of "killing off nationalities." Representatives of the French and British empires struggled to be heard amid the chorus of minority discontent and most likely wanted to broaden the discussion on the colonial problem. Curiously enough, however, it was because German agents thwarted this tendency that the Lausanne Conference did not become a forum on anticolonialism or a lectern from which colonized countries could finally vent their frustrations. Throughout the conference, the Germans pressured the delegates to attack openly only the Russian Empire, not in order to pacify their French and British enemies, but to forestall a general indictment of the imperial states, which would have been disastrous for the Hapsburg Empire.

The social democrats, the only émigré group from the empire that did not take part in the conference—they viewed the theme, the national problem, as devoid of interest and historically obsolete—were not blind to the dubious coalition of interests that used Russia as its scapegoat. Trotsky felt that the nationalities were being used by both sides as pawns: by the Central Powers as an instrument of foreign policy to clear the road to victory, and by France and England as a counter-revolutionary tactic to distract the masses with a false non-issue and steer them away from the revolutionary spirit that was everywhere on the rise.

The confusion of the discussions and the lack of tangible results cannot, however, belie the importance of the Lausanne Conference. Most important, it demonstrated that national minority movements in Russia were not the inventions of lost souls or émigré extremists, but rather arose from deeply rooted sentiments shared by many peoples. The open rebellion of the Kazakh tribes against conscription (which the empire tried to institute later that year) defined them as a dissident group of the Russian Empire and confirmed the lessons of the Lausanne Conference. No less crucial for Russia was the demonstration that what had been considered isolated currents of discontent in fact constituted an orientation common to all Russian peoples. After Lausanne, the idea of the solidarity of oppressed peoples, stemming from basic solidarity in the struggle, gained ground in Russia. It impressed Lenin, who saw in it a confirmation of his desire to enlist minority groups in the cause of revolution. It led Germany to adjust its as-yet uncertain policy to national realities. And most important, the Lausanne Conference was the first hint of the great movement of solidarity by the oppressed, a movement that, in the course of the twentieth century, has developed into a powerful current of thought and action. The solidarity of the oppressed, which made its first appearance on the world stage at Lausanne, foreshadowed the third-world Marxism of Sultan Galiev, at the Baku Conference, and of Mao Zedong. The idea that the class struggle was not the only historical link uniting people of different nations, but that a worldwide chasm separated "proletarian peoples"—oppressed as peoples—and oppressor peoples, first took root in 1916 in a peaceful Swiss city. Nearly forty years later, the Bandung Conference was to echo these themes first advanced on the banks of Leman Lake during the First World War.

Poland Caught between Germany and Russia

Poland had been at the heart of the Lausanne discussions. All free and dominated nations looked to Poland as the test case, and for this reason German policy was concentrated there. In August 1916 the Central Powers recognized the need to define the legal status of occupied Poland, but a hypothetical separate peace with Russia[31] stalled the discussions. On 5 November 1916 the matter reappeared on the agenda. The Central Powers issued a joint statement announcing the reestablishment of the Polish state. Such as it was, this Polish state was severely reduced in terms of both territory and sovereignty, which posed a panoply of problems to Russia and to Poland's promoters as well. The new Polish state was confined to the Russian part of Poland. Its sovereignty was limited by the Central Powers, who relegated to themselves the right to decide its political form—a constitutional, hereditary monarchy[32]—and the powers it would possess. The Polish state was master neither of its foreign policy nor of its armed forces, which were placed under German control. For the Central Powers, the establishment of a rump Polish state had the drawback of seriously reducing the chances for a separate peace, but it had its advantages as well. Russia, which had not honored its promise of autonomy, was now in a weak position, for it did not have the power to decide the nationalities' fate. The Austro-German armies could draw from the new state a manpower reserve equivalent to approximately three divisions. And, finally, the Russian border was pushed back from the German frontier, in consonance with the desire the new German chancellor had harbored from the beginning of the war.

Russia was not alone in regarding the creation of the new state as an affront. Other national groups in the empire were opposed, and the Poles themselves were by no means unanimously in favor of the decision. The Lithuanians had always maintained that they did not endorse a greater Poland in which their own rights would be forgotten, because it was quite possible that Russia would be the better guarantor of their interests.[33] To appease them, the Germans gave the Lithuanians certain assurances, which had the countereffect of upsetting Poland. Berlin replied that Poland's status was not yet definitive, that the border question was still open, and that Lithuanian interests would be taken into account when the final decisions were made, but this statement came too late to placate the Lithuanians, and it was too bald to leave the Poles undisturbed. Moreover, Polish politicians and the population at large were far from enthusiastic about accepting the Austro-German restrictions.

The Central Powers, ignorant of the desires of the Polish people—for they had only consulted with isolated figureheads[34]—restored a Polish state that did not conform to the people's wishes. Both supporters of the Allies and the Polish socialists greeted the 5 November decision with grave reservations. The Allies' supporters did not accept a Polish rump state. The Austro-German initiative led them to conclude that a ruling state should not decide the status of the nationality groups under its domination. The precedent thus created proved that neither Austro-German nor Russian authorities could control the national problem; an appropriate resolution required an international settlement. The Polish nationalists came to hope that an Allied victory would lead to the establishment of a true and sovereign Polish state. Although the Austro-German initiative was designed to satisfy, albeit partially, Polish national aspirations, in the final analysis, far from winning Polish sympathy, it helped turn Polish nationalist support toward the Allied powers.

For their part, the Polish socialists did not applaud the newly decreed independence of Poland, despite the blow it dealt to the Russian Empire. While they were pleased that Russia, along with "all the imperialists who noisily defended nationality rights" had been outmaneuvered by the Central Powers, the decision of these powers, motivated by purely selfish considerations, worked to the detriment of the true, that is, the social, interests of Poland.[35]

The Bund was indignant at the creation of a "Polish state that would encourage the development of chauvinism and anti-Semitism and help to undermine proletarian solidarity."[36] Social democracy, the Bund believed, should under any circumstance oppose the formation of new national states as vehicles for minority oppression rather than for liberation. Their shared opposition to the Polish state reconciled the estranged brothers of Polish socialism—the Social Democratic party of the Kingdoms of Poland and Lithuania and the left-wing Polish Socialist party—which issued a joint declaration decrying Poland's pseudo-independence, which reduced it to "the level of Senegal, and made the state a purveyor of colonial regiments for Prussia and Austria."[37] The fears of the Polish socialists were not borne out, but neither were Austro-German hopes fulfilled by Poland's military contribution to the war. Only a few hundred men were sufficiently inspired to defend the new state by joining the ranks of the German army.[38] The projected new divisions never materialized.

The main consequence of the Austro-German decision was that it lent the Polish problem an international dimension. It also had the effect of multiplying dissension among the Allied powers, whose solidarity was already seriously shaken by constant rumors of a separate peace.

A Polish deputy to the Duma, Filasiewicz, summed up the situation on 15 November 1915 by invoking the fairly widespread hostility to the unilateral creation of the state—which, to all intents and purposes, was a German protectorate—but he pointed out that Russia could never recreate the situation that had existed before the war. The multinational empire had ceased to exist.[39] Comprehending the consequences of the Austro-German decision and in an attempt to regain the upper hand, the Russian government took a clumsy and belated approach that only dramatized its defeat. Russia declared that the maneuver by the Central Powers was illegal, hence without effect; that Poland's destiny had been decided early in the war; that autonomy had been promised and would be granted within the framework of the empire. But far from satisfying the Poles, this declaration made them rise up all the more vehemently against Russia. By 1916 autonomy was a yearning of the past, and the time for special statutes had long since lapsed. The Russian declaration also had an unexpected effect on Russia's relations with the Allies. The French, British, and Italian governments interpreted it literally and voiced their support, thereby placing the Polish question under their joint aegis. It was a victory for Poland but a resounding defeat for Russia.[40] Amid all the protests, the League of Non-Native Peoples welcomed the Austro-German decision and saluted the 5 November declaration as an outgrowth of the Lausanne Conference. The announcement of Polish independence spurred the League to greater activity, and in the *Bulletin of Russian Nationalities*, published in Berne (where Ukrainian aspirations were especially promoted), it called on Berlin to declare the independence of Lithuania and the Ukraine as well.[41] From its first issue, the *Bulletin's* pro-Ukrainian slant angered Poles and Lithuanians, who protested to the League. The Poles felt that the *Bulletin* gave short shrift to Polish issues, the Lithuanians[42] that its position on the Ukraine was overly advantageous to Russia.

The years 1914 to 1916 were decisive in the development of the national problem. By the end of 1916, the Russian Empire, despite military setbacks and territorial losses, appeared still powerful and united. In fact, it would never again be an empire, and was in the process of disintegration. Its national minorities, which had in 1914 limited their demands to cultural and political autonomy, began advocating separatism, previously the exception, not the rule.

Development did not occur everywhere at the same pace. Separatism was demanded by those national groups whose strategic territories became the target of German policies aimed at the disintegration of Russia. Along the Central Asian periphery of the empire, minority-group consciousness was slower to dawn. We should not underestimate the dissimilarities between Poland, which rejected any restriction on its sovereignty, and Turkestan.

The consequences of the steps taken by Germany to sow discontent among émigré groups and institute even the partial and nominal "restoration" of the Polish state were far more enduring than German policy-makers ever imagined. First, a new solidarity was created among dominated peoples—a precarious solidarity, anchored in economics no doubt, but one that often neutralized previous rivalries. Slowly but surely the feeling solidified among peoples that they shared a common destiny. The more backward national groups were also aware that a precedent had been created in Poland that they could use to their own advantage to demand identical concessions of rights. Again, the Lausanne Conference was significant in this respect: for the first time, the isolated, individual demands of national groups were spread on a canvas that stretched across the entire empire. In addition, as a result of the Austro-German initiative, national problems took on an international dimension. Prior to 1914, most minority-group leaders thought that emancipation was necessarily linked to a change in the Russian political system. But by 1916 they were convinced that domestic political change alone was not sufficient to guarantee their rights, and that they must look to other national groups for protection—not to one group, but to many, in order to balance the scales. In 1914 Poland learned the same lesson that Georgia had in the nineteenth century, that the protection they sought might easily transform them into a protectorate. In realizing the need for international arbitration, Russia's minority movements followed a path parallel to that of the large European states.

P. Renouvin and J.-B. Duroselle have underscored the fact that in the prewar years, European governments were reluctant to interfere openly in the domestic affairs of other states.[43] At that time every state was so attached to its sovereignty that it hesitated to disturb any other state's sovereignty. After the war broke out, the opposite was true— and the Russian Empire's domestic crisis played a part in this; it was then that the idea of seeking international protection for minority rights began to take root.[44] Beginning in 1916, peoples of the Russian Empire dreamed of international arbitration and tried to get any state interested in their destiny to agree to it. By acting on the Polish affair before Russia did, although in pursuit of completely different goals, Germany actually pushed the smaller national groups in an international direction.

CHAPTER 4

The Nationalities:
Yeast for the Revolution

In the prewar years, the controversies between Lenin, the Austro-Marxists, and Rosa Luxemburg's colleagues had been confined to questions of theory or to problems related to party organization. Lenin had considered Russia to be still in the capitalist stage of the bourgeois revolution, when the destiny of minority peoples could not yet be decided. The war upset this tranquil outlook. Lenin then became convinced that the national conflicts could hasten the march of history and pave the way for the revolution. The national question came to occupy a new place in his strategy. Russian social democracy was divided over Lenin's attitude toward the war, and over his desire to use nationality groups in order to expedite the country's collapse. Most European social democrats disagreed with him. But Lenin was beyond hesitation, so great was his certainty that the conflict crippling Europe was sure to radically change the political situation.

Debate: The War and the Nationalities

Lenin had hoped for war yet had not dared to believe that it would come.[1] In 1913 he had written to Maxim Gorky: "A war between Russia and Austria would be very profitable to the revolution. But it's not likely that Franz-Joseph and Nicky will give us that pleasure."[2] Nevertheless, war had broken out. After a brief stop in Krakow, Lenin arrived in Berne, where he met with many Russian social democrats scandalized by his revolutionary investment in his country's defeat.[3] Plekhanov, who believed it was necessary to defend the country, was baffled. Not even Trotsky, who wanted a war "without victors or vanquished," could endorse Lenin's extremist views. Still, Lenin was implacable in pleading his cause: the defeat of imperial Russia and its army, which was responsible for the oppression of Poland, the Ukraine, and many national groups, was in the interests of the working class.[4] Lenin's arguments at Berne were incorporated into a resolution that he sent to Kamenev to be read by the Bolshevik deputies in the Duma. Their premature arrest prevented them from following Lenin's directives, but there can be no doubt that amid the patriotic fervor of the autumn of 1914, Lenin's position would only have discredited him, even in minority-group circles, for the war led them, for a time, to rally around Russia.

Lenin was correct in linking the national problem to discussions about the war. He found confirmation of his thinking in the attitude of the great powers, for the self-determination of peoples was a slogan that all powers, from the beginning of the war, had used against their enemies. The Allied Powers, the Central Powers, and later President Wilson all claimed to champion the cause of the oppressed nations and to be ready to help them win their liberation. The self-determination of peoples was a catchword of world politics in 1914. How could the social democrats, who for the most part acted in solidarity with Russia,[5] avoid taking a stance on this issue? Should they leave nationality emancipation in the hands of the governments they had always fought? With the exception of the Bolsheviks, the socialists did not know how to adapt to an unforeseen situation. Under very different circumstances, Social Democracy in Germany clung to the philosophy of Marx and Engels—then a half-century old—on the need for great historic formations, thus ignoring the national problem in 1914 and rejecting Lenin's ideas. The British Labour Party, which supported the British government, and the social democrats of the Austro-Hungarian Empire, who supported imperial war-mongering, shared the same attitude. The adherence of socialist groups to the most patriotic positions enraged Lenin, who mounted a masterful campaign to counter the reigning confusion of values. The first victims of his attack were Kautsky and the leaders of the Second International, who had, in Lenin's words, opened the door to "social-patriotism."[6]

In his "Manifesto on War" published on 1 November 1914, Lenin analyzed the positions and desired goals of the various belligerent nations, and declared that although it could not be determined which outcome would prove most favorable to the proletariat worldwide, it was clear that the defeat of the Russian Empire would promote the cause of the Russian proletariat and hasten the revolution.[7] His efforts to impose this idea at the Zimmerwald Conference in September 1915 were unflagging, but he was opposed by a majority who believed in "peace at any price" while being divided on the means to achieve it, whereas Lenin sought to make the war degenerate into a civil war.[8] He fought the compromise adopted at the conference and called on the European proletariat to fight for peace on the basis of the self-determination of peoples, without annexation or indemnification.[9] In place of "peace at any price," his watchword was "civil war."[10]

Lenin and the Self-Determination of Nations

As the debate on the war became more heated, the national question took on new urgency. Lenin's view remained consistent with the opinion he had expressed in 1914; now he accentuated even more the right of peoples to secede. In September 1914 he spoke of the need to dismantle the empire by detaching all its peripheral regions.[11] He hammered home the same theme in his analysis of how the Russian proletariat could recover its national pride,[12] the subject of an article published a short time later. Lenin's emphasis on national struggles, even as he predicted the potential victory of the proletariat, set him apart from his political peers and caused a serious rift in the Bolshevik party. For many, the possibility of a rapid social revolution rendered the idea of separate national states meaningless. Now more than ever, they argued, Marxists should not be concerned by national conflicts.

Lenin was at loggerheads with the Polish left. In November 1915, in a debate strangely reminiscent of his prewar arguments with Rosa Luxemburg, he faced a group dominated by Bukharin, Pyatakov, and Eugenia Bosch, who accused him of diverting the proletariat from its class interests and sapping its strength. Bukharin and Pyatakov believed there were only two possible scenarios for self-determination in Europe: territorial annexation in time of war, or the disintegration of an existing state. In either case, the proletariat was the victim. In the first scenario, self-determination would be confused with the defense of the state and serve counterrevolutionary interests; in the second, self-determination would turn the proletariat away from the class struggle and undermine proletarian unity, only to further advance bourgeois objectives.[13]

In fact, the left wing of the Bolshevik Party considered self-determination desirable only in colonial countries, where the revolt of the masses would cripple the country's ruling classes. Not a question of socialism or socialist aims, it was the bourgeoisie rather than the proletariat who would spearhead the struggle and indirectly help the working class by weakening their common enemy.[14] Radek published a series of articles in April 1916 defending this point of view.[15] His analysis of the world situation contained two observations: oppression of nationalist groups was increasing everywhere, and national-group interest did not, in the end, coincide with working-class interests. Thus socialist strategy, he argued, should be oriented accordingly to oppose all imperialist annexation policies and their corollary, policies of national oppression. But on no account should socialism support struggles for the establishment of new borders or for the recovery of former borders modified by imperialism. Radek, like Rosa Luxemburg, Bukharin, and Pyatakov, recognized that such reasoning was relevant in Europe but not in the colonies. The slogans he proposed were "liquidation of the national states in Europe" and "liquidation of the colonies elsewhere."[16] Did self-determination have a place in socialist society? Radek thought not. If capitalist society was by definition oppressive, socialism was the absence of oppression. Self-determination would have no meaning in the era of socialism because the classes responsible for national oppression would not exist. To link self-determination to socialism was as ludicrous as to link it to capitalism.

Radek's two propositions, that in a capitalist society minority-group interests could not be protected, and that in a socialist society they would cease to need protection, betray a profound misapprehension about the nature of both socialist and capitalist societies. In his substantive criticism of Lenin's positions he also declared, for tactical reasons, that the national issue, more than any other, divided the proletariat and diverted its energy from its fundamental goal.[17]

Lenin fought unceasingly for his views. The controversy of 1914–15 revealed that his main tactical concern was to avoid weakening the Bolshevik Party's position in relation to other parties in the Russian Empire. Thus, he did not suggest that the party's national program be eliminated; rather, that its demands for national groups should merely be limited to the oppressed minorities. This was not an innovative policy, and here Lenin was still following the approach laid out in his prewar writings, placing the national problem within the framework of the Russian Empire and making concrete proposals applicable to that framework. He radically modified his position in April 1916 with the publication of "The Socialist Revolution and the Right of Nations to Self-Determination,"[18] which was the first of his articles to examine the national issue on a world scale, and which identified three types of countries with respect to self-determination: the advanced capitalist countries of Western Europe and the United States, where progressive bourgeois national movements had come to an end; the two multinational empires of Eastern Europe, where national struggles were intensifying—"the tasks of the proletariat in these countries . . . cannot be carried out without championing the rights of nations to self-determination"; and, finally, the colonies and semi-colonial countries with their combined population of 1 billion, where bourgeois-democratic movements were just beginning. As Lenin stated, "Socialists must not only demand the unconditional and immediate liberation of the colonies . . . they must also . . . assist their uprising—or [support] revolutionary war, in the event of one."[19] By broadening the national problem and discussing it in global terms, Lenin gathered fuel against his colleagues and momentum for the future of his movement. His argument linking the national problem to imperialism and introducing the struggle for rights of oppressed people as a stage in the revolutionary movement was cogent and consistent. Furthermore, at a time when nationalist agitation was on the rise everywhere, not just within the Russian Empire, Lenin's worldwide program glossed over Russia's particular, historically backward character and placed his country at center-stage in the world revolutionary movement.

The Conditions for Self-Determination:
Who Represents the Nation?

Having defined socialist responsibilities with regard to national movements, Lenin next clarified his definition of the right to self-determination, that is to say, the conditions under which this right would be exercised, and its goals and limitations. The right to self-determination was not an empty formula. As far back as 1913 Lenin had discussed how it would be exercised in Russia and had proposed universal suffrage.[20] But he immediately added clauses limiting its scope, on the theory that the right to self-determination was not a universal right; in Russia it was applicable only in certain well-defined cases where there was geographical justification. Secession was possible only for the nationalities living along the periphery, not for those enclosed in the interior. And what future lay in store for the latter? A federalist solution was rejected, and separation considered physically impossible; the only acceptable form of autonomy was the official variety of the party program, which merely prohibited national discrimination and supported the right of the national cultures to develop in an internationalist domain. Thus the first problem with Lenin's proposal for self-determination was that it was only applicable to a limited number of national groups. No less important was the problem arising from the application of this principle. From his first mention of the issue in 1913, Lenin was extremely clear on this point.[21] In "each concrete case," the party was to decide whether the principle of self-determination applied. Lenin's designation of the party as supreme arbiter and conscience keeper of the masses was perhaps logical, but it contradicted other remarks he had made indicating that the desires of the nationalities should be the deciding factor. Citing the example of Norway, Lenin had written: "The decision came from the region in question. When Norway separated from Sweden, Norway alone decided."[22]

In Lenin's eyes, to disregard the right of the interested parties to decide their destiny freely was "trickery." But Lenin never clearly indicated the proper strategy to follow, for he never specified who *really* represented the rights of a small nation in deciding to be free. Was it some national-group institution, or the party that embodied the workers' will? Lenin highlighted the party's responsibility in deciding each case, "adopting the point of view of the interests of society's general development and the proletariat's class struggle for socialism."[23] Yet this guideline did not stipulate how the matter was to be decided: via regional organizations or by the entire party, a centralizing and unifying apparatus designed to solder together rather than to divide? What criteria would the party use? Whose will would be heeded: that of the proletariat, the nation as a whole, or the parties of the minority peoples—whichever parties they might be—that represented the national movements? In response to these thorny questions, Lenin either sidestepped the issue with pleasantries or reassured his interlocutors that the party could not be mistaken.

While the conditions justifying secession were vague, Lenin's preferences on the application of the principle of self-determination were abundantly clear. He always maintained that self-determination "was only an exception to our general premise of centralism," and that "nowhere is secession part of our plan."[24] Lenin rejected the idea of federation as incompatible with the interests of the proletariat at every historical stage—capitalism, dictatorship of the proletariat, socialism— and as contrary to the interests of socialists because it hampered economic integration and ran counter to democratic centralism. Al- though after the revolution a federalist solution in some very limited cases might be preferable to other alternatives that perpetuated the op- pression of peoples,[25] Lenin believed that the best solution to the or- ganization of the state was unity based on democratic centralism.

His position was strengthened by the fact that the two options for na- tions that he proposed, separation or unity, were unequal in nature and duration. The right to secede, even if obtained by perfectly legal means, could always be revoked. In any event, the option to secede would be exercised by the bourgeoisie or by a proletariat with a weak class con- sciousness. But a proletariat in a position of strength would naturally decide the question of self-determination in terms of its class interests and join forces with the proletarian state from which it was separated. Yet, any union forged in the course of a revolution would be irrevoca- ble, because the choice would have been made at a time when class in- terests predominated. How, then, could such a union be torn asunder?

Correctly exercised, self-determination would lead to a large, cen- tralized state. In the capitalist phase a large state was preferable, perhaps even indispensable, to the proletarian revolution.[26] After the revolution a national state would be necessary. All peoples comprising such a state would join freely and be assimilated, and it would become "a centralized, monolingual state."[27] The nationalist tendencies of non- Russian social democrats exasperated Lenin. His reply to the Ukrain- ian Lev Yurkevich, who wanted to "develop national culture among the Ukrainian masses," was "Assimilation is progress."[28] Assimilation was Lenin's solution to all national problems and, above all, to the most complex one—the Jewish problem. The final phase of national evolu- tion and one of the principal goals of socialism[29] was not only the economic but also the political and ethnic fusion of all nations.[30] Still, Lenin warned, it was a slow, complex process, and national minorities could not be coerced, nor could their will be disregarded. Only recogni- tion of their rights would permit them to transcend minority conscious- ness.

In sum, Lenin's insistence on the national issue certainly seems to have been a tactical choice based on his analysis of the conditions most propitious for the development of the Russian revolution, and despite criticism from his opponents on the left, his choice condemned the na- tional minorities to rapid dissolution. From 1917 on, his theory of self-determination, both as a weapon in the struggle for the destruction of the empire and as a solution to the aspirations of minority peoples, was put to the test of the facts. The facts bore out the accuracy of Lenin's tactical calculations but at the same time shed light on the contradictions inherent in his theory, which he was compelled to revise in the face of concrete events.

CHAPTER 5

The Self-Determination
of Nations versus the
Self-Determination of
the Proletariat

From Theory to Practice

For many long years Lenin had grappled with the issues without being able to confirm his hypotheses. The reality of revolution in 1917 made him deal daily, and not in thought alone, with the national problem.

The toppling of the monarchy in February 1917 infused the people of every social strata and nationality in Russia with high hopes. As revolution spread throughout the territory of the old empire, minority peoples expected the Provisional Government to decree their emancipation. But the Petrograd Soviet merely declared that it favored national cultural autonomy, an idea by then surpassed by the events and the inflamed passions of the time. The February leaders, paralyzed by the war—general dislocation throughout Russia did not help the war effort—adopted the legalistic approach of holding all major problems in abeyance until a constituent assembly could be elected. Such a "wait and see" attitude first disappointed and then exasperated Russia's minority peoples. During the summer the nations began to turn away from the revolution, which had not taken the initiative in responding to their aspirations, and embarked on a solitary venture that at times out-

distanced the revolution and at times tried to keep Russia's great up-
heavals at arm's length. The failure of the Provisional Government to
address the national question was obvious and all the more stark because the political parties now in power were the same ones that in the
past had incorporated federalism into their programs.

Aware of the confusion reigning among the national minorities,
Lenin imposed his theses on the party for the first time and thus succeeded in gaining the support of the national minorities against the
Provisional Government. Previously, he alone had advocated the right
to secede. In April, at the Party's Seventh Congress, the issue took on
larger proportions. Stalin, the *rapporteur* on the national question, defended the right to secede but qualified it by stating that the party
should recognize the right of nationality groups to secede from Russia.
He added: "The right of nations to separation should not be confused
with the idea that the nations must *inevitably* become separate. . . . For
our part, we have the duty of making our position known, for or
against the right to separation, taking first into account the interests of
the proletariat and of the proletarian revolution." "As far as I am concerned," Stalin declared, "I would, for example, oppose the secession
of Transcaucasia because of the situation prevailing in Transcaucasia
and Russia, and because of certain facts of the proletarian struggle."

Pyatakov and Dzerzhinsky vigorously opposed Stalin's view, on the
grounds that separation only served the interests of the bourgeoisie,
who would use it to crush the revolution. Lenin retorted that a refusal
to recognize the right of separation would cause the Bolsheviks to perpetuate Great Russian chauvinism. In the end, the party acceded to this
argument and by a vote of 56 to 16, with 8 abstentions, adopted Stalin's
theses, which contained four points: the right to secede; extensive regional autonomy for nationality groups that did not secede from Russia; laws to guarantee minority rights; and party unity.

The Bolsheviks were careful, no doubt, to leave some questions unde-
cided. When would self-determination begin, after a peace settlement,
or as soon as the nations were given the power to decide? And, above all,
to which nations would the right of self-determination apply? Despite
their prudent silence on these matters, the Bolsheviks' endorsement of
Lenin's ideas signaled a significant change in Russian politics.

After the takeover in October, the Bolsheviks came into direct contact
with the national problem. Until then the issue, subject of many debates, had been used to weaken their adversaries decisively and to
seize power—although, as Sukhanov has shown, rather than seize
power, the Bolsheviks actually stepped into a power vacuum. Back in

April, the Bolshevik Party had endorsed the right of peoples to secede because it had recognized the explosive potential of the issue. But they modified none of their previous ideas, and their internationalist orientation remained the same. The move had been a tactical concession to the demands of the moment; it committed them only nominally, for in April they were still far from holding the reins of power.

In October 1917, everything changed: now the Bolsheviks were in charge and had to make decisions. The stances taken months before molded to a significant degree the situation that developed. The change was brutal. In a matter of months Russia experienced the end of an empire and two revolutions. After years of stagnation and hesitation, history was on the run, and the Provisional Government was not able to keep pace. Like the adversaries they replaced, the Bolsheviks were forced abruptly to face facts. They had to revise the ideas, hopes, and promises previously made at a distance and to determine whether the theories elaborated in the tranquillity of libraries and on the shores of Lake Leman bore any relation whatsoever to Russian reality in October 1917. How were they to reconcile the belief, nestled in every Bolshevik's heart, that a proletarian revolution would surpass and erase all national borders, with their earlier promise to national minorities that the proletarian revolution would work to the benefit of their emancipation? Once the revolution triumphed, how were they to reconcile an intangible principle of Marxism with their earlier tactical positions? In October 1917, the Bolsheviks could not dissociate their ideology (a utopian ideology, as Mannheim defines it) from their promises, for they owed their existence to both.

The history of revolutions frequently illustrates that when revolutionaries' ideas triumph, theoreticians are replaced by men of action, who then become statesmen. The Bolsheviks had been seasoned theoreticians when, overnight, they were transformed into statesmen, and over time they endured as such. But in order to do so, they had to strike a balance between ideology and concessions to reality.

War, the "midwife of revolutions," unleashed an explosion of national sentiment with implications that even Lenin had not foreseen. The internationalization of national issues not only affected the status of the empire but also, from 1917 on, burdened the relations between the Bolsheviks and the national minorities. Once the national groups seeking self-determination could appeal to foreign states to support them, it was no longer a question of whether a particular social class or the society at large ought to demand self-determination. The interest of foreign powers in Russia's national minorities—whose yearning for emancipation had found an echo everywhere, even as far away as America—only strengthened their resolve and lent it a more radical orientation.

The self-determination proposed by Lenin, who had no model to follow, caused the complete territorial disintegration of the empire. Cut off from territories of economic and strategic importance and subject to a veritable state of siege, the Bolsheviks' domain was rolled back to exclusively Russian areas.

Watching the industrialized countries of Europe in the hope that they, too, would blaze up in the revolutionary fire, Lenin nonetheless recognized the need to protect Bolshevik territory. The relations between the Bolshevik state and the emancipated national minorities could be examined later; otherwise, the state, while revolution raged, would risk being overwhelmed by minority demands. In the early years of power, the Bolsheviks were becoming fully familiar with a revolutionary process that baffled all attempted predictions. Because a European revolution did not follow, it became necessary to establish a confident and stable place of origin from which the waves of revolution would spread and swell. A small Soviet state doing battle with many simultaneous demands and hostilities was certainly not desirable.

The steady rise of nationalist feelings and their entry into international politics against the Bolshevik state required a response from Lenin and his comrades that they were not prepared to make. Given that the demand for self-determination was at once a domestic and an international problem, what decisions had to be made? It is easy for the historian who decodes the sequence of events after the fact to find in them a clear pattern, the suggestion of a consistent policy. But in history we must try honestly to fathom the actors' intentions. Were the Bolsheviks' actions inspired by ideas, by their previous analysis? Was their policy shaped by reality? Did they maintain control over the national problem? Or, swept along by events, did they try to resolve the day-to-day problems and limit the damage?

This is not the place to rewrite the history of Russia's national disintegration, which Richard Pipes has already done in peerless fashion.[1] Instead we will take up our story of Lenin, now surrounded by an empire in ruins.

"Protected" Peoples and Self-Determination

By February 1917, the two national groups capable of demanding full independence had done so. Due to their past, their social structure, and their political experience, the situation of the Poles and the Finns even under the empire, had been unlike those of other national minorities. Lenin was well aware of this, but hoped that in time of revolution, class solidarity would prove stronger than centrifugal tendencies.[2]

Polish independence was gained by October 1917.[3] The world war and the German occupation had resolved the Polish problem in the absence of any initiative by the Russians. To some extent, all those in positions of responsibility after the fall of the Russian Empire—from the Provisional Government to Lenin—accepted this solution because the Polish question had been on the international agenda for more than half a century. In this regard Lenin demonstrated his ability to adapt to reality. He admitted that Polish independence was the outcome of German policy. But in the summer of 1918, seeking to regain the initiative, he proclaimed that Bolshevik desires for the self-determination of peoples and the self-determination of Poland were closely linked.[4]

The Finns demonstrated just as great a desire for independence, but the Bolsheviks were reluctant to grant them the right to secede. In the fall of 1917, Finland seemed to be in a revolutionary stage, as Lenin defined it. A well-organized social-democratic party, supported by the Russian army stationed in Finnish territory, seemed capable of channeling the desire for self-determination into a decision to unite with Russia, not separate from it. If separation were to be permitted, the Finnish bourgeoisie would have an advantage over the existing proletariat. The Bolsheviks in this case were divided over what course to follow. In response to the Finnish government's demand for separation, the *Sovnarkom* (Council of People's Commissars, presided over by Lenin) issued a decree on 18 December 1917[5] recognizing the existence of the independent state of Finland, a procedure that had been skirted in the case of Poland. But Stalin intervened in the debate held by the Central Executive Committee (VCIK), the body charged with issuing the decree, to say that political recognition of this type was an aberration. Faced with a choice between bourgeois and proletarian aspirations, he said, the Soviet state was favoring the former. For this reason, shortly after recognizing Finland's independence, the Bolsheviks began to foment another kind of self-determination, that of the working class. On 15 January 1918, a council of people's representatives, with the help of the Red Army, which was still stationed there, seized power in Helsinki. The revolutionary government, led by Kullervo Manner, ex-President of SEIM, comprised fourteen ministers, including Edvard Gilling at the ministry of finance, Eero Hayjatainen at the war ministry, Otto Kuusinen at education, and Irjo Sirola at foreign affairs.

The government proclaimed the Socialist Workers' Republic of Finland and on 1 March 1918 signed a friendship treaty with the Soviet state.[6] The Soviets enthusiastically greeted the revolution in Finland as a link in the chain of revolutions expected to be forged to the west of Russia. On the eve of the "Helsinki Coup," Lenin declared to a congress of railway workers, "A revolution is about to break out in Finland."[7] And some days later, before the Third All-Russian Congress of Soviets, he declared: "A short time ago, the bourgeois press was constantly howling that we are destroying the Russian state, that we do not know how to govern, and for this reason all the nationality groups— Finland, the Ukraine, and so on—want to separate from us. We kept quiet, convinced that our principles and acts would demonstrate better than words our true goals and hopes. We were right, our ideas have triumphed in Finland."[8]

The Bolsheviks played a clear role in the revolution in Finland. Lenin and Trotsky, his foreign affairs commissioner, often reiterated their interest in a new model of proletarian power.[9] The Mannerheim government, recognized by Russia in the 18 December decree, reacted to the Bolshevik action by appealing to Germany for help. A few weeks later, with German intervention, the Socialist Workers' Republic of Finland was abolished, and its leaders were in exile in Moscow.

The failure of the revolution in Finland was the first in a series that included Germany (Berlin and Bavaria), Hungary, and Austria. The Finnish revolution, the first of five foreign revolutions supported by Russia between 1918 and 1920, collapsed for both domestic and international reasons. German intervention was decisive in breaking up the revolutionary government and then reestablishing the authority of Mannerheim's government, but the weakness and inconsistency of Finnish socialists also played a part. The Communist Party of Finland was not founded until August 1918, after the Communists' hopes for regaining power had been dashed. The Helsinki revolutionaries had been social democrats who believed in legality, democracy, and parliamentary formalism; they proved incapable of fighting their compatriots who were succored by foreign aid.

The case of Finland illustrates the Bolsheviks' confusion at the time. In a matter of weeks they first reluctantly accepted self-determination, then encouraged a revolution challenging that self-determination, and finally recognized the failure of the revolution and the misguided moves that had led to it.[10] Finland gained its independence not through Lenin's belief in his own principles, which he did not hesitate to betray, but thanks to German military might. This experience indelibly marked the two countries' future relations and served as a lesson to other peoples seeking self-determination: to be successful they had to appeal for support to a third state.

Further confirmation of the need for outside support can be seen in the relations between the Bolsheviks and the Baltic countries, even though the three Baltic states won their independence only after long detours. In Estonia and Latvia, the Soviet governments of October 1917 were swept out of power by the German military advance. Then, after the German defeat in November 1918, national governments were established. In Lithuania, a pro-German national government was created in February 1918; when the Germans departed, it was unclear who would retain power. The Bolsheviks then shifted from the idea of national self-determination to the idea of self-determination for workers only, which had been partially experienced in Finland some months earlier. In a long article published by *Pravda*,[11] Stalin favored this approach, and Bolshevik policy reflected this view. In Estonia, too, after German troops withdrew, a Soviet Republic called "The Commune of the Workers of Estland" was established. It was recognized on 7 December 1918[12] by the RSFSR (Russian Socialist Federal Soviet Republic), and the *Sovnarkom* decided to aid it militarily and financially.[13] In Latvia, a government of workers' deputies, landless peasants, and *strel'tsy* headed by Stuchka, was formed on 4 December 1918, and the republic's independence was declared[14]; as occurred with the Commune of Estland, this government was recognized and assisted by Russia.[15]

However, in all these cases, the Soviet governments were to be ephemeral due to British pressure. Britain, whose fleet was present in the Baltic, supported the reestablishment of national bourgeois governments in Estonia and Latvia. Civil war prevented the Bolsheviks from intervening because Yudenich was using the Baltic states as his base of operations. When the Bolsheviks finally emerged victorious, both states retained their independence. To foment new revolutions there or to integrate the republics into Russia by force would have been problematic because Britain would have opposed such moves. Moreover, in these areas the Bolsheviks could not claim that the RSFSR's security was threatened. Yudenich's Great Russian program provoked such hostility in these two states that, clearly, no danger was pressing on the Soviet state from the shores of the Baltic. Finally, the Soviet state was beginning to think about foreign trade.[16] If necessary, the cities of Riga and Tallinn could serve as intermediaries between the still-isolated RSFSR and the capitalist powers.

Most important, one must consider that when the RSFSR recognized the sovereignty of the Baltic states and their borders through the peace treaties of February and August 1920,[17] Lenin believed that a new revolutionary upsurge was imminent. Discouraged by the failures that he had witnessed in Hungary and Germany in 1919, he projected that a new revolutionary vigor would develop within the next year. Against the advice of many of his colleagues[18] and though he had opposed the Berlin adventure, Lenin decided that the war in Poland should be transformed into a revolutionary war. Expecting a revolutionary uprising throughout Europe,[19] he did not want to divert forces to reconquer the Baltic states, whose bourgeois regimes were at any rate fated to be short-lived.

To an even greater degree than that of Estonia and Latvia, Lithuania's destiny hinged on the international situation. The national government that had been supported by the Germans fell when Germany lost the war; it was replaced by a provisional revolutionary government headed by Mitskevich-Kapsukas,[20] recognized by the RSFSR on 22 December 1918.[21] In February 1919, the Union of Lithuania and Byelorussia was proclaimed. A common government was established in Vilnius on 27 February.[22] The union made sense in light of the federalist links then existing between the RSFSR and Byelorussia. Thus, although Lithuania was not recognized, it entered into an extremely close alliance with the RSFSR in early 1919, just as the two other Baltic states had done. Once again, exterior events—the Russo-Polish war— interfered with the *rapprochement*. When the Polish troops took Vilnius, the Soviet Republic of Lithuania-Byelorussia ceased to exist. And when the Polish army retreated, Lithuania, which was not in favor of reincorporation into the Soviet orbit, asserted its right to independence,[23] which the RSFSR recognized in the peace treaty of July 1920.

By 1920, Poland, Finland, and the Baltic states were sovereign states whose independence was not contested by the Soviet state until international conditions enabled them to challenge the treaties and agreements of that era. With the exception of Poland, which managed from the start to keep Bolshevik influence at bay, the other states gained rather than conquered their independence. Through steady international pressure, the German occupation, the Polish war, and British policy forced the Bolsheviks to let these countries interpret self-determination in their own way. Depending on the circumstances, the Bolsheviks themselves interpreted it differently, declaring that self-determination could be decided by nations when they were sufficiently strong; or when, supported by foreign forces, they could impose their desired status; or when, according to the will of the workers, it appeared possible to influence the domestic policy of a national state and support a revolutionary government.

Above all, they hoped that a European revolution, set off by the Bolshevik offensive in Poland, would render the acquisition of independence ineffectual. In August 1920, after failing to sow revolution in Poland, the time came for the Soviets to withdraw, and Lenin reassessed the situation in international terms. A *modus vivendi* had to be found in the west; Soviet borders had to be secure, trade negotiations initiated. To achieve these ends, it was necessary that capitalist countries not be alarmed by a Soviet policy of territorial reconquest. Furthermore, Lenin hoped that self-determination—a status recognized more than granted—would create, between the RSFSR and the capitalist world, buffer-zones of states well-disposed toward the Soviet state, zones that would act as protective armor for the revolution.

The self-determination proclaimed by Lenin was thus practicable on Russia's western borders because international conditions demanded as much. For as long as revolution in Europe was delayed, the powers of the European continent supported any nations desirous of independence in the hope that they would serve as protective armor against the revolution.

Ephemeral Self-Determination

The Bolsheviks often placed the Ukraine and Finland in the same category. Prior to 1917, Lenin had recognized their right to independence.[24] But by January 1918 he saw things differently: "Our ideas are now triumphing in Finland and the Ukraine."[25] A closer look will reveal that the two places were lumped together only for a time, and that the confusing situation in the Ukraine furthered the Bolsheviks' policy changes.

On 19 November 1917 the Ukraine's *Rada*, in what appeared to be a victory for the Ukrainian intelligentsia's federalist ideas developed at the turn of the century, established a republic without availing itself of the right to separation.[26] But a breach began to open between Ukrainian political forces. Frightened by the chaos in Russia, the *Rada* proclaimed independence on 28 January 1918.[27] Earlier, the First Congress of Ukrainian Soviets, which had met on 12 December 1917, had denounced the petty bourgeois tendencies of the *Rada* and had claimed to represent the Soviet Republic of the Ukraine, "an integral part of the Federated Republic of Russia."[28] In a telegram to the *Sovnarkom*, this Ukrainian government, established in Kharkov, called itself "the identity of the interests of the Ukrainian and Russian peoples."[29] It imposed its authority in the main cities of the Ukraine, thereby limiting the *Rada's* sphere of influence. Thus, the self-determination of the working classes, assisted, to be sure, by the Bolshevik troops, seemed to have quickly prevailed over strictly nationalist aspirations. Lenin's optimism during this period is understandable. Even so, the international situation was to upset relations between Petrograd and the Ukrainians. Unable to resist Bolshevik pressure, the *Rada's* leaders appealed to the Central Powers. In Brest-Litovsk, where Trotsky was discussing peace conditions, representatives of the *Rada* claimed the right to negotiate separately and on 9 February 1918 reached a separate peace. The Ukrainian Republic, established by the *Rada* in November 1917, was recognized by the Central Powers.[30] But at the same time the Red Army took Kiev, the seat of the *Rada* government, which fled to Zhitomir. In fact, the Ukrainian Republic ceased to exist. Once again a rupture among the spokesmen in Brest-Litovsk altered the situation. German troops moved into the Ukraine, took Kiev, and put an end to the Soviet Ukrainian government. After years of vacillation, Germany declared it was in favor of Ukrainian separatism, which would deprive Russia of rich resources and open the Ukraine to German penetration.[31] The Treaty of Brest-Litovsk committed Russia to recognize Ukrainian independence. Here again, the meaning of self-determination was different from what it had been elsewhere.

But Germany's desire to dominate in the Ukraine became evident immediately. The Germans replaced the *Rada*, which had defended national interests, with a government of their own creation. They supported the hetman Skoropadsky, who abolished all the social reforms of the revolutionary period.[32] The Ukrainians were hostile to a conservative power that accepted foreign domination. The German defeat and the fall of the hetman after the German troops decamped did not simplify Ukrainian political life, but rather further complicated it by multiplying centers of authority.

A national republic with a Directorate whose party leader was Petliura and whose president was Vinnichenko was established in Kiev. To protect Ukrainian independence, the Directorate appealed, without great success, to the French forces in Odessa.[33] The national republic managed to survive until the end of the civil war; a "Western State of

Ukraine" existed in Galicia until the collapse of the Central Powers; it was then incorporated into the Ukrainian Republic. Until that time, the Ukraine lived through two bloody years. The French army, General Denikin's White army, the Red Army, and Makhno's anarchist movement all stripped local governments of their authority. In this chaotic situation, the Soviet state was competing with other states. What action could the Bolsheviks take, and to what end?

The steps taken reflected the disorder reigning in the Ukraine. Even to talk of "Bolshevik policy" is a misnomer because diverse points of view were violently opposed to one another. Lenin at first advocated two conflicting forms of self-determination and then, after the Ukraine was occupied by German troops, became exclusively concerned with the security of the Soviet state. In 1918 the Ukraine was the point of assembly for all the adversaries of the Bolshevik regime. As it was no longer feasible for Bolsheviks to spread revolutionary ideas there, it was preferable to neutralize those in power, even a figure like Skoropadsky. For this reason Lenin sent Rakovsky to establish contact with the hetman and negotiate a peace treaty.[34]

But Lenin's desire to reach an accord in the Ukraine conflicted with the insurrectional policy being carried out by Ukrainian communist organizations of which Pyatakov, founder of the first Soviet Republic of the Ukraine, was the principal architect. Here the inherent contradictions of Bolshevik policies became evident. One was a policy of self-determination; the other, of party organization. Hostile to the self-determination desired by Lenin—and motivated by a desire for efficiency rather than by nationalism—Pyatakov advocated an autonomous organization of Ukrainian communists, on the theory that an autonomous party would be better equipped to oppose the German occupation and eliminate the Skoropadsky government. Pyatakov was convinced that the Bolshevik Party was too far away and too preoccupied with Russian problems to stop the Ukrainian communists.[35] However, his ideas were rejected not only in Russia by Lenin but more fiercely in the Ukraine by a communist group in Ekaterinoslav that insisted that the Soviet state's economic viability depended on large industrial centers in the Ukraine such as Kharkov, Ekaterinoslav, Krivorog, and the Donbass, and that these could not be surrendered to Ukrainian separatism. In the name of Russian and Ukrainian working-class unity, this group, made up of natives of regions with an industrial proletariat, rejected the ideas of separation and of an independent party.[36]

The two factions clashed in April 1918 at the constituent congress of the Ukrainian party in Taganrog. Pyatakov proposed the creation of an independent party; there was a counterproposal to form a Ukrainian section of the "Russian Bolshevik Party." A compromise solution prevailed: Skrypnik added the word "Bolshevik" to the Ukrainian Communist Party.[37] Thus the adherents of an independent organization and those favoring attachment to the Bolshevik Party were reconciled.

Lenin could not tolerate such a controversy: he feared German reprisals against the Soviet Union in response to the actions of the Pyatakov group. In the name of a "Soviet Government of the Ukraine," Pyatakov had called Ukrainians to general insurrection, and his followers were organizing raids in the occupied territories of the buffer-zone between the Russian and the German forces. More than anywhere else, the situation in the Ukraine clearly illustrated how the interests of independent nations, or of the proletariat that stood to benefit by independence, could conflict with the interests of the Soviet state. In the summer of 1918 Lenin had no means of imposing his will on the Ukrainian communists, and this convinced him more than ever of the need to centralize communist organizations. A few months later, his theory was proved right, for the Ukrainian uprising organized in August by Pyatakov and his friends met with disastrous results.[38]

At the Ukrainian Communist Party Congress in Moscow in October 1918, Lenin established the direction and tactics that the party was to follow. Stalin was placed on the Central Committee of the Ukrainian Communist Party as the liaison with the Bolshevik Party.[39] Pyatakov and his friends retained their posts but had to accept their subordination. Lenin succeeded in substituting for the policy of popular uprising a prudent policy of working-class agitation, and with regard to other matters considered it best to wait for the occupation to end.

With the defeat of the Central Powers, the Treaty of Brest-Litovsk became void and Russia could begin to redefine its relation to the Ukraine. Once again, Bolshevik policy varied depending on where it was to be carried out. The government formed by Pyatakov in Kursk distributed land to the peasants and to nationalized businesses.[40] A Soviet was formed in Kharkov.[41] Meanwhile, the Red Army was marching into the Ukraine. The Directorate (which was re-formed when the German troops withdrew) denounced Pyatakov's action and that of the Red Army, which was seen as a return to tsarist imperialism,[42] and declared war on Russia. This, however, did not stop the Red Army. The Soviet Republic of the Ukraine was reestablished under Rakovsky,[43] who, unlike Pyatakov, was prepared to follow Lenin's policy.

Throughout these turbulent years, the Ukraine still kept its independent status, but independence was held in check by Bolshevik authority over the Ukrainian party and by Russia's economic needs. At the Second Congress of the Ukrainian Communist Party, Lenin clearly affirmed the subordination of the Ukrainian party to the Bolshevik Party. In addition, to preclude the appearance of autonomist tendencies, he placed his followers in leadership positions in the organizations of the Ukrainian party. However, these efforts did not suffice to ensure a consistent or continuous policy. The difference between Russian and Ukrainian jurisdiction was not defined, nor was the role of parties in the two states made clear. As a result, Russian-Ukrainian clashes occurred repeatedly. Lenin's pressure on the Ukraine continued and resulted in rancor and considerable confusion.

The problem of overlapping authority was overshadowed by Russia's economic situation, which lay at the heart of the Russian-Ukrainian conflicts. When Rakovsky rose to power, the first task Lenin entrusted to him was to "feed the famished North." Given Russia's intolerable economic situation in 1919, it was imperative to control the Ukraine's rich agricultural resources. Some months later, Rakovsky wrote, "We entered the Ukraine when Soviet Russia was experiencing an exceedingly serious production crisis; we approached the Ukraine with the idea of exploiting it to the maximum to ease the crisis."[44]

Thus, in 1919 Lenin followed a two-tiered policy. Ukrainian independence was restored because he believed that Russia had to respect nationalist aspirations or pay the price in turmoil. At the Eighth Congress of the Russian Communist Party he doggedly opposed Bukharin and Pyatakov, who denied the need for self-determination on the grounds that it should apply only to the proletariat. Lenin's arguments against Pyatakov shed light on the contradictions of his own policy. Lenin stated: "When Comrade Pyatakov says that the Ukrainian communists bow to the directives of the Russian Communist Party, I don't understand the tone in which he says it—regretfully? I don't suspect him of such. But the sense of his speech was, Why have self-determination when there is an admirable Central Committee in Moscow?"[45] Lenin also conceded to Pyatakov that "he was a thousand times correct to say that unity is indispensable to us."[46] The resolutions of the Eighth Congress stated that the party had to be unified, that democratic centralism took precedence over national realities, and that "the Ukrainian central committees . . . are totally subordinate to the Central Committee of the Russian Communist Party."[47]

While concerned with organizational unity, Russia had pressing economic needs, which explains its permanent interventionism in the Ukraine. Lenin always insisted on his authority to decide defense matters, to give orders in the name of the party and the *Sovnarkom*. But the Ukrainian leaders whom he himself had appointed were opposed to this, claiming autonomy of action and quoting Lenin's own dictum that Russia must respect the sovereignty of states. Until 1920, Lenin held fast to the principle of sovereignty, defending it against those who tried to show him its drawbacks and the futility of applying it. Yet, at the same time, he constantly went against it in practice, driven by material and military exigencies. Thus, on 22 May 1919, he wired Trotsky that in order to take wheat away from the Ukrainians and resolve military problems, "we must send a trustworthy Cheka battalion, several hundred Baltic sailors interested in obtaining wheat and coal, a detachment of workers from Moscow or Ivanovo-Voznesensk, and dozens of serious propagandists."[48]

Lenin's centralist practices acquired a new dimension and a certain legitimacy in texts that heralded the birth of a unique organ in defense of the RSFSR, the Ukraine, the Baltic states, and Byelorussia. The Central Committee of the party decided that all army-related problems (Article 1) and all transportation-related problems (Article 2) would be placed under the sole authority of the appropriate bodies of the RSFSR.[49] The Central Executive Committee (VCIK) passed a resolution on 1 June 1919,[50] likewise providing for "the independence and capacity for self-determination of the toiling masses" and outlining unification measures.

The VCIK resolution, formulated in vaguer terms than the Central Committee's decision, paved the way for practices that took no account of legal independent status. In the civil-war period, because the urgency of the situation demanded the extreme centralization of decision making, Lenin and Trotsky treated the Ukrainian political and military organizations as mere couriers; Lenin had always said that after Denikin's defeat the Ukrainians themselves would determine their relationship to Russia; in fact, after Denikin's fall Moscow refused to consider reviewing the unification measures, restoring the independence of various unified commissionerships (war and labor), or reconstituting the Ukrainian army. Moscow's desire to maintain its centralized authority was unmistakable when, in March 1920, the Central Committee of the Russian Communist Party judged the recently elected Central Committee in the Ukraine to be anti-Russian and, without deliberation or consultation, proclaimed its dissolution.

Soviet authority was reestablished in 1920 under deplorable conditions. Ukrainians retained the indelible memory of being subjected to economic exploitation and constant intervention from Moscow.

Self-determination in the Ukraine, as elsewhere, was exercised fully only when foreign pressure reinforced nationalist aspirations. The rights of self-determination were not restored in 1920, when Russia embarked on the path of international normalization. For having depended on vanquished Germany, far-away France, and Poland for support when Russia was gathering strength, the Ukraine lost the independence it appeared to have acquired in Brest-Litovsk.

The route of Byelorussia's political evolution in the years 1917 to 1920 was very similar to that of the Ukraine. However, the main difference was that in 1917 a true Byelorussian nation did not exist. Ethnographic maps attest to the fact that in the nineteenth century it would have been difficult, if not impossible, to identify a Byelorussian nation because of the great number of Poles, Lithuanians, and Jews who lived among the Byelorussians.[51]

To be sure, some intellectuals after 1905 affirmed the existence of a nation of western Russia (*Zapadnaia Rossiia*) distinct from Russia and Poland. But in 1917 those who twenty years earlier had appeared in the census as Byelorussians were still speaking some twenty different dialects, classified by linguists as belonging to four main groups,[52] each as different from the others as it was from Russian, Polish, or Ukrainian.

Byelorussian national sentiment, where it existed prior to 1917, was the creation of a small group of intellectuals who dreamed of a partially mythical national past in that they sought to restore a culture and language that had not truly existed. Moreover, where Byelorussian culture was promoted, it was not contrasted—as it was in the Ukraine— with Russian culture, but primarily with Jewish and Polish culture.

As had occurred in the Ukraine, from the time of Russian revolution to the winter of 1918, a Soviet government was established in Byelorussia, in Minsk. After the German advance put an end to Soviet rule, the *Hromada*, the only national party, which had been resoundingly defeated in the elections for the Constituent Assembly, called a national congress in Minsk. There it proclaimed the independence of Byelorussia and depended on German troops for protection. However, the Germans regarded Byelorussian separatism as insignificant, and if they conceded some administrative authority to the phantom government of Byelorussia, it was because they needed to use it as a go-between. Later the German troops were recalled, and the question of Byelorussia's future was left open.

Byelorussian Bolsheviks exiled in Russia during the German occupation had advocated union with—not separation from—Russia.[53] When they returned to Minsk, they realized that the idea of nationhood had not caught on with the masses, but had found resonance among those in managerial positions and among a small group of urbanized

Byelorussians. These sectors believed that though denuded of real authority, the ephemeral state had been a giant step forward. It had enabled Byelorussia to have relations with other states, above all with the RSFSR, as a state in its own right, rather than as a nonstate in a dialogue of unequals with a nation-state. Meanwhile, the Byelorussian Polophiles—or, more simply, the Poles—preferred that Byelorussia become integrated into Poland rather than into Russia,[54] and they invoked Pilsudski's Lithuanian-Byelorussian origin. The Byelorussian Bolsheviks, in their desire to short-circuit both separatism and the orientation toward Poland, argued that Byelorussia should be granted status as a nation, even if the masses were utterly indifferent. They easily succeeded in convincing the Bolsheviks in Moscow to respect the wishes of what in fact was a rather meager elite.

On 31 January 1919[55] the Soviet Republic of Byelorussia was born with Moscow's blessings. To be sure, its sovereignty was limited by the immediate establishment of "close [federative links] in the economic and political spheres with its big brother, the Russian state."[56]

The First Congress of the Soviets of Byelorussia, convened in Minsk on 2 and 3 February 1919, approved a hastily written constitution[57] and elected a Central Executive Committee with a Bolshevik majority (45 members), as well as two Bund representatives, two members of *Poale Zion*, and a Menshevik. Bolsheviks had been predominant in Byelorussia from October 1917, when they had obtained 60 percent of the vote in the Constituent Assembly elections, in contrast to just 25 percent in the country as a whole. Yet, in 1919, when the population was more conscious of what united them to Russia than of what conspired to keep them apart, why did the Bolsheviks prefer to make Byelorussia an independent republic, rather than incorporate it without further ado into Russia?

The Bolshevik attitude can be explained both by their ignorance of the realities and by the fact that independence had certain general political advantages. In 1919 the Bolsheviks were obsessed by the Ukraine— they tended to generalize the case there and apply it elsewhere. Lenin was obliged to react quickly to a new situation: he wanted to blunt separatist and Polish tendencies by surpassing the demands of the moment. Rather than resulting from clear policy, Byelorussian independence was probably decided in a hasty and uninformed manner. Still, there were distinct advantages to this decision. The Union of Byelorussia and Lithuania, approved in early February 1919 by the Congress of Soviets of both republics,[58] included independently minded Lithuania in a state in which the majority of the population was favorable to Russia. This binational state served Russian interests. On 31 May, the dual Republic's Defense Council (created on 19 April and made up of Mitskevich-Kapsukas, Unshlikht, and Kalmanovich) declared the military union of all Soviet Republics.[59] Thus, shrewdly proclaimed by two independent nations, the idea of union seemed to originate not from Russia but from nations seeking Russia's protection. It mattered little that when the announcement was made only independent Byelorussia was still in existence (as the war with Poland, which occupied Vilna, had detached Lithuania), in an area that had always regarded the Russian state as its big brother.

This episode exemplifies how useful Byelorussian independence was to Russia. Placed by its sovereign status in the same category as other republics, it became the agent of a *rapprochement* with Russia, which no other republic initiated; and, if the war with Poland had not occurred, Lithuania (whose independence had been dissolved, for the benefit of unity) would have been cut off from British protection, which was supporting national aspirations in two other Baltic nations. The armistice in October 1920, which was followed by the Riga Treaty, ended the Russo-Polish war and reduced Byelorussia to its original territory. The Second Congress of the Soviets of Byelorussia met in Minsk between 14 and 20 December 1920 to finish drafting the constitution of 1918,[60] thus closing the parenthesis of Byelorussia's union with Lithuania.

Despite this, Byelorussia retained its independence, even while deferring international jurisdiction to Russia. The Congress of Soviets decided that as big brother it behooved them to represent Byelorussia in negotiations with Poland, to resolve any border problems, and to sign all treaties pertinent thereto. It was a tall order, the eventual outcome of which was the general return of authority to Russia.

Byelorussia's self-determination was accomplished in an international context fairly similar to the one that had existed in the Ukraine and the Baltic states, but national sentiment in Byelorussia was not supported by any outside power, nor was it expressed more than sporadically by the *Hromada*. It was the Bolsheviks who wanted independence, which was only halfheartedly demanded by the Byelorussians—and in this case it was merely a passing phase—to illustrate "internationalism."

Finally, the evolution of the three states of the Caucasus—Georgia, Armenia, and Azerbaijan—was also closely influenced by international politics. When the Bolsheviks seized power, the situation in the Caucasus was complicated by the conflicts between neighboring regions and by the presence of Turkey, a keenly felt danger on the borders of Georgia and Armenia. Religion, culture, economic interests, and often the definition of borders[61]—nearly everything—divided the national groups that lived close to each other in the Caucasus. Within these borders, the course of independence was varied. In October 1917 a Caucasian commissariat, in which Georgians played a key role and over which Gegechkori, a Social Democrat, presided,[62] achieved unity in the region. The commissariat expected the Constituent Assembly to decide the future of Russia's nationalities. But the assembly's dissolution and its hostility toward the Bolsheviks led the government of the Caucasus to assume an attitude of independence from Russia, even if it did not yet have legal status.[63] The events that followed occurred as the Treaty of Brest-Litovsk was being signed. The Bolsheviks, acting as legitimate heirs to the tsars (a continuity of authority they denied elsewhere), agreed to cede Batumi and the ancient *vilayets* of Kars and Ardahan to Turkey, a unilateral decision made in the absence of prior consultation with Georgia and Armenia, the interested parties. Secession followed: on 25 April 1918 the Federal Republic of Transcaucasia was proclaimed.[64]

The political organization of the Caucasus initially was a juxtaposition of three systems: a federal republic, the Commune of Baku—Bolshevik citadel over which Shaumian presided—and those regions ceded to Turkey or under Turkish control. On 26 May 1918, one month after its creation, the republic exploded under the pressure of national rivalries and left in its wake three independent states, each dominated by one political party: Georgia by the Mensheviks, Armenia by the *Dashnaks*, and Azerbaijan by the *Mussavat*. The last-named was deprived of Baku, its principal center, where the Bolsheviks retained power until July 1918.[65] In the summer of 1918, Turkish troops suppressed Armenian and Azerbaijani independence. Even though in Azerbaijan a phantom government tried to play its cultural and religious solidarity with Turkey to advantage, Georgia preserved its independence, through a persistent search for outside support.

Georgia first expected help from Germany, whose Turkish allies were present in the Caucasus. The German-Georgian treaty of 28 May 1918[66] reveals the multiplicity of German intentions. Germany wanted simultaneously to obtain Georgian manganese, to control Georgia's oil route, and to treat the Russian state tactfully. In exchange for manganese deliveries and German presence in Georgia, Germany guaranteed that Turkey would not attempt to broaden the advantages acquired in the

Brest-Litovsk negotiations. But before granting a *de jure* recognition of the Georgian state, Germany, in an addendum to the Brest-Litovsk treaty (27 August 1918), succeeded in getting Russia, too, to recognize Georgia.[67]

Until September 1918 the Mensheviks in power in Tiflis balanced their independence in a subtle four-handed game. In proximate danger of Turkey and distrustful of the Bolsheviks, they used as trump card the economic and strategic advantages offered by their alliance with Germany—from Georgia, Germany could control both access to the Black Sea and the attempts of the Soviet state to be reconciled with regions rich in oil resources. But the Georgian Mensheviks, knowing also that Germany was interested in showing consideration for the RSFSR, played up the rivalries arising from access to national resources and oil deposits in the Caucasus. From these opposing economic interests the Georgians hoped to engender enough hostility between the two countries to encourage Germany to remain in the region.[68] Aware of its vulnerability, Georgia adopted a policy of granting concessions to Germany. But developments on the military chessboard soon dashed Georgian hopes. The defeat of the Central Powers was preceded in the Caucasus by the rapid advance of British troops, and the Menshevik government realized that an alliance with Britain was preferable to one with Germany.

In 1919 the situation in Georgia was more complicated than it had been when Germany controlled the region. British policy unquestionably favored Georgian independence, which led to Georgia's presence at the Peace Conference[69]; at the same time, however, the Allies were supporting the White generals, who held categorically that Russia's only future lay in reforging unity.[70] Thus, the Allies' conceptions were contradictory, and in more ways than one.

While Georgia, Armenia, and Azerbaijan (whose existence as a nation was restored after the Turkish collapse) wanted to preserve their independence, the Allies were troubled by the proliferation of little states the viability of which seemed doubtful. Rather than having many independent states in the Caucasus, they preferred a conglomerate similar to the federation that had existed in early 1918.[71] And so long as the White armies appeared able to impose their will, the Allies did not want to decide the fate of the Caucasus singlehandedly, or to dissociate its future from that of Russia.[72]

Denikin's defeat simplified matters. The Allied Supreme Council recognized the independence of the three Caucasian republics, but the republics, seeing that their temporary status (which had been tied to the war) was about to end, made one last attempt to step out of Soviet reach. Each republic sought powerful protection from the United States, Britain, or Italy,[73] or multilateral protection. The Caucasian republics were prepared to pay the price for their survival by surrendering partial sovereignty to a representative power in order to safeguard a national identity that could not be challenged by Russia.

Lenin had never declared that self-determination should be strictly applied in the Caucasus. The Commune of Baku was evidence in early 1918 that the Bolsheviks did not wish to be excluded from the region. Until 1920, the international situation counseled prudence,[74] but subsequent circumstances compelled the Bolsheviks to intervene. The British withdrew from the region, on which the Soviet states depended for survival. The Baltic states and Finland were different; Russia could not give up the Caucasus, which was the repository of its main oil supply and essential mineral resources.[75] As long as the illusion of a European revolution persisted, the problem was eclipsed by the expectation of foreign assistance. However, the expansion of revolution in Europe was never used as an argument to justify independence in the Caucasus. The Caucasus, even more so than the Ukraine, contained energy resources indispensable to Russia's economic development. When, as Lenin realized toward the end of 1919, Russia could no longer depend on its own resources, the reconquest of the Caucasus was pursued. Reconquest was swift in Azerbaijan, where a revolutionary military committee replaced the Mussavatist government in April 1920 and appealed to Russia for assistance.[76] On 5 July, in preliminary theses on the National and Colonial Question that were prepared for the Second Congress of the Comintern, Lenin declared that Azerbaijan already maintained federative ties to the RSFSR.[77] The actual accords between the two republics were not signed until three months later. But, in Lenin's mind, a *de facto* situation could be translated at once into legal terms.

Armenia's fate, which was directly tied to the power conflicts in Turkey, did not solidify until November 1920,[78] when a Soviet Republic was established. Domestic order was constantly endangered and had to be maintained by the Red Army.

During this period of reconquest, Menshevik Georgia managed to salvage its independence and once again benefited—remarkably—from the RSFSR's apparent neutrality. On 7 May 1920 the two states signed a treaty guaranteeing the recognition of Georgia; in exchange, Georgia recognized Soviet Azerbaijan.[79] The preservation and fortification of Georgian independence, as set forth in Article 1 of the treaty, which contains Russia's explicit admission that it had no right to interfere in sovereign Georgia, had three justifications. First, as in the past, the international situation was worsening for Russia: Poland posed a threat, and the Bolsheviks could not have sustained simultaneous military operations on their western border and in the Caucasus. Second, Georgia was headed by a Menshevik government, with which European socialists sympathized. Provisionally, the cautious measures of people like Henri de Man protected Georgia. Finally, Georgian national sentiment was very strong: the Bolsheviks knew this, and knew that force would be the only means to subdue it. In the spring of 1920, the use of force against a country that was drawing strong international sympathy would have been a gross miscalculation.

All the above reasons constrained the Bolsheviks to reassure Georgia and to wait. But in the meantime they were not inactive. The treaty provisions obligated Georgia to grant legal status to communist organizations, which were intent on destroying Menshevism. And the implements of the next Bolshevik offensive were fashioned: one organization of the party was assigned to Caucasian affairs, and the Eleventh Army was charged with maintaining order in the region.

By 1920, when the Soviet state was free of domestic dangers and foreign wars, the fate of most of the Russian Empire's former possessions was sealed. Some nations stood in the shadow of the great powers to ensure their independence. But international pressure did not suffice for the Ukraine, Byelorussia, or the states of the Caucasus. The postwar vision of the victors reached as far as the western borders of the Soviet state. Elsewhere, the withdrawal of occupation troops was accompanied by a slackening of interest in states' destinies. The oil of the Caucasus was too far away, the Ukraine's population was too Slavic, and Byelorussia was unknown. Deprived of outside support, these states experienced only fleeting independence, an independence that fluctuated with major military movements. And when the postwar map of the world was being redrawn and Britain was in the process of normalizing relations with a Russian state (which because it survived had earned a place in international politics), the destiny of some nationalities was dependent once more on Russia. The formal sovereignty of these states lasted only as long as the RSFSR deemed fit, or tolerated it. But the signs were mounting that pointed to the states' integration into a whole, the organizer and center of which was to be the RSFSR.

Self-Determination within the Russian Framework

The Third Congress of Soviets defined the institutions of the Federated Republic of Russia and began to regulate the transfer of jurisdictions within the federation, that is, the degree of autonomy accorded to its component parts.[80] The provisions adopted by the Congress were vague and only theoretical in scope; no decision was made about where or how they were to be applied. The nations along the periphery had already made known or were in the process of declaring their desire for independence. But the status of those nations that were more closely intermingled with Russia, and that had not yet voiced their national sentiments, was still to be decided.

When discussions on the future constitution began in the spring of 1918, opinions were divided between those who wanted a decentralized Russian state organized around economic needs, and those like Stalin who wanted decentralization to apply to the national minorities only.

With regard to national minorities whose geographic position or undeveloped national consciousness made extreme solutions unnecessary, the Bolshevik approach was empirical; policy varied according to circumstance and feasibility. Generally, the status of nationalities was decided solely by the Bolsheviks, and decisions emanated from the center.

The first experiment in federalist organization took place in a Moslem country. In March 1918, Stalin, then Commissar of Nationalities, claiming that the Tatars and Bashkirs had responded to the call of the Third Soviet Congress, proposed that a Tatar-Bashkir Republic be created.[81] A Commissariat of Moslem Affairs, initially conceived as autonomous but quickly reduced to a section of the Commissariat of Nationalities, was established to handle the day-to-day problems related to the creation of the republic. But with civil war raging on Tatar and Bashkir territory, there was local hostility to the idea of unification, amid a panoply of opposing views, all of which combined to toll the death of both the united republic and the Commissariat on Moslem Affairs, thus shorn of its principal task. One year later the collapse of Kolchak's armies restored the initiative to the Bolsheviks, who were not about to repeat the mistakes of 1918. The Bashkir national leadership, opposed to Bolshevik plans, had been associated with the White armies; but in the face of Kolchak's Russo-centrism, they later changed sides. In March 1919 Validov, their leader, concluded an agreement with the Bolsheviks that laid the foundation for the formation of an autonomous Bashkir state within a federation. However, the degree of autonomy provided in the 1919 accord was not completely consistent with federative status, because the Bashkir Republic was to retain total control over its domestic political system (only mines, factories, and railways were to be administered by a common system) and over its armies, although the armed forces were in the last instance subordinate to the federal commissariat.

The compromise of 1919 granted far more concessions than the Bolsheviks had contemplated, but it had the immediate dual advantage of separating the Bashkirs from the Whites and providing an alluring example for other national groups in the same alliance. In the long run, the Bashkir experiment could not last. No federal organization could leave such wide-ranging authority in the hands of federated units; moreover, the desire of Validov and his colleagues to form a Bashkir state (in which various national groups and many Russians lived) led inexorably not to a lessening of nationality differences, but to a deepening of Bashkir national sentiment.

In 1919 Lenin, in justifying the compromise before the party, invoked the necessity of offering the "Kirghiz, Turkmen, Uzbeks, and Tadzhiks, who until now have been under the influence of their mullahs" an example of internationalism and of the Russians' positive attitude toward them as ethnic entities.[82]

After the civil war the Bolsheviks were able to weaken the compromise. On 20 May 1920 a VCIK decree established the definitive form of Bashkir autonomy. The Autonomous Republic returned most authority to the RSFSR, and what little authority remained was relegated to the VCIK. The far-reaching autonomy of 1917 was reduced to authority in matters of local administration—less authority, Validov claimed, than the rights conceded to minorities in the darkest days of tsarist rule.[83] The fate of the Tatars in the Volga region and of the peoples in Daghestan and the Crimea was decided in 1920 in the same manner: Russia would regulate their status as autonomous republics with limited authority.

The cases of the German peoples of the Volga and the Kirghiz also illustrate the Bolshevik's pragmatism at this time. The Germans along the Volga posed a problem because they were a heterogeneous group, a product of foreign colonization. In order to treat them as a nationality, thus admitting that areas where German colonization had occurred were historically German lands, Lenin would have had to recognize a culture which he had always considered of marginal importance. The Bolsheviks were uneasy about this situation, as can be seen in their creation of special status, at least initially, for these people—the VCIK set up a "Commune of Germans of the Volga" that would consolidate "the Soviets from districts with a specific national character."[84] The Commune was attached to an administrative region on which it was completely dependent; all that was left in its own jurisdiction were cultural matters.

The other exception to the rule was the Kirghiz, a people of the steppes that was closely interwoven among a population of Russian colonists. Colonization had engendered conflicts over landownership, and, before the Kirghiz demanded recognition as a nationality, they demanded the return of confiscated lands. The Bolsheviks sought to reconcile two groups—one with a tradition of dominance, the other the bitter victims of despoliation—without dissociating themselves from either one. A solution was fashioned in Moscow, but no trace of any discussion on the subject can be found. A Kirghiz Revolutionary Committee, created by decree on 10 June 1919, was "parachuted" into the steppes.[85] Its task was to organize Soviet power while respecting the cultural rights of each community.[86] The ensuing conflict was so violent that in October 1920 the territory, notwithstanding its mixed population, was declared an Autonomous Kirghiz Republic. Although the Russians who had already settled there could preserve their landholdings, future colonization was prohibited.

Turkestan, on the other hand, gave the Bolsheviks the opportunity to carry out an unusual type of revolution—a colonial one. In this colonized area, which was governed as such, two parallel and irreconcilable revolutions developed after October 1917[87]: a proletarian revolution among Russian soldiers and workers in the area that had at its epicenter Tashkent,[88] and a nationalist revolution led by the educated bourgeoisie of Turkestan, which established autonomous power in Kokand.[89] The rivalry between the two powers in Turkestan could be contained easily, at first, because military strength was concentrated in Tashkent, and because it was only the local population that was sympathetic to the government in Kokand. This was not the case of the government that established power in the name of Turkmen around the same time in the Transcaspian region.[90] The Bolshevik government in Tashkent, unable to foment revolution in the emirates of Bokhara and Khiva,[91] unsuccessfully opposed the authorities in Merv, in Transcaspia, who appealed for help to the British forces stationed in Persia. At this stage—it was the summer of 1918—the revolution appeared doomed in Central Asia, where the Russian revolution was personified by the colonists, administrators, and workers who had lived in the territory for a long time and who, cut off from Petrograd at the outset of the civil war, interpreted Bolshevik policy as they saw fit. In Central Asia Bolshevism was a local, colonial phenomenon. The Bolshevik Party of Turkestan, made up of Russians who lived in a system of colonial relations, did not know how to practice a policy of self-determination. For them, the danger of nationalists, whether or not they were allied with the Whites, was as great as that of the Whites or of Great Britain. Thus, a colonial vision of the revolution and the desire to maintain the status quo—not to transcend nationality differences, but to protect Russian interests—characterized the revolution in Turkestan.[92] The Russian Bolsheviks, who had long been cut off from Turkestan by the civil war, were quite ignorant about the distant colony; they were more occupied with nations closer to the center of events. Petrograd did not evidence concern until after the civil war, in June 1919; and it was less concerned about Turkestan than about the strategic position of a colonial territory on the steppes of Asia, a territory that could become the outpost of the Asiatic revolution.[93] In October 1919 the Soviet government sent a mission to Turkestan headed by Kuibyshev and Frunze, who realized that the chauvinism of Russians claiming to be Bolsheviks was what had set the Moslems against revolutionary Russia, which they now identified with tsarist oppression.[94] The weakened Bolsheviks oscillated from one extreme to the other, first decrying Russian excesses, then condemning native excesses. The Kuibyshev-Frunze Commission carried out a purge in Russian communist circles and blamed chauvinist excesses on the "former" infiltrators in the party.[95] But these measures could not stem the tide of local discontent or the growth of the Basmashi opposition army.[96] Alerted by Frunze, the Soviet government then tackled local nationalism. A second commission, composed of Satarov, Kaganovich, and Peters, purged the Turkestani communists.[97] But Lenin, wishing to avoid the errors made elsewhere, moved to reassure the Turkestani population, even while excluding nationalists from political participation. The situation in Turkestan opened the debate over how to emancipate a colony without pushing it toward a nationalist revolution. The Baku Congress responded that the social revolution had to come before the nationalist revolution.[98] Soviet order had to be introduced in Turkestan without appearing to be just a variation on Russian domination. The solution adopted in Turkestan is interesting because it took an untrodden path. Everywhere else, with few exceptions, dominated peoples that demanded the right to self-determination in the end received a circumscribed right to federated state status, or local administrative autonomy. However, in the case of Turkestan, where self-determination as such was not alluded to, and where the Russian and Ukrainian sectors of the population fought to avoid separation, none of the previous solutions was satisfactory. Of two programs proposed in 1920, one reflected the nationalist sentiments of the Turkestani people and the other the central concerns of the Bolsheviks. On 23 May 1920 the Central Committee of the Russian Communist Party discussed the proposal made by the "Turkestani delegation" composed of T. Ryskulov, F. Khodjaev, and Bekh Ivanov to create an Autonomous Republic of Turkestan that would be integrated into the RSFSR.[99] This idea represented the aspirations of the Moslem groups of the region. Separation from Russia and degrees of autonomy were unimportant to them; what mattered was the unity of the peoples of Turkestan in a political-administrative entity. The second proposal, which was essentially centralist and ignored the problematic relations between indigenous and Russian populations and the multiplicity of indigenous groups, emanated from a commission of the Central Committee that was formed by Krestinsky, Sisherin, and Eliava. It represented an administrative solution designed to ensure firm control by the center over the periphery. On 20 June Lenin decided[100] that Ryskulov's project was to be avoided at all costs. He amended the second proposal so that it included measures to improve relations between Russians and native peoples. He recommended "sending to concentration camps in Russia all former members of the police, military, security forces, administration, et cetera, who were products of the tsarist era and who swarmed around Soviet power because they saw in it the perpetuation of Russian domination." In order that self-determination not seem a prolongation of the previous system, Lenin also recommended that the respective powers of the center and the periphery be strictly defined. In the end, local authority granted to Turkestan surpassed the hopes and demands of the native groups. The case of Turkestan, an Autonomous Republic in 1920 that later gave rise to various federated republics, was unique. Lenin was most prescient in 1920 regarding self-determination and unity in Turkestan. In a postscript to his remarks on the future of the region, he stated: "(1) We must establish a factual (ethnographic and otherwise) map of Turkestan, dividing it into Uzbek, Kirghiz, and Turkmen territories; (2) we must examine in detail the conditions for unity or separation in these three sections."[101]

In 1920, however, the issues of geographic separation and redistribution were only generally addressed. Because Turkestan had undergone a revolution protesting the perpetuation of colonial designs, and because it was far from the center and difficult to control, it received even more autonomy than it demanded. The principal problem was not its relation of autonomy with the center, but its relation with colonists and with the local Russian administration.

Between 1917 and 1920 the principle of self-determination was applied in a variety of ways, depending on individual conditions—geographic location, importance to Russia, international environment, strength of national movements—in the different areas where the desire for nationality recognition was expressed.

Of the strategies that the Bolshevik leaders adopted, some had been anticipated; others had been rejected at first and later endorsed. The policies they instituted ranged from accepted separation (Finland) to cultural autonomy (Germans along the Volga) to—the supreme heresy—national autonomy on a personal basis, as occurred with the Kirghiz in the decree of 10 June 1919. Apparent inconsistencies were also evident in the case of the Jews and in the Russian Far East.

The Jewish problem had always made the Bolsheviks uncomfortable. Prior to 1917 Lenin and Stalin had skirted the issue by denying it. There is no Jewish nation, they asserted, because the Jewish people's only characteristic is an attachment to a religious culture. After the revolution Lenin acknowledged that Jews had been oppressed under the tsarist regime, although he did not define Jews as belonging to a nation—rather they were a community that had been universally oppressed, irrespective of social criteria. For this reason, he stopped short of devising a comprehensive solution. He avoided a pronouncement on the future destiny of the Jews and did not grant them any particular political status; nonetheless, he recognized the need for Jewish representation in the Commissariat of Nationalities and for a Jewish section of the party to express and defend Jewish interests. Autonomy—on any basis—was not considered, but the existence of a Jewish *cultural* difference was implicitly admitted by the fact that Jews were included in organizations whose mission was to represent their culture.

The last case, no less extreme, was that of Siberia, where in 1917 small groups of primitive, dispersed peoples with no nationalist sentiment lived alongside Russian colonists. Self-determination was not at issue, but separation was, due to the region's domestic and international situation. Anti-Bolshevik governments multiplied in the shadow of Japanese troops, which landed in Vladivostok in April 1918, and Czech regiments, which occupied some territories in May 1918. French and British missions were also present. Despite the fall of Kolchak's government in January 1920 and the Bolshevik presence in the region, the Soviet government agreed for international reasons (above all, Japanese concerns) to the creation of a Far East Independent Republic, which endured and expanded its zone of authority until November 1922. Siberian separation from the RSFSR did not result from local demand but on account of the interrelations among forces in Siberia. Still, the area was categorized as a beneficiary of self-determination, which later enabled the Soviet state to review its status with the idea of reincorporation in mind.

The chaotic history of self-determination and of decisions that to a greater or lesser degree were improvised as the occasion arose should not mask the fact that from 1918 on, a consistent Bolshevik policy was taking shape.

Lenin repeatedly endeavored to detach the national problem from its international context and to reduce it to what it properly was—in his mind, an issue in which initiative ought to be taken by the Russian working class. Even his concessions must be understood from this viewpoint, which would explain why, while continuing to assert the right of peoples to self-determination, he spoke brutally of the need to retain Ukrainian wheat and oil, and metal in the Caucasus. Self-determination was an absolute right, except when it clashed with the future interests of the socialist state. Thus, in the final analysis, Lenin pursued the same goal as those who decried his policies—to preserve for the present and the future the power of the working class by subordinating or joining to it the rights of nations.

Part Three

A Tough Compromise: Diversity and Unity

CHAPTER 6

A Parliament for Nationalities

The *Narkomnats*: An Unstable Institution

The Second All-Russian Congress of Soviets decided on 25 October 1917 to create a Commissariat of Nationalities (*Narkomnats*)[1] under the authority of Stalin, the People's Commissar, aided by two assistants, one of whom was Felix Seniuta,[2] a former shoemaker. The commissariat was composed of sections headed by local nationals.

On 15 February 1918 the leaders of the national sections were given decision-making power and assembled in a Collegium.[3] By June 1918 it had sixteen members.

The Commissariat of Nationalities was managed until February 1918 by Stalin and his two assistants, who attended to matters in order of urgency. Later they were replaced by the national base that demanded a voice within the framework of the Collegium and wished to supersede the power of the commissar.

This contentious situation was remedied by a reform of 9 June 1918[4] that limited the Collegium's capacity as a national parliament with decision-making power: membership was limited to nine, and unrepresented nationalities were given advisory status, except in discussions directly concerning them, in which they had voting rights. The party's Central Committee and the Council of People's Commissars of the RSFSR ratified the choice of representatives to the Collegium and arbitrated any conflicts occurring therein.

The complex organization of the Commissariat of Nationalities, or *Narkomnats*, changed over time.[5] In 1918 it was composed of eight commissariats, or *Natskom*, and eleven departments, or *Natsotdel*. Almost all commissariats and departments were headed by a commissar from the nationality group represented in the official proceedings, except for the rare occasion when small nationality groups could not provide acceptable leadership and were represented by Russians.[6]

It was not always clear by what criteria the nationalities fell into one or the other category. Poles, Latvians, and Armenians had a commissariat, whereas Ukrainians had only a section. The most curious cases—because they suggest that theory had to be adapted to reality—were the commissariat of Jewish Affairs[7] and that of the Moslems of Russia.[8] Neither Jews nor Moslems were classified, in Marxist terms, as nationalities, yet reality obliged Soviet authorities to grant them nationality status. Seventy years later, the difficulties that this concession engendered still endure.

The *Narkomnats* had specialized offices for agitation and propaganda; for relations with the *Natskom* and *Natsotdel*; for drafting decrees common to all commissariats; a press department and offices for international relations and statistics.[9] At first these offices consisted of one or two employees, seated at a *table* (the name it was initially given), whose task it was to furnish information in their domain. On 14 April 1918 Stalin created a Central Information Bureau,[10] an apparently innocent reform but one that considerably weakened the nationalities. The Bureau was to centralize statistical data and factual material on the political, cultural, economic, and social life of Russia's nationalities as well as of the nationalities that remained separate from Russia. Under the pretext of coordination, the Bureau took custody of documents that were later used in defining the relations among nations in the Soviet state, thus preventing the national representatives from participating in any discussion of the state's organization.

The Commissariat of Nationalities evolved a great deal in a matter of months. The growth of national representation made it into a parliament, but at the same time its powers were steadily reduced, while the means of centralization multiplied.

The Purpose of the *Narkomnats*

The transformation of the *Narkomnats* paralleled the general evolution of Bolshevik policy. Until 1920 it played a minor role, to such an extent that although Stalin was Commissar of Nationalities, he left his assistants in charge of implementing day-to-day decisions.[11]

The creation of national commissariats came about as a result of the German occupation of national territories. After the German invasion, numerous inhabitants of Poland, the Baltic states, the Ukraine, and Byelorussia fled. The *Natskom* was in charge of refugees and their eventual destinations when their country of origin opted for independence (Poland), and also had more authoritarian functions. Cultural or military nationalist organizations were sprouting up all over Russian territory.[12] The national commissariats oversaw these, and thus managed and controlled any nationalist groups who were worrisome to those in power.

The nations that had chosen to separate from Russia were subject to greater control. The *Natskom* claimed to represent all its subjects or associations that remained on Russian soil; it set separatist tendencies against unifying tendencies, thereby challenging the validity of Lenin's acceptance of secession. Many tendencies coexisted in the *Narkomnats*: some national cadre were attentive to the needs of the group they were presumed to, or in fact did, represent; but there were also adversaries of secession who were harsh critics of a policy they considered useless, especially when it generated federalist proposals.[13]

One of the major activities that the Commissariat carried out abroad was to mobilize the resistance of former subjects of the empire who lived in occupied territories. In 1918 it published newspapers in 20 languages; two years later, in 60. In the first three years of its existence, 700 titles appeared, with 12 million copies in print.[14]

Among the propaganda organs was a Russian language daily, *Zhizn' Natsional'nostei*, first issued on 15 February 1918 as the official newspaper of the Commissariat, with articles on policy and, occasionally, discussions of in-house trends. Stalin contributed many important articles.[15]

In the early years, in addition to its leadership and propaganda activities, the Commissariat initiated two projects that were to fail. Assigned the task of laying the groundwork for Tatar-Bashkir union and defining their relation to the center, the *Narkomnats* called a meeting in Moscow from 10–16 May 1918 of thirty delegates for a constituent congress of the republic. For the first time, the nationalities were to have a forum for discussing concrete problems of autonomy, including its meaning and scope.[16] The civil war put an end to these discussions, which had turned bitter, and to the entire project.

The second undertaking was the creation of national minority military organizations in the Red Army. In February 1918 the Moslem Commissariat proposed to the *Narkomnats* Collegium that Moslem regiments be sent as reinforcement into Moslem regions. Wary of steps that might spur nationalist desires more than revolutionary unity,[17] Soviet leaders vetoed the idea. A reduced commission of three members of the *Narkomnats* Collegium and some aides to the commissar of defense discussed this idea irregularly without ever reaching a conclusion.[18] Lenin's conviction was unshakable, and he accepted no argument: within a federalist framework, defense was properly within the jurisdiction of the federation.

At the end of the civil war, with the return of territories and the development of the state, it seemed the *Narkomnats* might play a different role, which led Stalin to fashion new reforms. Four decrees transformed the hybrid organ into the official intermediary between local governments and the central power-structure.

The decree of 6 May 1920 modified the structure of the *Narkomnats* and the representation of nationalities.[19] A Council of Nationalities, a representative body placed under the chairmanship of the commissar, was created, a true "parliament of nationalities" with elected representatives. The commissariats all became national departments, complemented by a Department of Minorities representing nonterritorial ethnic-group interests. The exception was the Jewish Commissariat, *Evkom*, which became *Evotdel*, a department, despite the territorial dispersion of the Jewish people.

A decree of 30 October 1920 defined the authority of the Commissariat.[20] For any problem affecting the republics or the national regions, the local departments were to act in conjunction with the Commissariat. Thus, in matters concerning them, the nationalities could participate in decisions emanating from the central power.

A decree of 6 November 1920 charged the *Narkomnats* with centralizing and channeling toward the central government all demands from nationality-group representatives, and of sending out from the center to the periphery the credits, decisions, or means of any sort that the RSFSR put at their service.[21]

Lastly, a 20 December 1920[22] decree stipulated that the *Narkomnats* would be permanently represented in the governments of the republics and the autonomous regions of the RSFSR, as well as in the independent republics with which the RSFSR normalized relations through bilateral treaties.[23]

The *Narkomnats* acquired substantial authority, and the decrees seemed to give nationalities a way of participating in the development of national policy in the RSFSR; however a closer look at the texts and at Soviet practice reveals that exactly the contrary was the case. From 1920 on, the *Narkomnats* worked toward centralization, to the detriment of both the nationalities that were already integrated into the RSFSR and those that were still independent. Previously, the nationality groups of the RSFSR had had direct access to the Central Executive Committee (VCIK), where they often would plead their causes and contact representatives. Laxity, the absence of precise guidelines ruling bilateral relations, and multiple rungs of authority had given the nationality groups a certain autonomy. However, once the *Narkomnats* was restructured and endowed with wider authority, even if it still resembled a national parliament, it became the mandatory mediator in relations between the center and the national territories. These relations became uniform, and the center acquired greater authority. Meanwhile *Narkomnats'* representation in local governments[24] gradually changed to interference, much to the annoyance of the local authorities.

Stalin tried to reduce tensions between *Narkomnats* representatives and local authorities by strictly defining the parameters of his assistants' task: they were to supervise the application of RSFSR national policy, facilitate relations between RSFSR organizations and local organizations, and make bimonthly reports on local conditions[25] to the *Narkomnats*.

The crucial provisions concerning *Narkomnats* representation furnish proof of Russian desire to control the republics. At the outset, *Narkomnats* representatives were agitators espousing pro-Soviet propaganda that ran deeply against the grain of the local authorities.[26] The 20 December decree granting them quasi-diplomatic status infuriated the independent governments even more, for past experience with the representatives had inspired little faith. By empowering the *Narkomnats* to maintain a presence in independent states, Soviet power seemed to erase the distinction between independent states and those territories that were incorporated into the RSFSR. Even as the policy of bilateral alliances was in its infancy, a blueprint of the future was being drawn up: the plan was for independent states to become part of a federalized whole. This was the true intention behind the *Narkomnats*: more than a forum for nationalities, it was to be a symbol of future federation and the implement for attaining that goal. Created in the federation's image, it assured national representation on its Council and established not only a hierarchy among nations but also a hierarchy of status in relations between national territories and the center.

In 1922 the organization of the *Narkomnats* was modified one last time. By this date the Soviet state was established, and it needed a common economic and social policy more than it needed national representation. The statutory provisions of 27 July 1922 highlighted not the national departments whose usefulness was fading, but rather the functional departments whose staff and authority were to be augmented: agriculture, economic structures, education, social security, defense, et cetera. In practice, the departments developed at an uneven pace because they were subject to the changing priorities of the central authorities. Interest moved first from one sector to another, with expansion in one area occurring at the expense of the recently abandoned one.

Once union was achieved, there was no further need for the *Narkomnats*. All its officials deplored the chronic shortage of personnel, the lack of material means, and general indifference to their activities.[27] Stalin himself was an episodic commissar, moving from one task to another and returning to the *Narkomnats* only to reorganize it or resolve conflicts.[28]

In 1924 the USSR came into being, and the *Narkomnats* easily slipped into oblivion, as its historians say, "having accomplished its mission." Only the Council of Nationalities—whose only action from its founding had been to organize the first All-Russian Congress of Nationalities in December 1920, survived the restructuring. In the new era, the constitution of 1924 transformed the Council into the second chamber representing nationalities in the bicameral parliament of the USSR, a function later ratified by the basic laws of 1936 and 1977.

The *Narkomnats* in the Field: The Example of Central Asia

To understand how the *Narkomnats* functioned, we must look to the field. Central Asia provides the best example for study purposes, because the *Narkomnats* was more active there than elsewhere due to pressing problems and the atypical status of the region.

Until 1920, Central Asia escaped Russian power. A kaleidoscope of configurations existed there: nationalist and colonial revolutions;

Soviet power and independent states (Bukhara and Khiva); historic, identity-conscious nationality groups (the Uzbeks, for example), as well as small nationality groups with no identity consciousness, or no means to express it. The Autonomous Republic of Turkestan was accorded special status, and its governmental bodies included a Commissariat of Nationalities, created in 1918[29] and theoretically independent of the *Narkomnats*. The latter, meanwhile, had at its disposal substantial means for intervention in the republic, and it used them liberally. Temporary official representatives were sent to advise local authorities on specific problems such as establishing institutions in the new republic. Until the dissolution of the *Narkomnats*, these emissaries sent by the center played a vital role in local government, alternating advice and pressure. Their activities placed them in constant friction with local officials, who accused them of undermining local autonomy.[30]

But the representatives of the *Narkomnats* acquired a larger role in 1922 when their offices became permanent organizations attached to local government, which ensured the center of control.[31] The *Narkomnats* representative or the leader of its delegation participated in an advisory capacity in the meetings of the Turkestani government. Any divergences in policy between the center and the Republic of Turkestan caused pressure to be exerted on the Turkestani government and resulted in an immediate report to the *Narkomnats*.[32] Whenever the *Narkomnats* judged the affair to be serious, a veritable commando would arrive to reinforce the *Narkomnats'* regional delegation under directives from the center to impose a policy alignment on the local level. More than intervention in local government, the *Narkomnats'* function was to serve as active liaison between local authority and the Soviet government and to further the integration of Turkestan. After 1920, any local demands had to be channeled through the *Narkomnats*; "nationalities' embassies" were established under its auspices.

Official representation for the Republic of Turkestan was installed on 1 April 1921. The representatives were to bring problems in the republic to the attention of Moscow through the *Narkomnats*, and to relay to the republic any instructions or suggestions from the center. In 1922–23 alone, representatives from Turkestan, via the Commissariat, referred 1,200 files on local problems to the appropriate organizations of the RSFSR.[33] These files actually represented any local problem for which the RSFSR's help or agreement was necessary (for instance, the establishment of an agricultural bank in Central Asia, which began operations in 1923[34]).

In 1922, while the federation was progressing, a radical change took place in the relations between the center and the periphery. The *Narkomnats* lost control of their representatives in the republics, who were invited to deal directly with the appropriate ministries of the RSFSR,[35] but was assigned the new task of organizing federal committees devoted to the unification of principles and procedures to be followed in various domains, economy and education especially.

The *Fedkomzem* (Federal Committee for Agricultural Problems) held its first meeting in November 1922 and settled down to the business of drafting a property code.[36] Turkestan, where "the problem of agricultural organization is of key importance and should be considered a priority,"[37] was first on the agenda. The Committee soon attacked the problems of irrigation and the settlement process,[38] which required much on-site explanation and propaganda work. To this end, the Commissariat acquired Western Cultural Editions, which published political and pedagogical newspapers and brochures in all the languages of Central Asia, and controlled the local editions as well.

Narkomnats activities in Turkestan, whether carried out in the center, the periphery, through temporary or permanent representatives, or through relations with the local commissariat, offer myriad examples of overlapping functions. Many organizations worked simultaneously to resolve the same problems, which enfeebled the consistency and efficiency of the whole. A close examination reveals that despite the permanent disarray, controls by the center over the periphery were proliferating.

The *Narkomnats*, an acceptable instrument of control because it was by definition the voice of the nationalities— their parliament—was also efficient in surveying outlying national territories and reporting to the central authority. In the early 1920s, in a charged climate of pitched nationalist passions, the center was not in a position to go to the field to gather the information needed for defining policies and identifying resources. The national commissariats, however, were prepared to do this work. Their curiosity and activities were accepted by their fellow citizens, who were not aware that the census and inquiries were carried out not on local initiative but as part of an overall plan aimed at integration with the USSR.

The persistent and polymorphous intervention by the *Narkomnats* in the national regions—as we have seen in Turkestan—was not always welcomed; local authorities often rebelled against such interference. Given the friction caused by an organ personifying the national groups themselves, direct intervention from the center would have been even less well received. This instrument of control also served as a screen to protect the future relations between the center and institutions in the periphery.

The disappearance of the *Narkomnats* was greeted with indifference, for the peoples that the "nationalities parliament" was supposed to represent never really identified with it. The repeated reforms of its structure also lessened its capacity to represent the nationalities in a meaningful way. Despite its failure, various questions remain about its role. Did the Bolsheviks have a clear design in mind? Did the *Narkomnats* seek to surpass its founders' intentions and assume its own role? What place did it occupy in the Soviet political system from 1918 to 1924?

In creating the *Narkomnats*, the Bolsheviks meant for it to become a platform for nationalities, as can be seen by the status of Jews in the Commissariat. Lenin believed that the national question could be resolved by giving priority to the aspirations of nationalities and ethnic groups. But he quickly saw that the road to effective action was not always paved with good intentions. Centrifugal tendencies were strong; nationalism grew; despite national egalitarianism, anti-Bolshevik alliances formed—all of which contradicted his optimistic forecasts and added fuel to the arguments of those who criticized what they called his "national liberalism."

The *Narkomnats* did not become a forum for national reconciliation: national groups were antagonistic toward it and defied all initiatives emanating from the center. Moreover, the national cadre who worked in the *Narkomnats* were more Bolshevik than nationalist, more disposed to unity than to division. Thus Lenin paid the price for a largely improvised policy. *Narkomnats* cadre were recruited in a haphazard manner, depending on the whims of the available personnel in the capital, and their tasks were ill-defined. The failure of the *Narkomnats* in its early stages explains why Soviet leaders abandoned it in less than one year and relegated its business to their representatives. Stalin was called away on other missions; Lenin was absorbed in trying to end the war and the counterrevolution, and was occupied in organizing the world revolution, that is to say, the Comintern.

Left to their own devices, the *Narkomnats* leaders, especially the emissaries, sometimes abused their discretion by creating their own policy. Emissaries often behaved as authoritarian figures and were prone to excessive intervention (in contradiction to the flexible policy Lenin advocated), thus compromising the prestige of their institution. The manner in which they relayed nationalist demands to the RSFSR also undermined the institution. Conceived by Lenin as a means to simplify and rationalize contacts, the *Narkomnats* begat leaders who stressed control, barriers, and uniformity, thereby betraying Lenin's original intent.

In the final analysis, then, what exactly was the *Narkomnats*? More than a ministry in charge of specific problems, it was actually an adjunct of the Communist Party: following the example of the party, it worked toward unity and against diversity; like the party, it went beyond, or attempted to surmount, more limited tasks and attempted to take on all the problems of the nationality groups revolving around Russia. It was this global vision that made for the originality and importance of the institution. Despite hesitations, contradictory action, its unwieldy nature, and the defects of the apparatus—and notwithstanding its modest accomplishments and failures—its universal vision earned the *Narkomnats* a place in the history of the early steps taken toward a multi-ethnic Soviet state.

CHAPTER 7

Diversity: The Federal State

A Transitional State for a Transitional Period

Before revolution erupted in Russia, Lenin studied Marxist canons for a clear idea of the political organization of a revolution. His reading notes, which formed the basis for "The Marxist Theory of the State"[1] and "State and Revolution"[2] and were written in January–February and August–September 1917, respectively, contain some practical proposals for the year 1918. Engels believed that revolution naturally and inevitably did away with the state[3]; Marx, in his "Critique of the Gotha Program," alluded to "the future state of Communist society"[4]; yet Lenin, adopting neither view, looked to evolution over time, which would separate the *transitional* post-revolutionary phase from the stage at which communism would be fully realized. Lenin's thinking revolved around this *transition period*, and his ideas on the organization of nationalities can be understood only in this context.

In his prerevolutionary writings focusing on the transition period between revolution and the passage to communism, Lenin posited that the state would no longer exist in its primitive form but would take on a provisional political form "between state and nonstate, in other words, ceasing to be a state in the proper sense of the term."[5] The transitional stage corresponded to the dictatorship of the proletariat, or the "half-state." Prudently, Lenin made no statement about the duration of the transition period or the longevity of the political forms that would emerge at that time; quite the contrary, he underscored the impossibility of placing precise temporal limitations on the historical process or of trying to predict its concrete forms.[6] He believed, however, that a state that had ceased to exist as such would begin to wither away; as a state in transition, it would experience progressive weakening, not further development.

Lenin posited the creation of a new kind of state from the moment the revolution began. His "Decree on Peace,"[7] read to the Second All-Russian Congress of Soviets on 26 October 1917, encapsulated his visions of events and expressed his hopes for the future. Addressing his appeal not to governments but to peoples, he condemned all forms of national oppression (multinational empires and colonial states) and defined a world of political relations based on popular, national inclinations and not on the existing power-structure. He also outlined a young "State of Soviets"—a springboard for a revolutionary state destined to spread with each success of the revolution—a state without nationalities and without borders, which would contain seeds of the universal state.[8]

Lenin's ideas at this stage foreshadowed subsequent definitions of Soviet law. By linking the state and the revolution, he redefined the territory over which the state had authority. The territory of the socialist state was not fixed or inviolable, it was an elastic revolutionary space that expanded with continuous revolutions. Lenin stressed the relationship between the territory of the socialist state and historic conditions: "We must not consider the union of any *foreign* territory as annexation, for socialists in general sympathize with any effort to eliminate borders between nations and to establish larger states. *Any* violation of the status quo is not necessarily annexation, for that would be evidence of a completely reactionary spirit and would make a mockery of the fundamental concepts of historical science. The same is true of *any* unification that takes place through war and violence when the interests of the majority of the population are at stake."[9]

What of the nationalities in such an open, fluid, socialist state that spreads to include other territories where the revolution triumphs? The "Declaration of the Rights of the Peoples of Russia,"[10] published on 2 November, proclaimed "the equality and sovereignty of the peoples of

Russia," the right of peoples to self-determination and to secession, even to the establishment of an independent state. The text implicitly posed the problem of the domestic political organization of Russian territory. Would the transitional state be centralized or federal? The declaration clearly stated that the alternative to secession was "the voluntary and honest union of the peoples of Russia." But beyond that, the conditions for union, and the form of the state that would unify these peoples, remained undefined.

Despite his hostility to federalism, Lenin realized early that, in practice, federation could for a time help to resolve the national problem. In "State and Revolution," Lenin did not retract his assertion that a centralized state was the political organization most suited to the transitional stage, but he cited Engels, who had believed that federal organization of a state might under certain conditions be "a step forward."[11] Furthermore, Stalin, who had recently been appointed Commissar of Nationalities, stated on 30 November 1917 that the power of the Soviets was not hostile to the idea of a federal republic.[12]

But the disintegration of Russia in 1918 demanded that some viable space be safeguarded, and that the examples of Finland and the Ukraine not be followed by all non-Russian peoples. At Stalin's insistence, Lenin, impelled as well by his own sense of reality, repudiated his early ideas and made the federal principle the foundation of the Soviet state. Article 2 of the "Declaration of the Rights of Workers and Exploited People" of 12 January 1918 declared, "The Soviet Republic of Russia is constituted on the basis of the free union of free nations as a federation of national Soviet Republics."[13]

The decision to join the federal republic was entrusted to "workers and peasants of each ethnic group, who shall make an independent decision within their own Soviet organizations." It was then up to them to express their conception of their future and "the bases on which they intended to participate in the government and in the various federal institutions."[14] This declaration defined for the first time the form of the Soviet state. Recognition of the federal principle enabled Soviet power to enlarge its territorial base without violating the national rights of other peoples. A short time later, Lenin defined the type of relations that were to be established among nations belonging to the federation: not decentralized domination in the "mode of the ancient Roman empire," but an egalitarian union the basic foundation of which was the clear interest of the working classes.[15] Such interest might give rise to various types of associations—to union with revolutionary Russia, or to a constellation around Russia of diverse federations of free nations.[16]

The 12 January declaration also spelled out the forms of union with Russia: self-determination was the birthright of all workers and was to be exercised within the Congress of Soviets. The ambiguity of Lenin's prerevolutionary writings was thus replaced by a definite doctrine in which the Congress of Soviets was the seat of decision making. In the declaration as well as in his speeches, Lenin placed special emphasis on the egalitarian ideology that was at the heart of the choice of federalism for the newly instituted Russian power-structure.

But the federation conceived by Lenin was a means and not an end; transitional in nature, it would enable Russia to await world revolution as a viable state. Federation was a necessary phase on the road to unity and to the transcendence of national differences in the country's interior. On a multitude of later occasions, Lenin's remarks would hark back to his basic orientation, and to his conviction that only unifying, centralizing structures could satisfy the real long-term interests of the working class. "The federation of nations," he wrote in March 1918, "is a stage toward a *conscious* and closer unity of the workers, who will have learned *voluntarily* to rise above national conflicts,"[17] and subsequently he referred to "federation as a stage on the way to voluntary fusion."[18] The Soviet state, while federal, was above all founded on *democratic centralism*, which counterbalanced the concessions the Bolsheviks were forced by circumstance to make after the revolution. Lenin stated: "In reality, federation . . . does not contradict democratic centralism. Federation is a stage on the way to democratic centralism."[19]

Lenin's frequently stated reluctance to assign an absolute or definitive value to federal status was particularly evident in the constitution of 1918.[20] The text of the first Soviet constitution was prepared by the constitutional committee that had been created on 1 April 1918 and was chaired by Sverdlov. In July, a special commission of the party's Central Committee, under Lenin's leadership, produced a final text that combined the basic text of the Sverdlov Commission and a draft prepared by the Ministry of Justice. On 10 July 1918 the Fifth All-Russian Congress of Soviets unanimously adopted the constitution, which was promulgated on 19 July.

The constitutional corpus[21] was composed of two texts: a slightly amended version of the "Declaration of the Rights of Working and Exploited People" and the provisions setting forth the organization of the federal republic.

E. H. Carr has justly pointed out that the term "federation" or "federal" does not appear in the constitution of 1918 except in a discussion of general principles and in the formal title of the new state.[22] R. Pipes states more emphatically that the word "federation" is never mentioned in the constitution,[23] a statement belied by the constitution's Article 11. Both historians are right to focus attention on how parsimoniously the Soviet founders used the term. Yet the greatest discretion was displayed when it came to the political form and functions of the federal system. In fact, the constitution of 1918 established an organizational system that was relatively decentralized, whose large administrative units—regions, or *oblasti*—could at the time "be characterized by a particular way of life and national composition" (Article 11).

Although the constitution carefully defined the power-structure, it did not express the desire for national representation. Jurisdictional problems arising out of federal status did not appear until Article 49, sections C(b) (establishment and modification of borders) and D (entry of new members into the federation and recognition of the right to withdraw from the federation). The federation's flag, mentioned in Article 89, seemed to symbolize an already unified society; it made no allusion to its multinational status.

The institutions of the federated entities were described as local institutions. There is reference to local Soviets (*mestnye sovety*), regional Soviets (*oblastnye sovety*), provincial Soviets (*gubernskie*), districts (*uezdnye*), rural districts (*volostnye*), and organs of Soviet power (*organy Sovetskoi vlasti*), but there is no mention of larger national institutions. The federal state was organized on the basis of territorial administration, and the federation seemed limited to the voluntary cohabitation of peoples, on the one hand, and the statement that all nations have equal rights, on the other. This restrictive version of a federation is understandable if one considers the circumstances under which it was devised. In the summer of 1918 it was not known in which territories the constitution could be applied. The Baltic states, most of the Ukraine, and Byelorussia were in German hands; Turkestan and Siberia were out of reach, separated from the Bolsheviks by hostile troops. Moreover, Lenin still believed that a greater revolution was imminent and would open all of Europe to the Soviet state. In the interim, while awaiting such events, how could federal ties and separate jurisdictions have been strictly defined?

Many Roads to Federalism

From 1918 to 1922 the federation developed in one of three ways: republics or autonomous regions (the difference between them was not always clear) joined the federated republic; bilateral alliances were formed between independent republics and the RSFSR; and individual federations were established as a prelude to their integration into the Soviet state.

In 1919 Soviet power was sufficiently entrenched to initiate a policy of integration of regions and republics into the RSFSR. In March, the RSFSR and the Soviet Bashkir Republic, with Validov at its head, signed an agreement whereby Bashkiria would receive protection against Kolchak, who had abolished by decree the autonomy of the republic.[24] This was illusory protection: In May 1920 the RSFSR denounced the agreement and incorporated Bashkiria, to which Tatary was added, and, a month later, the autonomous Chuvash region as well.[25]

At the same time, the collapse of the Kazakh Alash-Orda[26] (the national government formed in the steppes by the Kazakhs) enabled the Soviet authorities to take a similar action in that region. The most interesting episode concerned the Kalmyks, a Buddhist Mongol people, who were essentially nomads and cattle-breeders and who lived to the west of the Caspian Sea. This group of widely scattered people had a turbulent history. On 22 July 1919 the Council of the People's Commissars invited them to seek self-determination under the protection of Soviet power and to join the Red Army in fighting Denikin.[27] The invitation itself revealed how Soviet policy had changed with regard to small national groups. Addressing the Kalmyks, Lenin called on them to convene a "workers' congress" that would decide on the future of the whole national group. (Although rejected in theory, the idea that self-determination belonged solely to the working classes lay behind this invitation.) The Kalmyks' Workers' Congress met and received aid from the *Sovnarkom* of the RSFSR, which assigned a commission to take charge of organizing the application of the right to self-determination.[28] On 25 November 1920 a Kalmyk Autonomous Region was created and incorporated into the RSFSR.[29] In the meantime, the RSFSR incorporated the Commune of Karelian workers (August 1920), the Kirghiz Autonomous Republic (August 1920), and the Mari Autonomous Region (early November 1920).

The profusion of inextricably interwoven ethnic groups in the Caucasus posed such enormous problems that Stalin personally had to attend to matters of administrative organization. On 13 November 1920, at the Congress of the Peoples of Daghestan held in Temir Khan Shura, he declared that self-determination implied respect for traditions and for the particularities of the region's peoples but "not their separation from Russia."[30] Four days later he repeated the same remarks to the "mountaineers" of Terek at their congress in Vladikavkaz. Insisting on the need to preserve the character of each ethnic group and to reduce the rivalries arising out of the nationalist parceling of the Caucasus, Stalin highlighted the need for territorial and administrative reorganization.[31] On 20 January 1921 a decree of the Central Executive Committee created two autonomous republics—Daghestan and the Mountaineers' Republic (*Gorskaia*)—and incorporated them into the RSFSR.[32] The group was completed with the Republic of Crimea (October 1921), the Buryat Mongol Autonomous Region (January 1922), the Karachay-Cherkess and Kabardino-Balkarsh Autonomous Regions (January 1922), the Yakut Republic (April 1922), the Oirak Autonomous Region (June 1922), and the Adygei Autonomous Region (July 1922).[33]

By 1923 the RSFSR had seventeen autonomous units, some of which enjoyed purely administrative autonomy, while others, considered republics, had a degree of political autonomy—or at least these relations with the RSFSR existed in principle. In practice, there was little difference between the jurisdiction of republics and that of regions. Their status was decided by the conditions under which their integration had been carried out (external pressures, nationalist leaders). In the years 1919–23, local authority was held in check by the constant intervention of the Russian Communist Party and the *Narkomnats*.

The second path to integration was that of establishing bilateral relations between the RSFSR and independent Soviet republics. In addition to those able to attain lasting independence—Finland, Poland, the Baltic states, and, temporarily, Georgia—several other nations, ones generally mistrustful of the RSFSR, organized themselves into independent Soviet republics. On 10 October 1920 Stalin published an article in *Pravda* that amounted to a plan of action designed to address the national question. The article enumerated the consequences of the fact that revolution had not spread in the West. Stalin maintained that in order to save the Russian revolution, relations between Russia and its former far-flung possessions had to be cemented, and, that some viable manner of organization had to be devised. He listed the possible solutions, from local autonomy to broad political autonomy, or a system of contractual relations that could be applied to the seven independent republics.[34] A complex system of bilateral treaties[35] was then put into effect, gradually tying these entities to the RSFSR and limiting the scope of their authority. Curtailed sovereignty was especially clear in the case of the agreements signed on 30 November 1920 between the RSFSR and Azerbaijan. The "Agreement on Military, Financial, and

Economic Union,"[36] signed by Chicherin and Shakhtakhtinski, commissar of justice in Azerbaijan, stipulated (in Article 2) that the two countries were committed to achieving unity as soon as possible in six areas: military organization and military leadership; organizations governing the economy and foreign trade; supplies; rail and water transportation; post and telecommunications; and finance.

Supplemental agreements dealt with the material conditions for this unification and, significantly, required Azerbaijan to establish its own production plan in accordance with that of the RSFSR while making prices of raw materials and manufactured products in the peripheral republics conform to those of the center (Articles 1 and 5 of the supplemental agreement on economic unification).[37] Finally, the RSFSR was to be represented in the areas undergoing unification by vote-casting plenipotentiaries (Article 6 of the above-cited agreement).

The Russo-Ajar accords are noteworthy for their laconic wording. The goals of unification are contained in a heading only, and the introductory paragraph makes a cursory mention of the need to respond to common interests.

The treaty between the USSR and the Ukraine, signed on 28 December 1920,[38] was of an entirely different nature. It began by invoking the right of peoples to self-determination, independence, and sovereignty. Furthermore, although Article 1 defined the signatories' commitment to military and economic unity, Article 2 emphasized that previous dependent relations did not create any hierarchy between the two states. In Article 3, the agreement provided for the unification of seven Ukrainian and Russian commissariats: war and navy; Supreme Council of National Economy; foreign trade; finances; labor; communications; post and telecommunications. A certain balance was established in that the unified commissariats were part of the governmental machinery of the RSFSR, but were represented in the Ukraine by representatives who came under their own government's control (Article 4). In the end, although the unified commissariats were placed under the authority of the All-Russian Congress of Soviets and the Central Executive Committee of the RSFSR, the Ukrainians were included. In his analysis of the treaty in a thesis devoted to Rakovsky's policy in the Ukraine,[39] Francis Conte underscores that, at this time, the Ukraine maintained a Commissariat of Foreign Affairs independent of the USSR. He offers two explanations for this anomaly: Soviet desire to weaken the Ukrainian governments in exile by making the Soviet Republic of the Ukraine subject to international law, and the desire to use the Ukraine on the chessboard of international politics. Beyond a doubt, Rakovsky's strong personality would not have tolerated being placed at the head of a phantom state; he wanted to act with a high degree of independence, even if he was partial to certain Ukrainian nationalist currents. But there were two other, more profound reasons for different institutional status in the Ukraine. Above all, one must consider the conditions of the Russo-Ukrainian *rapprochement*. After three years of independent political activity, it was difficult to reabsorb the Ukraine into Russian unity. With one decree after another, the RSFSR had transferred the powers of the various Ukrainian Commissariats to their Russian counterparts, emptying the Ukrainian Republic of all substance. The December 1920 treaty thus ratified a practice that had been followed already for months previous. The Soviet leadership recognized the gap between the egalitarian ideology it continued to espouse and the policies directed toward restoring unity, and, in this difficult case, it endeavored to limit its intervention to areas that were deemed essential— economy and defense—while backing off in those areas, such as foreign affairs, that symbolized formal independence. Indeed, from 1920 on, the Ukraine's foreign policy (treaties signed with Germany, Poland, et cetera)[40] was but a pale reflection of the foreign-policy decisions of the RSFSR.

Prudent empiricism made basic needs the focus of the unification effort and worked to preserve appearances, but the Bolshevik perspective on international relations in the early years of the revolution will help explain Bolshevik policy in the Ukraine. From 1917 to 1921, Lenin and the Bolsheviks in general thought of foreign policy in terms of the cause of world revolution; they considered the Soviets' foreign-policy organizations to be instruments of the revolution, as attested by the confusion reigning after 1919 between the organizations of the Comintern and those of the *Narkomindel*, the Commissariat for Foreign Affairs.[41] First Trotsky and then Chicherin were occupied with how to advance the revolution in the West. So long as the Bolsheviks cherished the hope that a new revolutionary tide was rising, they would give little attention to the Commissariat for Foreign Affairs. Rakovsky himself was no stranger to this confusion of tasks: in 1919 he was both the leader of the Ukrainian government and in charge of the southern department of the Comintern. These two institutions had their headquarters in the same place, and Rakovsky was assisted at the Comintern by Angelica Balabanova, who at that time was both a member of the Secretariat of the International and minister of foreign affairs for the Ukraine.[42] Until the 1920 Polish offensive in Kiev, there were few differences in organization and accomplishments between the Southern

Bureau in Kiev and Rakovsky's Ukrainian government. The Polish attack on Kiev forced the Southern Bureau to retreat to Moscow, after which it disappeared as a separate department of the Comintern. It was not until the summer of 1920, after the failed revolutionary war in Poland, that the Bolsheviks, mindful of the need to safeguard the increasingly isolated Soviet state, began to provide adequate instruments for enabling the state to carry out its functions. By the Third Congress of the Comintern in 1921, Lenin and his principal collaborators were acting as statesmen and had withdrawn from the world revolutionary organization, which from that time forward had its own staff.[43] But when the Russo-Ukrainian treaty was concluded, autonomy in foreign affairs was virtually an abstract notion, for at this time there was no concrete foreign problem requiring a concrete response by the Ukraine.

A few weeks later a similar pact was made between Byelorussia and the RSFSR, with nearly identical terms[44] with one exception. An addendum to the Russo-Ukrainian treaty had specified that "in the Congress of Soviets, when matters extraneous to the unified commissariats were being discussed, the other contracting party had only an advisory vote."[45] This clause, which seems to curtail Ukrainian rights in the organizations of the RSFSR, is missing from the treaty with Byelorussia. Does this mean that Byelorussia was more closely integrated into the RSFSR. Undoubtedly, for a supplemental accord on financial problems, signed in June 1921, introduced a representative of the RSFSR with voting power into the Byelorussian Republic's government and subordinated the Republic's financial organizations to the authority of the Russian government.[46]

Statutory differences among the first three republics that were signatories to bilateral agreements have only comparative importance. All the republics were in a position of real independence, from the RSFSR beginning in early 1921, a shift that produced no major confrontations in the periphery.

Georgia was cast in a different mold, and there the Bolsheviks' task was quite another matter. Instead of a Soviet-style government prepared to negotiate with Moscow, Georgia was a nation determined to maintain its regained independence. And the Georgian state could not be accused of counterrevolutionary maneuvers because it was led by Mensheviks.[47] However, Moscow considered independent Georgia, located as it was on the very doorstep of the Soviet state, to be an outpost for the Allies. The Georgian Mensheviks were carrying out continuous international activities and had obtained the *de jure* recognition of several states—even, as we have seen, a *de facto* recognition by the

Bolshevik state in the treaty of May 1920.[48] European social democrats went to Tbilisi to see "real socialism" in power[49] and suggested that the RSFSR should end at the Kura River. The right to self-determination was being asserted in Georgia in a way that proved particularly nettlesome to the Bolsheviks once they reestablished their authority, in 1920, in the other two states of the Caucasus, Armenia and Azerbaijan.[50] But how could the unification policy spread to the rest of the Caucasus if a Georgian social-democratic enclave subsisted?

The Bolsheviks agreed that Georgian independence weakened their southern flank, but were divided on what remedy to apply. It was then that Stalin became the most vehement advocate for decisive action in his native land, invoking the urgency of the international situation and geopolitics. As to the first, he declared: "Georgia is like a girl with many admirers. We, too, must take advantage. The Allies want to build an alliance there against us. Of course we cannot force the Georgians into our camp, but we can help weaken the Georgian government, and with some effort we can hinder the formation of an aggressive alliance between Georgia and the Allies. After that, we shall see what is best to do."[51] He added, from a geopolitical perspective: "The Caucasus is important for the revolution because it is a source of raw materials and food products. And due to its geographical position between Europe and Asia, between Europe and Turkey, its economic and strategic routes are particularly significant."[52]

Stalin's remarks reveal the new perception that was dawning in the domain of Russia's relation to the national territories. In 1917, the revolution consisted of the establishment of the Soviet state. In 1921, the Soviet state, like other states, was beginning to organize its strategic needs and economic resources, both of which required the recovery of areas lost in 1917.

Three elements favored the reintegration of Georgia: the presence in the Caucasus of the Eleventh Army, which retook Baku in 1920[53]; the 7 May 1920 treaty between the RSFSR and the Republic of Georgia, with a secret clause compelling Georgia to legalize the Communist Party and give it full freedom of movement; and the existence of the *Kavburo* (Caucasian Bureau), which worked in cooperation with the Eleventh Army.[54]

Thus Georgia was under pressure from both sides—under communist pressure from within, under *Kavburo*-Army pressure from without. The *Kavburo*-Army pressure intensified in the latter months of 1920, when Ordzhonikidze and Kirov prevailed on Lenin to send the Eleventh Army to the rescue of the Georgian communists.[55] On 20 January

Chicherin, then minister of foreign affairs, took action on the Georgian situation without consulting Lenin. He accused the Georgian government of engaging in repeated violations of the 7 May treaty and called for military intervention to end a domestic insurrection.[56] After lengthy discussions in the Central Committee, Lenin gave the *Kavburo* leaders the authorization to intervene. The Eleventh Army's invasion of Georgia began on 15 February and ended on the 25th, with the fall of Tbilisi and the proclamation of the Soviet Republic of Georgia.[57]

The case of Georgia is interesting for a number of reasons. First, it demonstrates that Soviet leaders in 1921 were concerned about *control*. In January, disagreement over this subject had divided the Central Committee.[58] Stalin, Chicherin, and the *Kavburo* had all been in favor of invasion, against a hesitant Lenin[59]—the difference of opinion was rooted in their analyses of the consequences of a military operation, not in their basic approaches. Stalin and the *Kavburo* wanted to use the instruments of integration that already existed in the Caucasus (party organizations, the army), which they judged powerful enough to quash local resistance. Chicherin was concerned with the West's response, but recalled that Lloyd George had assured Krasin that England considered the Caucasus to be within the sphere of Russian influence. Lenin feared a series of international consequences. A British reaction could endanger Soviet security and ruin Lenin's efforts to integrate Russia into the international community, which he deemed to be indispensable. But Turkey also gave him pause, for Turkey and Russia were in the process of negotiating what later became the friendship treaty of 16 March 1921.[60] Lenin judged peace with Turkey to be more desirable for Russian security than control over a weakened Georgia, which at any rate would have to cede to Russian demands in order to preserve its independence. He was also apprehensive about the reaction of the Georgian people, but his main concern was the international security of the Soviet state—its objective was to reassure, not frighten, the capitalist countries, or so he gave his colleagues to understand, and he reassured them on this point.

The Georgian affair casts a sharp light on the instruments of centralization. Lenin's directives had been ignored in Georgia not in the wake of a particularly violent confrontation, but because the extant political structure enjoyed a considerable degree of autonomy. Stalin had always used the *Kavburo* to argue his point of view and the allegedly popular Georgian demands, the truth of which Lenin had never been able to ascertain. The *Kavburo* had been established to represent the party in the periphery and to work toward reconquest, but in the end it had proved difficult to manipulate. In the same way, the Eleventh Army had completely escaped the authority of Trotsky, commissar of war,[61] who on 21 February 1921—one week after the invasion—was still inquiring into the conditions under which the decision to invade had been made.[62] Moreover, Lenin had agreed on the 14th to the invasion, by which time it was already two days old.[63] At any rate, in order to cushion the risk of international reaction, the Bolshevik leaders portrayed the Georgian affair as a conflict between Georgians and Armenians that had produced unrest, which the Eleventh Army had been called in temporarily to quell: this was the explanation Lenin gave to the Soviet on 28 February. But the Georgian communists who prepared locally for Soviet intervention—Orakhelashvili, Budu Mdivani, Filip Makharadze, and A. Gegeshkori—made no mention in their message of any conflict with the Armenians, which proves that the affair was entirely fabricated by the *Kavburo*.[64]

Although he agreed to it, the pressure exerted on Georgia and the activities of the poorly controlled officials there did not sit well with Lenin. Until that time, relations between the Soviet state and the nationalities had been decided in Moscow; in the case of Georgia, however, the initiative had slipped away from the Soviets, and to a great extent their hand had been forced by the political and military authorities in the Caucasus. The gulf between Soviet authority and the local Caucasian group led Lenin to strengthen safeguards and recommend caution. His telegram of 2 March to Ordzhonikidze discloses his concerns: "We must carry out a specific policy of concessions to the Georgian intelligentsia and small merchants; we must even accept sacrifices so that the latter may continue business activity. It is immensely important to look for an acceptable compromise to form a bloc with Jordania or with other Georgian Mensheviks who before the insurrection were not totally opposed to the idea of a Soviet organization in Georgia under certain conditions. I beseech you to remember the domestic and international conditions that require that the Georgian communists not apply the Russian *Shablon* [model] but discover specific, intelligent, and flexible tactics."[65]

The crisis ended on 21 May with the signing of a bilateral treaty. Three treaties fit into this pattern—Khiva, 30 September 1920[66]; Bukhara, 4 March 1921[67]; and Armenia, 30 September 1921—thus reconciling Russia with the former possessions that it had lost for a time.

The treaties were formulated differently where different relations of power existed, but all, except for the ones pertaining to the two former emirates of Central Asia, were in response to the situation that prevailed in 1921 or to the exigencies imposed on the RSFSR. All the treaties were drafted as classic alliances between equals, not as agreements creating hierarchical relations, and they all covered two principal areas, economic and military matters. In the economic sphere, shortages were the main concern; in the military domain, unity already existed, having been forged by the Red Army over the course of the civil war. However, unity of diplomatic action was not stipulated in the treaties. Until 1922 the Ukraine was the only nation that maintained its own ties to foreign powers in the name of particular interests.[68] But the political and economic overlap resulting from the treaties was so strong that no Soviet republic could entertain the notion of an independent foreign policy. This was seen on 18 March 1921 when the Riga treaty was signed, ending the war in Poland, where various republics had sent largely fictitious representatives. Although the Ukraine had had two envoys in Poland, Poland had received only a single Russo-Ukrainian delegation, which suggested that the Ukraine enjoyed semi-federal status. Certainly Moscow was trying to preserve appearances. Thus the Soviet-Turkish treaty of 1921, which resolved border disputes in the three Caucasian republics, was negotiated by Russia alone, with a proviso for participation in the second stage of negotiations by the republics in question. The republics signed the Kars treaty a short time later, thus indicating that their position was the product of a dialogue with Russia.[69]

At the first large international meeting, the fiction of the republics' diplomatic capacities was revealed to be utterly transparent. When the RSFSR alone was invited to the 1922 Genoa conference, the republics of the former empire discussed what attitude they would adopt. The Ukraine did not want to abandon its sovereignty: the Politburo of its communist party declared on 23 January 1922 that although a "common diplomatic front of all the Soviet republics" was desirable, Ukrainian delegates would consent to be part of the Soviet delegation.[70] This was a vain struggle. On 22 February 1922 representatives of the eight republics attended a meeting at the Kremlin, after which they agreed to "entrust to the RSFSR the mission of representing them, of defending their interests at the conference and signing in their name any documents."[71]

On the same day, Kalinin, president of the All-Russian Central Executive Committee, emphasized that such a mission confirmed the provisions adopted by the Central Executive Committee on 27 January.[72] Thus, without waiting for the republics to delegate international powers to it, Russia confiscated their authority. The alliance defined by the bilateral treaties now bore a striking resemblance to union.

Union Imposed

At this time, communists who hitherto had not been suspected of hostility toward Moscow were showing nationalist inclinations. This renascent nationalism had three centers. In Central Asia, Basmashi military resistance was growing, and—even more serious—dissidence was spreading within the Bolshevik Party. Sultan Galiev, the Tatar leader, repudiated the Marxist concept of proletarian internationalism in relations between unequally developed nations.[73] In Georgia, Bolsheviks such as Filip Makharadze and Budu Mdivani, architects of the February 1921 intervention, moved closer to nationalist positions.[74] All these crises had their source in the policy of regional unity imposed by Moscow. Lenin, who had been hesitant about military intervention in Georgia, was most adamant about unity. Economic necessities were a priority; building up the whole was more important to him than fortifying the framework of the republics.[75] Total economic disorganization throughout Russia in 1921 demanded both a loosening of constraints— thus the birth of NEP (New Economic Policy)—and the rational use of existing resources. Moreover, economic unity would facilitate political solutions, which in turn would harmonize the status of all the republics. Indubitably, beginning in 1921 the Soviet republics adopted constitutions aligning their political systems with the structures of the RSFSR.[76] But the provisions concerning interrelations among republics betrayed profound disagreements. Whereas Armenia endorsed associations between regions,[77] Georgia contemplated treating all Soviet republics equally and, instead of regional unity, preferred that all territories enter on an equal footing "in one Soviet Socialist Republic as soon as the conditions necessary for its foundation are created."[78]

On 16 April 1921, under pressure from Moscow, the republics of the Caucasus moved to unify management of railroad transportation (woefully disorganized) on the RSFSR model and according to its rules. Similarly, foreign trade was unified in 2 June 1921. In Moscow it was thought that having these common institutions would pave the way for complete unity. In practice, the economic conditions in the Caucasian republics changed very little, because the unity they had hoped for was hampered by different currencies, customs barriers, and local desires to persist in particularism. Once again the *Kavburo*, in conjunction with the central leadership, decided the outcome. Ordzhonikidze was sent to the Caucasus[79]; the *Kavburo* met in Baku on 3 November with Molotov and Dzerzhinsky, and decided to draft a federal program. The discussions took place between Moscow and the *Kavburo* rather than between the *Kavburo* and the capitals of the republics in question. Lenin considered the matter of Transcaucasian unity to be finally resolved, but was concerned about the nature of the links between the Transcaucasian federation and the RSFSR.[80] The Georgian communists, however, followed more timidly by their Ajar counterparts, became indignant. On 25 November 1921 Budu Mdivani wired Stalin, "The partisans of immediate federalization . . . take no account of the existing forces and the actual situation."[81] Filip Makharadze protested the principle and methods to be used, although he did not question the pace of federalization proposed by the *Kavburo*. In his 6 December 1921 report to the Central Committee of the Bolshevik Party and to Lenin he wrote: "Federation imposed from above will be nothing but an additional bureaucratic apparatus that will be wholly unpopular with the masses and remote from them. . . . It would be better to maintain contractual ties, to unite our economic efforts without organizational fusion or formal subordination."[82] After criticizing the content of the *Kavburo*'s plan, he deplored the methods: the federal process was being imposed "from above" by violence. Complaints about the latter had been inundating Moscow. Georgians were appealing to the Central Committee and to Stalin. On 13 December 1921 A. Svanidze wrote to Stalin, "Ordzhonikidze is holding the heavy bludgeon of central authority over our heads."

Throughout the crisis Lenin backed the *Kavburo*. He was kept informed by Stalin, but their discussions were confined to details. The federation's constitution would have to be established "from above"— the *Kavburo* and a special commission on federation were installed by 8 December 1921—yet would also have to be agreed on by the base, that is, the Soviets, elected on a federal platform. The elections that took place in the three republics between 1921 and 1922 became a battle for and against Transcaucasian federation. In the face of those opposed to federation, Ordzhonikidze brandished the flag of internationalism and warned of the danger of factionalism, which had been prohibited in March 1921 by the Tenth Congress of the Communist Party. To oppose a federation that was deemed necessary by the Bolshevik Party was, he said, in and of itself participation in divisive activities.[83]

These threats made any opposition untenable, when, in February 1922, after the elections, Ordzhonikidze announced that the time had come to begin organizing the federation. The opponents of federation, isolated in their parties and under pressure from the *Kavburo*, capitulated. In Tiflis, on 11 and 12 March the Conference for the Unity of the Caucasus adopted a federal statute comprising thirteen points,[84] and the Federation of Soviet Socialist Republics of Transcaucasia was born, as an institution responsible for the business of foreign relations, defense, finance, foreign trade, transport, information, domestic security, and the economy. The federated republics maintained their sovereignty in other spheres, which were greatly reduced. The organization of federal and local powers, as well as the association between the two levels, followed the pattern already set down in the RSFSR. Article 13 of the 12 March accord, which served as the federal constitution, provided that relations between the Transcaucasian Federation and the RSFSR be defined by treaty.

In actuality, a series of accords signed over the following months set the stage for the federation's economic integration into the RSFSR and relegated international representation to the RSFSR (on 8 April 1922 tariff barriers were eliminated; on 12 May telecommunications were unified; on 10 November the presidium of the Transcaucasian communist organization recommended to the Federal Council that the federation's foreign representatives be recalled and that Caucasian interests be represented by the RSFSR).

The federalization of the Caucasus and the 12 March 1922 treaty clarified the views held by Lenin and Stalin, who were in agreement at the time on the scope of sovereignty within the federation. Ordzhonikidze aptly summed up their viewpoints. He said that sovereignty should be defined not in a static way "by the attributes each nation gains once and for all, but as a dynamic movement in which unity is a guarantor of sovereignty for all, not the guarantor of diversity."[85] If Ordzhonikidze did not define the formal nature of the process to which he alluded, it was because the Bolsheviks in 1922 were sensitive to the dynamics of unity more than to the particular means whereby to achieve it. But their general intent was clear.

The Caucasians protested the prospective political unity. The Georgians, who even after March 1922 were the most violent critics of Russian policy, denounced its voluntarism. Mdivani declared that even if the economic situation demanded that sovereignty be restricted, it did not follow that real economic cooperation required political unity. Moreover, he argued, economic unity did not exist in 1922; there was not even any cooperation, so why erect federal structures? Makharadze added his voice to these criticisms: "Your union is a corpse that you will not be able to revive."[86] Thus, Georgians were opposed to the idea— which was endorsed and largely put into practice by the Bolsheviks— that a revolution could begin at the superstructure level (in this case, the bureaucratic organizations of federal authority) without taking into account the state of the society, its needs, and its aspirations. Federalization was imposed on the republics of the Caucasus because the instruments to achieve it were at hand: the *Kavburo*, an emanation of the Bolshevik Party, was there to interpret centralist concepts in the Caucasus, against the wishes of the local communist parties. The *Kavburo* used the same arguments that had led the Tenth Congress to prohibit factions and to transpose the Russian solution to the periphery. In fact, Ordzhonikidze maintained that the rush to forge federal bonds was justified by the excessive concessions that had been granted in 1921, and to prove his point he cited the theses of the Eleventh Party Congress, which retreated from NEP.

With the problem of the Caucasus settled, even if for a short time, the Soviet leaders had gathered the territories that had been dispersed for a five-year period into a constellation of states revolving around the RSFSR, with Moscow at the center. For example, an area as important as Baku depended for all its economic decisions on the direct authority of the organizations of the RSFSR. The central Communist Party thus achieved total authority over the communist organizations of the periphery. In the eyes of the outside world, the differences between the Soviet republics and the RSFSR became blurred. By the fifth anniversary of the Russian revolution, the institutionalization of territorial unification was on the agenda.

The Constitutional Conflict:
The Definition of Federation

In 1920 Lenin defined his vision of the future relations among Soviet republics: "In recognizing federation as one of the transitional forms to complete unity, it is indispensable to make federal links even tighter."[87]

At this time, when Lenin spoke of federation, he did not have a precise model in mind but rather believed that practicality had to serve as the basis for defining federal links.[88] He also identified two federal realities, the *contractual* reality of the RSFSR's relation to the sovereign republics and the *organic* reality of the autonomy of the national entities integrated into the RSFSR. In fact, Byelorussia and Turkestan represented yet a third model, one that combined contractual relations and autonomy.

But contractual differences aside, attitudes and actions mattered more. Whereas some states—Byelorussia, for example—seemed to accept the development of federal links and the dynamic concept of the federal system, others—especially Georgia—blocked the development of common institutions. In Georgia, the division of the communist party into pro-federationists and anti-federationists had the effect of paralyzing the contractual relationship. The federal system was propagated in an authoritarian way from the center. The persistence of conflict in the Caucasus and the setbacks encountered in the Ukraine caused Lenin to consider accelerating federation and fully developing the common institutions so that the two would have the same status. In 1922 he declared to the Eleventh Party Congress: "An independent Ukrainian republic is all well and good. But as far as the party is concerned, the republic sometimes—how shall I say it—takes liberties that we would do well to shatter. For there are cunning people there and I won't say the C.C. is deceiving us, but in a certain way it is slipping away from us."[89] At the preceding year's Congress, Stalin, *rapporteur* on the national question, had stated that the party's policy of unification should lead to the formation of a federation on the RSFSR model, which in turn should serve as a model for a future world federation of socialist states. Stalin here unveiled his concept of federation, which was soon to become a subject of controversy with Lenin. On 13 January 1922 he wrote to Lenin, "Some comrades propose organizing the unification of all the independent republics around the principle of autonomy."[90] But, he added, it would be ill-advised to embark on this enterprise on the eve of the Genoa conference.

On 10 August 1922 a commission composed of Stalin, Kuibyshev, Molotov, Ordzhonikidze, Rakovsky, and Sokolnikov, who represented the federation, with Agamaly-Ogly (Azerbaijan), Miasnikov (Armenia), Cherviakov (Byelorussia), Petrovsky (Ukraine), and Mdivani (Georgia) representing the republics, settled down in Moscow to draw up plans for the federation.

Stalin had a prominent position as the project's drafter. One month later he presented his colleagues with a text containing the ideas he had espoused at the Eleventh Congress, that is, to use the RSFSR model for the federation. The RSFSR now included new national groups with autonomous status; the federation could be formed via "formal adherence" to the RSFSR by Soviet republics, which would become autonomous republics. The power structure of the RSFSR (government, Central Executive Committee) would serve as the organizations of power for the federation.

Stalin's text was sent to the central committees of the various parties in each republic. Azerbaijan and Byelorussia approved, noting that the law conformed to the existing reality. Armenia followed suit. The

Ukrainians, without criticizing the draft, expressed their preference for the status quo. The reaction in Georgia was explosive. The central committee there rejected the text and asserted its desire to safeguard the republic's sovereignty. The presence in the Central Committee of the Georgian party of Ordzhonikidze, Kirov, and Sokolnikov was not enough to dissuade the opposition. Lenin, who was ill at the time, did not find out about the project and its controversies until the end of September, when the various republics were firm in their positions. At that time he opposed Stalin, accusing him of moving too quickly.[91] Lenin condemned the idea of autonomy and proposed something completely different: for the federation to unite equal republics, not republics under RSFSR domination. "I hope," he wrote, "that the meaning of this concession is clear; we recognize ourselves as equal in rights with the RSS of the Ukraine, et cetera, and we enter into a new union, a new federation on equal footing. . . . It is important not to provide grist for the mill of the advocates of independence [nezavisimtsy]."[92]

For such equality to be effective, the federation would have to have its own power-structure, beyond that of the individual republics or of the RSFSR. Lenin suggested the creation of an Executive Committee and a Council of Commissars of the Federated Peoples. He also decided to follow the affair personally. Despite his evident ill humor,[93] Stalin amended his draft, incorporating Lenin's comments, and presented it on 6 October to the Central Committee as a "more precise" formulation of the original project.[94] Lenin's final comment on the affair, in a note to Kamenev, was to "declare war to the death on Great Russian chauvinism" and to emphasize the need for "a Russian, a Ukrainian, a Georgian, et cetera, each in turn, to preside over the Central Executive Committee of the Union."[95]

On 6 October the compromise project signed by Stalin, Ordzhonikidze, Miasnikov, and Molotov was sent to the Central Committee, which approved it.[96] It appeared that the troubles between the peripheral republics and the center were over, but this was not the case. First Stalin's submission to Lenin's "national liberalism," as he wrote to the members of the Politburo, had been only superficial. More so than Lenin, Stalin was attached to the centralist conception of relations among Soviet nations. Lenin certainly agreed in principle, but he opposed Stalin's methods: if Lenin favored equal status for all nations, it was not for the nations' benefit, but in order to avoid acrimonious relations with them. Lenin's concerns were the same in October 1922 as they were in 1913: to give oppressed nations the confidence in proletarian internationalism so that national sentiment could be replaced by class solidarity. Lenin's objection to Stalin was that he was "too rushed" and did not understand that the non-Russian nations had yet to surpass the stage of national loyalties. He condemned Stalin's approach not as misguided but as inopportune; if applied too soon it ran the risk of "providing more grist for the mill of the advocates of independence." The advocates of independence, especially the Georgians, evoked no tenderness in Lenin; in the conflict that erupted between them and Stalin over the Transcaucasian federation, he supported Stalin.

Stalin's attitude was equally revealing of his real thoughts. If he accepted Lenin's criticism and revised his draft, it was only out of a realistic conception of the connection between the law and a *de facto* situation. Given that the preexisting distribution of forces in the old tsarist empire had led to the RSFSR's preeminence in the federation, he endeavored to have this position of strength legally codified. He resigned himself to surrendering the point because he was convinced that, at any rate, egalitarian formulas would not change actual inequalities. The RSFSR was and would continue to be the fulcrum and focus of the federation.

The new version of the federation plan was accepted by all the national parties. However, Georgian leaders demanded that their nation be admitted with the same status as the Ukraine rather than through a Transcaucasian federation in which its rights as a republic would be limited. Stalin and Ordzhonikidze, his representative at Tiflis, insisted that Georgia enter the Union indirectly and that the Transcaucasian federation become a federated republic, thereby reducing each republic of the Caucasus to an autonomous entity.

Stalin and his supporters had two principal arguments. First, they claimed that the complexity of nationalities in the Caucasus and in each republic justified a federalist organization of the region, designed to neutralize nationality clashes. In an article titled "Why Should Georgia, Azerbaijan, and Armenia Join the Union of Republics through a Transcaucasian Republic?"[97] Miasnikov maintained that the conflicts among minorities in the Caucasus were so serious that a mediating organization—regional federation—was necessary so that Moscow, the federal center, would not be swamped by these groups' mutual recriminations. Ordzhonikidze even cited the example of an "idiotic tsarism" that had "understood that a unifying administrative center should exist in the Caucasus to be a buffer between the nationalities and the central power."[98] The second argument used against the Georgians was egalitarianism. Georgia's geographic position was so important that its privileges would persist unless it joined a Transcaucasian organization, for no Soviet republic could hope to maintain privileges within the greater Union.[99]

But even more than with arguments, Ordzhonikidze fought the local communist leaders in Georgia by the rules. While Ordzhonikidze purged the communist party apparatus in Georgia, local leaders appealed to Lenin, Kamenev, and Bukharin, accusing Moscow's envoy of sowing anarchy and using violent means—even physical violence—against them. Lenin, who believed that the federal solution would resolve these difficulties, replied in a scathing telegram[100]: "I am surprised by the indecorous tone of your note . . . . I resolutely condemn your attacks against Ordzhonikidze and I insist you submit your problems, in a decent and loyal tone, to the secretariat of the Central Committee of the Russian Communist Party."

Bukharin and Kamenev were no more sympathetic. Yet the Russian leaders were clearly concerned by the rash of complaints from Georgia and decided to dispatch an investigatory committee. The committee, however, designed by Stalin,[101] and headed by Dzerzhinsky, with Mitskevich-Kapsukas and Sosnovsky as assistants, had minimal contact with the rebels and ignored Ordzhonikidze, who went to the extreme of physical violence against his opponents. The committee blamed the crisis on the nationalists.[102]

The crisis shocked Lenin, and probably aggravated his worsening health. By November he gave no credence to Stalin or Dzerzhinsky's explanations and decided to gather his own information. Before his envoy (Rykov) and aides submitted their detailed report, Lenin drew his own conclusions from the affair and began to reconsider the problem of interrelations among the national groups.

On 30 December 1922 he drafted the notes[103] that were later sent to Trotsky (in March 1923) and represented his final theoretical contribution to the national problem. The notes were meant not for publication but to clarify his position at the Twelfth Party Congress, where he hoped the situation would be resolved. He began with an admission of failure: "Before the workers of Russia, I am terribly guilty of not having dedicated sufficient energy to the famous question of 'autonomization,' officially called the Union of Soviet Socialist Republics." The solution of the national question in it present form, he wrote, reduced "the freedom to leave the Union, which is our justification, to a mere scrap of paper" and left the minorities at the mercy of that one-hundred-percent Russian product, the Great Russian chauvinism that characterizes the Russian bureaucracy." What was needed was to protect the minorities against the Russian *derzhimordy* (a character from Gogol' who embodied the brutality and stupidity of the bureaucrat). This letter, together with the notes he dictated to his secretaries in the days before his last stroke,[104] testifies to the new direction Lenin's thoughts were taking. He acknowledged the imbalance between large- and small-state chauvinism and was troubled to see Russian communists restoring the positions of great power occupied by bureaucrats under the old regime. Stalin, Ordzhonikidze, and various fellow travelers, like their predecessors, were becoming *velikoderzhavniki* (imperialists) and *derzhimordy.* On 7 March a last stroke left Lenin incapacitated. Two days earlier he had entrusted the Georgian dossier[105] to Trotsky, and the next day he announced his support of the Georgian communists ("Disgusted by Ordzhonikidze's brutality and the complicity of Stalin and Dzerzhinsky, I am preparing my notes for a speech"[106]) but time ran out before he could complete the project.

Although the Georgian affair distressed Lenin, it did not slow the march toward unity. On 21 November 1922, although Georgia was opposed, the special commission of the party's Central Committee publicly announced the date projected for the definitive text of the constitution and the formal ratification of the Union. On 30 November the Politburo adopted the text of the "fundamental principles for the establishment of the Union," which stipulated in Article 1 that the Transcaucasian federation would join the Union. Both the Politburo and the Central Committee, which on 18 November had ratified the former's decision, ignored Georgian resistance to these measures.

The republics lost no time falling into line. On 13 November the Seventh Congress of Soviets of the Ukraine announced its approval of the Union of Soviet Republics and the Ukraine's membership.[107] The same day the Transcaucasian Federal Republic had formed, adopted a constitution, and voted to join the Union.[108] On 18 December Byelorussia followed its example.[109] Finally, on 30 December the USSR was born of the treaty uniting the RSFSR and the three republics of the Ukraine, Byelorussia, and Transcaucasia.[110]

The Constitution of 1924

The first constitution of the USSR, drafted by a commission of twenty-five members with Kalinin at its head, was adopted by the Executive Committee (VCIK) on 6 July 1923 and approved by the Second All-Union Congress of Soviets on 31 January 1924. The constitution's cornerstone was the principle embodied in the 30 December treaty: Union as a contractual act, the voluntary association of states with equal rights, with the right to withdraw voluntarily from the Union. In joining the Union, the states did not give up their national sovereignty, and the Union did not possess a system of state control distinct from the individual state's sovereignty.

The sovereign states gave the federation considerable authority, as elaborated in chapter one: international representation, defense, modification of borders, domestic security, foreign trade, planning, transport, telecommunications, budget, currency, and credit. The federal organizations consisted of the All-Union Congress of Soviets, the Central Executive Committee and its chair, and the Council of People's Commissars. The Congress of Soviets was to be elected indirectly by limited public suffrage. The cities would elect delegates at the rate of one for every 25,000 inhabitants and the provinces, at one for every 125,000 inhabitants. The All-Union Congress of Soviets was to meet annually, but in practice would meet every two years.

Between Congresses, state authority was to be assured by the Central Executive Committee, a bicameral body composed of the Council of the Union and the Council of Nationalities. In the republics the Central Executive Committee was to contain only one chamber, made up of representatives elected on a territorial basis. The 414 members of the Council of the Union were to be elected by the Congress from the representatives of the federated republics, in proportion to their population. The Council of Nationalities would be composed of five representatives per federated republic or Autonomous Republic; one per Autonomous Region of the RSFSR; and one each from the Adzhar Autonomous Republic, the Abkhazian Autonomous Republic, and the autonomous regions of the Caucasus (southern Ossetia, Nakhichevan, Upper Karabakh), respectively. The Central Executive Committee was to meet three times a year. In between, the presidium of twenty-one members would assume responsibility. The Council of Peoples' Commissars was empowered with both executive and administrative, and certain legislative functions. The Peoples' Commissariats managed the branches of the government, and to a greater extent than the other organizations of power represented the federal structure of the Soviet state. Three types of Peoples' Commissariats coexisted in the constitution of 1924: *federal commissariats*, existing only at the level of the Union and dealing with problems of the federation; *unified commissariats*, existing both at the local level (in the republics) and at the federal level, with the federal level coordinating and directing the action of the corresponding commissariats in the republics (thus the Supreme Council of National

Economy, and Food, Labor, Finance, and Workers' and Peasants' In-
spection commissariats existed on both levels); and, lastly, *commissariats of the republics*, in charge of domains not reserved for the Union or
the common authority of the Union and its members.

The constitution of 1924 was a closed and defined, durable legal
framework, unlike the constitution of 1918, which had been left open-
ended in contemplation of future changes. In 1924, though the constitution framers had considered the Soviet state to be still in transition,
they endowed it with the attributes of a traditional state. In Title II, the
constitution listed the four federated republics; hence the new state corresponded to an enclosed territory. It is true that Title I allowed for the
possibility that other republics would join the Union, but the notion of
capitalist encirclement was alluded to. The opposition between the
socialist state and the hostile capitalist world presupposed the existence of safe borders, provided in the treaties of the years 1920–21. Thus
the constitution unified two contrasting tendencies: the aspiration for
universality, which lent the Soviet state an open, offensive, and transitory character; and the desire to preserve what was already established,
which led the state to withdraw, adopt a defensive attitude, and affirm
its permanent character. This fundamental contradiction also exists in
federalism, the linchpin of the organization of the Soviet state.

The constitution of 1924 was a federal constitution, even though the
terms "federal" and "federation," used in the 1918 constitution, were
absent from the new text. Despite this silence, the characteristics of
federalism are unmistakable: the constitution of 1924 consecrated the
union of legally equal and sovereign nations, free to enter into or secede from the federation, a right they retained forever; federal jurisdiction was granted by the desire of the nations— without the nations'
consent, neither their right to leave the Union, nor the ability to modify
their borders, nor the balance between federal and national jurisdictions could be altered; and, finally, the existence of two chambers and a
parliament reflecting the multinational composition of the Soviet state
were indicative of federalist construction.

Thus, in a strictly formal sense, the constitution of 1924 satisfied national aspirations and founded a Union in which nations coexisted
under generally accepted principles. But did the inclusion in the constitution of national rights make the Soviet state a true federal state? It
falls to the jurists to answer this question, and they have given totally
contradictory opinions. But beyond the legal debates, we must
examine the extent to which the framework of the Soviet constitution

fulfilled national aspirations. In this regard, it bears noting that the constitution granted a range of statutes to the various nationalities, a diversity of solutions in some ways reminiscent of the tsarist regime's multipronged approach. Four republics existed in 1922, six in 1925 (Uzbekistan and Turkestan as separate from the RSFSR); of the first four, two were already federal republics (RSFSR and Transcaucasia). Even those sovereign nations that joined the Union did not all enjoy the same degree of sovereignty within the Union. Besides the large national groups, the constitution recognized various types of autonomy adhering to minority peoples, depending on their classification as Autonomous Republics, Autonomous Regions, or territorially dispersed ethnic groups. Everything from national sovereignty to cultural autonomy fit into the complex constitutional construction of 1924. In some cases, reduced autonomy was justified by the numeric or cultural weakness of the national group—the Arabs in the Caucasus or the Buryat peoples, respectively. In other cases, a national group's geographical position rendered sovereign status permanently out of reach, for sovereignty was illusory for those not bound to the Union by a border. Thus, the Bashkir people, who had evidenced their desire to exist as a nation, could never hope to advance beyond the stage of political and cultural autonomy. Statutory differences prevailed where aspirations for nationhood—juridical sovereignty—were held in check by the federation's need for territorial cohesiveness. These inequalities weakened the scope of the federal system and encouraged latent national discontent. What compensation could limited sovereignty offer if the rights of all the peoples of the USSR were supposed to be equally represented in the federal whole?

It also bears noting that although its transitional nature was not articulated in the text, the constitution of 1924 was the product of a particular stage, and the concessions that the constitution granted to national groups were tied to that stage. The Soviet state was announcing a definitive occurrence—the triumph of the revolution and the complementary revolution of economic and social structures—but the federal structure of the state reflected a provisional situation characterized by the belatedly aroused consciousness of national groups' rights and national particularities. Yet the entire *raison d'être* of the revolution and the Soviet state was to enable its constituent peoples to surpass the stage of national aspirations. Herein lies one of the fundamental contradictions of the Soviet constitution of 1924. The federal system was expected to function only in the short term, to further the withering away of national sentiment and the replacement of the federal system with another. The state's status was ambiguous and uncertain—transitional or enduring?—but not the nations comprising it or the federation itself: both were believed to be transitional, fated to disappear. Yet concessions had to be made to local conditions—the national heterogeneity of Russian territory—and the demands of the time—capitalist encirclement was sharpening nationalist conflicts, as Lenin repeatedly pointed out. Federation was seen above all as a pedagogical instrument, a school of internationalism.

Hence, while discussions concerning the reality or the purely formal nature of the constitution of 1924 surely have legal significance, they will not help us to understand Bolshevik intentions. To decipher these, we must reformulate the question and ask: What in the federal system can be interpreted as evidence of a final objective?

Beyond its federal provisions, the constitution of 1924 contained basic provisions that promoted increased unity, and for the interim it set up a system of control emanating from the center to the periphery. Via the federal constitution, the Bolsheviks were hoping to move toward international unity, but they also had to prevent federalism from disintegrating—for fear that the burgeoning centrifugal forces could consume the unitary objective. The constitution of 1924 was a response to the need to move beyond federalism and the need to preserve it. The areas of federal jurisdiction were very important. At the same time, everything worked in favor of constant federal intervention in the ill-defined and insufficiently protected areas supposedly within the republics' domain. The constitution was clear about the Union's responsibilities (Title II, Chapter I), but the republics' particular spheres of interest were never identified, and the constitution contained no statement, as would have been logical, that whatever did not fall into federal domain was to be deemed to lie within the republics' jurisdiction. The opposite was in fact the case: Chapter IV (Articles 13 to 29), which dealt with federal authority, foresaw the possibility that federal organizations would overstep their jurisdictional boundaries. The absence of a regulatory mechanism to distribute authority between the republic and the federation; the Supreme Court's ability to intervene as final arbiter of the legality of the republic's decisions (Chapter VII, Article 436), without a counterpart to control the legality of federal decisions; the general affirmation of the primacy of the constitution and federal rules over the constitution and local rules of the republics in case of conflict—these elements all favored centralized decision making and promoted control by the central leadership over the local authorities in the periphery. The constitution did not disguise these centralizing elements or the desire to reinforce controls for two reasons. One reason was circumstantial and had to do with the economic concerns of the Soviet leaders. The economy required a certain degree of centralization, and in the 1920s the primary goal of the Soviet authorities was to get on a firm economic footing. Thus, the constitution provided for economic affairs above all to come under federal control. The second, and deeper, reason was the pedagogical function it was expected that federalism would fulfill. Because federalism was a temporary concession to undeveloped social consciousness, it had to be transfused throughout with a unitary, internationalist perspective, of which the Union was a first phase. Consequently, the authors of the constitution of 1924 did not want to emphasize its local ramifications; rather, they proclaimed its common, unifying elements.

From 1917 to 1924 an important evolutionary process took place: egalitarian ideology still lay at the heart of Bolshevik thought, but what changed was the way it was put into practice. In 1917 this ideology translated into the nation's right to choose its destiny. In 1921 and continuously thereafter, it translated into the right to equal participation in the revolution of changing structures and mentalities.

Common destiny took primacy over individual inclinations, and common destiny implied a tightening of control, a centralized organization of Soviet society within a fortified framework. Democratic centralism, which enabled Lenin to forge an efficient revolutionary instrument, underpinned the construction of the Soviet federal state and gave it its true meaning.

CHAPTER 8

Unity: The Communist Party

The equilibrium of Soviet institutions depended on two apparently contradictory goals—temporary diversity and ultimate unity. The state, guarantor of minority-group rights, was reinforced by the structure of the Communist Party, which from the center to the periphery ensured respect for working-class interests. But in the year 1918, the party was not prepared to be grafted onto a federal state. Lenin had always balked at applying a principle of national equality to party organization, yet the party's centralized structure and steadfast internationalism could not fulfill his intentions. Adjustments had to be made so that nationality groups would not perceive the internationalist party as exclusively Russian, or as a vehicle of centralization.

The Communist Party of Turkestan: A Compromise between Nationalism and Centralism

Bolshevik actions were aimed at keeping regional communist organizations under a central authority so that the center would be able to control the periphery. This control presupposed the existence of infra-structures adapted to different regions. In places lacking communist or-ganizations— Central Asia was an extreme case—the party had to be-come decentralized and create local organizations with an "indige-nous" coloration.

In 1917 the Bolshevik Party in the Moslem peripheral regions had few members, all of whom were Russian. The party's "colonial" attitude to-ward the natives only resulted in further alienation.[1] With the revolu-tion, bureaucrats and colonists swelled the party's ranks; for these atyp-ical militants the party came to represent Russian interests in a colonial milieu. Lenin's orders from Moscow were to develop the party in Cen-tral Asia and involve the local population, but only the first part of his directive was actually carried out. In the early months of 1918 local party organizations multiplied in Turkestan. They recruited new mem-bers and elected standing committees, but recruitment efforts, at the mercy of the civil war, were plagued by endemic personnel changes and stringent membership requirements.

How could the native population be attracted to these organizations? At the party's first regional Congress, in December 1918, Klevleev, the principal *rapporteur*, proposed that the Koran be used to promulgate communist ideas.[2] His suggestion was adopted despite vigorous op-position; thereafter, newspapers and the basic communist texts were disseminated in local languages as well as in Russian. It was also de-cided that local communist cadre would be quickly trained and inte-grated into the state apparatus, and youth organizations formed. One may well wonder toward which social class these recruitment efforts were directed, for the delegates assumed that the proletariat in Moslem areas was essentially Russian, and they feared that the peasantry would "sooner or later lend its support to the counterrevolution," an analysis that discouraged the development of a local party.

Relations between local party organizations in Moslem areas and the central party were fraught with tension, and the manner in which thorny issues were resolved in Turkestan was long a serious impedi-ment to party development throughout the USSR. The central leader-ship considered two approaches: the creation of a party—preferably Moslem—to act as an umbrella federation for all existing organizations in Central Asia and be represented in the Russian Communist Party, with equal status,[3] or the integration of such an organization into the Russian Communist Party.[4] The latter model was adopted, a portent of the hierarchical relations that obtained after 1924 between local parties in the republics, all of which followed a similar evolution, and the Communist Party of the Soviet Union.

Lenin's watchwords, the necessary "de-Russification" and "indigenization" of the party, ignited debates in Tashkent on party organization. The controversy was troubling to the central leadership because it was not an isolated case. The Tatar Sultan Galiev, one of the highest officials in the *Narkomnats's* Moslem Commissariat in Moscow at the time, was charged with attracting the Moslem masses to the Bolshevik Party. But, doubtful that a unitary party would fulfill nationalist aspirations, he founded (in March 1918) the Moslem Communist-Socialist Party, independent of the Russian Communist Party, with membership open to all, regardless of previous communist affiliation. Some months later it became the Russian Party of Moslem Communists (Bolsheviks), maintaining its independence from the Russian Communist Party.[5]

In both Moscow and Tashkent the Communist Party was splintering into separate organizations predicated on ethnic, territorial, and religious schisms. With Stalin as its strategist, the Russian Communist Party reacted swiftly by creating a *Musboro*, a Central Bureau of Moslem organizations, to manage all existing party organizations in Islamic territories.[6]

Turkestan was to be the testing-ground for the *Musburo*, whose first mission was to transform a predominantly Russian organization into a Moslem-controlled party in order to make it an attractive model.[7] In May 1919 the *Musburo* convened the First Conference of Moslem Organizations in Tashkent. At the time, a Basmashi revolt, supported by the population, was at its height. The Soviet authorities in Tashkent, most of them Russians, felt besieged.[8] The conference was in a double bind, embroiled in a conflict on the one hand between the Russian Communist Party (represented by the *Musburo*) and the Soviet authorities in Turkestan; and between the local Soviet and the local population on the other. The Soviet in Tashkent attempted to bar Moslems from the conference, but the *Musburo* insisted that they be represented and called upon all "those whom the Basmashis attract with their lies" to attend.[9]

The confrontation brought the concerns of local organizations to the forefront. In the end, the conference advocated the establishment of a Soviet Republic of United Turkestan, to include the Turks of Russia and the Caucasus, thereby reviving and draping in a red flag the pan-Turkestani dream long cherished by Moslem reformists in Central Asia.[10] The Moslems wanted the *Musburo* to create a state of all Turkic peoples, one that would be too burdensome ever to be assimilated by Russia. The scope of their plans was especially far-reaching because of the extensive representation at the conference—108 organizations had sent delegates.[11] When the discussions came to a close, a regional committee of the *Musburo* was elected with several Moslem members, including nationalists such as T. Ryskulov. This development proved alarming to Moscow but did not provoke any immediate response: in 1919 the center could not exert pressure on Turkestan because it was controlled by Basmashi guerrillas.

The Russian communists in the region correctly analyzed the need for native membership in the party. "Indigenization" programs caused a wave of natives to swell the ranks of the party in the hopes that their greater numbers would give them a position of dominance. Of the 248 delegates at the Third Congress of the Communist Party of Turkestan (1–15 June 1919), 128 were natives.[12] Attendance at the Second Conference of Moslem organizations in September 1919 confirmed this trend. Ryskulov, the *Musburo* representative, was the spokesman for nationalist aspirations, which figured prominently on the agenda. Words quickly led to action. At the following conference a few months later it was proposed that Turkestan become the Autonomous Turkish Republic, and that the Turkestani Party, which had previously been affiliated with the Russian Communist Party, be reconstituted as an independent Turkish Communist Party.[13]

The stunning advances made by the Turkestani national independence movement in forming separate communist organizations demonstrated to Moscow that the creation of the *Musburo* had been a mistake, for imbuing the party with a nationalist hue had led to its disintegration. Moscow's immediate response was to scrap the *Musburo*,[14] and create in its place the Turkish Commission, *Turkkommissiia*, with a mandate to eliminate nationalist deviations within the Turkestani Communist Party. Members of the Commission were handpicked by Lenin; no Moslem was among them.[15] Some weeks later, the Communist Party sent its own representatives to purge local organizations.[16] The targets of the purge were dyed-in-the-wool nationalists and "Great Power chauvinists" who "intend to prevent access to the party by non-proletarian natives."[17]

At the Fifth Regional Party Conference (12–18 January 1920), Ryskulov called for action on the previous resolutions concerning the Turkish Republic and the Turkish Party. Now that the objectives of "indigenization" had been accomplished, there was a Moslem majority at the conference, and the Moslems backed Ryskulov. On the ruins of the

Turkestani Party organization, the conference erected the Turkish Communist Party, and Ryskulov demanded that the Russian Communist Party recognize the fait accompli.[18] Moscow's response on 8 March 1920 was brutal. The time for compromise had passed: the only Communist Party was that of the Republic of Turkestan, "incorporated as a regional organization (*oblastnaia*) into the Russian Communist Party." The Republic of Turkestan had autonomous status—period. Purges of local party organizations followed, providing the center with subsequent justification. In 1922, in what was only the beginning, more than 15,000 people were expelled from the Communist Party in Turkestan. Many others were forced to resign. The sweep of the purges was very broad, given the fact that in 1922 the organization totaled fewer than 20,000 members (see Table 1).[19]

TABLE 1.   National Composition of the Communist Party
of Turkestan in 1922[20]

Nationality	Number	Percentage
Russian	9,424	49.7
Kazakh and Kirghiz	4,409	23.3
Uzbek	2,021	10.7
Turkmen	867	4.6
Tadzhik	421	2.2
Tatar, Karakalpak, etc.	1,803	9.5
Total	18,945	

After the purges, the party was rebuilt. The new criteria for recruitment were: numerical strength—the party had to be large enough to constitute a political force; a carefully maintained balance of national and Russian elements; and respect for the region's predominantly agrarian social structure.[21] Although recruitment efforts appeared to take account of national origin, the end result was the opposite of its intended effect. The natives of the region were peasants, the workers were Russian; the latter played leading roles in the party whereas the former only rarely rose to positions of responsibility. The developing native elite became partly denationalized, for only by so doing could it act as a liaison between the local population and the party. At any rate, Russian or European cadre dominated the organization and ensured that the party would maintain links with the Russian Communist Party. Close relations were reinforced by the center because of Moscow's pre-

TABLE 2.   Social Composition (incomplete data) in 1922[22]
of the Entire Party, without Distinction
as to Nationalities

Class	Percentage
Peasants	67
Workers	20
Employees	6.5
Miscellaneous	6.5

TABLE 3.   Organization of the Communist Party of Turkestan in 1922[23]

Type of Organization (by Cells)	Number	Percentage
Rural	568	57
Soviets	294	30
Military	51	5
Commercial	38	4
Transport	30	4

vious errors and the uncertain outcome of changes in NEP. Lenin emphasized the need for exceptional vigilance.[24] On 20 June 1920, to facilitate control, the Russian party created the *Turkburo*, a bureau in Turkestan that was to promote an indigenization policy. Previous spontaneity had proven intolerable; therefore, policy had to be controlled by the center. Lenin wanted to make it "an example for all the East"[25] Later, on 1 February 1922, when problems between the RSFSR and the popular republics in Central Asia, Bukhara, and Khiva became exacerbated, the *Turkburo* was suppressed and replaced by the Central Committee's Bureau on Central Asia (*Sredazburo*).[26] The name change was significant. At the time the RSFSR was beginning to unify Central Asia under one banner, and the name "Turkestan" was considered dangerous because it evoked pan-Turkic aspirations of the period 1917 to 1920. "Central Asia" designated a geographical, not a historic-cultural reality. The function of the *Sredazburo* was to carry out a horizontal unification of the nation's regions under the vertical authority structure of the party. Not surprisingly, the local leader of the *Sredazburo* was Ordzhonikidze, a specialist in the political unification of the party, whose expertise had already been employed in the Caucasus. In October 1922, over 150 Russian communists were sent to Turkestan to assist him.

The example of Turkestan illustrates the party's role as the vehicle of unification. While recognizing the region's particular characteristics—its quasi-colonial status, its distance from the center, the historical and cultural universe to which it belonged—the Bolshevik Party devised a policy to hold a growing national movement in check; and by controlling the institutions of Turkestan it created relations of subordination. In 1922, when the Soviet federation was being formed, Turkestan was held up as an example for the other republics to follow (see Tables 2 and 3). Turkestan had stable state institutions; a national party composition, as Moscow directed, of militants and local cadre, thus demonstrating that Lenin's national policy was not purely hypothetical; and at the same time the Russian party and the local communist party were linked vertically, ensuring the cohesion of the whole.

The Communist Party in the Caucasus: Forced Unification

Lenin wanted national independent communist parties to be created in the Caucasus in order to "combat local chauvinism."[27] Many Caucasian social democrats opposed Lenin on this point because they did not welcome the prospect of factionalism along lines of national differences; but despite their disapproval three communist parties came into being in 1920—in Azerbaijan in February, in Georgia in May, and in Armenia in June. The three parties had the status of regional organizations within the Russian Communist Party (on a territorial, not a national-group basis) and were attached to the Caucasian Bureau (*Kavburo*), directed by a presidium comprising Ordzhonikidze, Stassova, Beloborodova, Nazaretian (secretary), and Budu Mdivani.[28]

The *Kavburo* was supposed to lay the groundwork for the unification of the Caucasus. Yet from the outset, it demonstrated authoritarian proclivities in solving the region's problems, which only sharpened conflicts, especially among the Georgians. Claiming that the demarcation of borders was within its jurisdiction, the *Kavburo* turned its attention first to border disputes, the subject of frequent international conflicts. This caused deep-seated resentment among those on whom its mediation was imposed. But the *Kavburo* was most active in the economic sphere in matters affecting the region's unity, interests, and structures, and progressively weakened local sovereignty. It decided unilaterally to dismantle the tariff walls and protectionist measures that each republic had erected; to integrate foreign trade into a unified organization that would act in conjunction with the corresponding Russian commissariat; and, finally, to create an Economic Council of the Caucasus, a symbol of unity, to be responsible for establishing communal structures. In all this, the republics' desires were ignored; *Kavburo* strategy was to present them with the fait accompli of irreversible situations.

After the Caucasus was unified economically, it had to be unified as a political entity. For Lenin, political unity already existed. Speaking of the republics of the region in October 1921, he designated them collectively by the term "Caucasian Republic."[29] In November 1921, when the *Kavburo* was working toward the creation of a federation of the Caucasus, the Russian Central Committee's only concern was to be kept informed of the relationship the federation would have to the RSFSR.[30]

In February 1922 the *Kavburo* disappeared and a new organism, the Transcaucasian Regional Committee (*Zakraikom*) of the Russian Communist Party, was put in its place. The name change was not accompanied by any change of personnel; the former leaders of the *Kavburo* simply became the presidium of the *Zakraikom*. The constancy of staff reflects the constancy of intentions, but the name change was not merely cosmetic. First, the incessant conflicts with local communists obliged the central leadership at least to appear to take widening local discontent into account. Second, once economic unity was achieved, the Russian Communist Party organizations had to adapt to the new configurations of the region. The *Kavburo* was at the service of the Central Committee only for a limited purpose; the *Zakraikom*, in contrast, was a regular and permanent construct: with its establishment, the national parties were integrated and unified in one supreme regional organization that represented them before the Russian Communist Party's Central Committee. The party's organic unity, evidenced by the change, preceded—and presaged—its political unity. Beginning in the summer of 1922, the *Zakraikom* purged the Georgian Communist Party.[31] The casualties were heavy: 37 percent of the militant members of the party were expelled,[32] and the three parties were prevailed upon to recruit new members in accordance with the rules laid down at the Eleventh Congress of the Russian Communist Party.

In December 1922 the Transcaucasian federation was created[33] and instantly transformed into a federated republic[34] to "consolidate unity." The Georgians' desperate resistance did not impede the implacable progress of Stalin's plan.

When Lenin's notes on the Georgian affair were published, historians concluded that he roundly condemned all the activities of the *Kavburo* and the *Zakraikom*.[35] However, certain periods and problems must be distinguished from others. In February 1922, when Lenin took a keen interest in the Georgian affair, he did not oppose the lines of Ordzhonikidze and Kirov; he was ill-disposed only to the methods they used and their consequences. He condemned the reigning lack of respect among communists, the brutality, the discussions or arguments won by violence.[36] He was apprehensive that Great Russian chauvinism would permanently poison the relations between the RSFSR and the non-Russian republics.[37] For Lenin, the lack of party spirit indicated the dangerous degradation of the party itself; the lack of internationalism, an endangerment to the Soviet state. But Lenin's scrutiny of the issues was not equal on both accounts. Where it was a question of the party, he developed fundamental principles; where it was a question of the nations, his interest was purely strategic. This led him to reject not the content but the form that the *Kavburo* and *Zakraikom* activities assumed. He entrusted to Trotsky the task of opening discussion on this point at the upcoming Party Congress.[38]

We must not lose sight of the fact that Lenin was in the minority on Georgian matters in the Politburo and the *Orgburo*, the highest party organs, whereas the Politburo was clearly in agreement with its representatives in the Caucasus. On 21 December 1922 the *Orgburo*, called upon to arbitrate a conflict between Georgian communists and the *Kavburo* (later the *Zakraikom*), concluded that Lenin's policy was being correctly interpreted, but that the Georgian Communist Party had distorted his directives to mean unconditional support for Georgian sovereignty. This harsh judgment worried Lenin and moved him to alert Kamenev, a member of the Politburo—to no avail. At the Second Congress of Communist Organizations of the Caucasus, which met between 19 and 23 March 1923—on the eve of the Twelfth Congress of the Russian Communist Party—Ordzhonikidze, who presented the *Zakraikom*'s political report, justified its action on the grounds of regional rivalries and national particularism. By approving the report—and it had no choice, given pressure from the center—the Congress strengthened the party's centralist theses.[39]

On the eve of the Twelfth Congress, *Pravda* opened its columns to exasperated party members from the Caucasus, but closed the discussion with a contribution from a Georgian who declared that unity had not been imposed by Moscow, but rather had been unanimously determined by the workers of the three republics.[40] The policy imposed on the Caucasus was cited as an example of the self-determination of the working classes! Despite Bukharin's support of the Georgians[41] and the stormy debates at the Twelfth Congress, which condemned both Great

Power chauvinism and national deviations,[42] the party did not reiterate the idea that federation was a necessary sign of progress.[43]

At the Twelfth Congress, with Lenin's final notes on hand, after hearing complaints from the Caucasus the delegates confirmed Lenin's minority position and expressed party satisfaction at having pursued an unambiguous policy. Rather than repeat the experiment of Central Asia, where the party in effect vacillated between enforcing centralism and encouraging decentralization, in the Caucasus the party worked tenaciously and continuously at organizing centralization. Lenin's hesitations came too late to affect a process that was by then drawing to a close. At any rate, he did not seriously question the concept of centralization, but its pace and methods.

The Jewish Section:
Differentiation for the Purpose of Assimilation

After the revolution, the Jewish community posed a problem for the Bolsheviks.[44] Although the Jews had no territory of their own, they were recognized as a nationality group and given organizational representation in the *Narkomnats*. In 1917 the Jewish community was a marginal society; to integrate it fully into Russian society, a transformation on all fronts was necessary. By definition, the Jewish Commissariat represented particular interests; it was not created to socialize the community for the purpose of carving out a place for it in the Soviet state. The task of socialization fell to the party, but the Bolsheviks were ill-equipped to work in a Jewish milieu. The fact that several Bolshevik leaders were of Jewish origin masked the community's antipathy toward the party. For a long time Jews had been more attracted to the Bund and to Menshevism. The few hundred Jews who belonged to the Bolshevik Party were generally assimilated and indifferent to the community in which they had been raised. Moreover, as historian Zvi Gitelman has rightly noted, in their education and desire to become assimilated the Bolsheviks of Jewish origin were strangers to Jewish society and not in a position to influence its development.[45]

Dimanshtein, the Commissar on Jewish Affairs, declaring that new organizations were needed to reach the Jewish masses and to counteract the influence of Jewish political parties, proposed that Jewish organizations be created within the Bolshevik Party. Although Lenin recognized some problems as being particular to the Jewish community, he did not endorse Dimanshtein's suggestion. For his part, Sverdlov flatly opposed it: any such program would only repeat the Bund's mistakes; moreover, a separate Jewish organization would open the door to the federalization of the Bolshevik Party.

In January 1918, frightened by the distance separating nonassimilated and working-class Jews from the party, Lenin, over Sverdlov's objection, called for the creation of Jewish sections in the party. Such a decision might appear paradoxical from a man who had opposed not only the Bund but also the very concept of separate organizations and the idea of cultural autonomy, but like all Lenin's decisions of the period, its logic was based on immediate necessity. Previous opinions notwithstanding, Lenin searched for a way to reach a group that until then had been impervious to his influence. His earlier convictions crumbled in the face of a reality that could not be ignored. Yet here again Lenin's concession was provisional. *Evsektsiia* (*Evreiskaia Sektsiia*), the Jewish section of the party, had a temporary mission: to mold Jewish Bolsheviks, reconcile them to the party, and then integrate them, after which the Jewish section as such would cease to exist.[46]

The evolution of the *Evsektsiia* justified Sverdlov's fears more than it confirmed Lenin's calculations. From the very beginning the section suffered, predictably, from the lack of cadre, which caused some overlapping in staff with the Jewish Commissariat. The section defined itself more as a Jewish than a Bolshevik organization. Dimanshtein, a veritable orchestra conductor, gathered around him the intellectuals who could translate Bolshevik literature into Yiddish, edit newspapers, and so on—activities that absorbed all available goodwill: as a result, the *Evsektsiia* had to draw its cadre from the same core group. This confusion became apparent at the *Evkom-Evsektsiia* joint conference organized in Moscow in October 1918. Thirty-one out of sixty-four delegates were Bolsheviks, most of them Commissariat and provincial subdivision functionaries. Dimanshtein was confronted with the delegates' demand that Yiddish be the official and exclusive language of the conference. He also had to defend the position that the Jewish section was not an autonomous Jewish party but a department of the Russian party.

The section's recruitment problems highlighted the ambiguity of its identity. Jews who joined the party after January 1918 (when the section was created) had to become members of the Jewish section. The two advantages of this practice were that the *Evsektsiia* became a focal point for all Jewish communists, and at the same time greater membership assured the section of financial autonomy.[47] However, the party wanted from the start to keep the section within well-defined limits: it was to be a provisional organization for those whose cultural background alienated them from the party. Assimilated Jews in the party supported the decision to limit recruitment for the *Evsektsiia* to those for whom language was a barrier to membership in local organizations; assimilated elements would not stop using Russian or enclose themselves in what they saw as the vestiges of a milieu they had rejected.

Disagreements multiplied. After hesitating for a time, the Russian Communist Party opted to create national communist organizations on a territorial basis (on the Turkestan model), and the Jewish section, lacking a territorial base, found itself excluded. It became reattached to local party organizations, a cause for bitterness that later nourished Jewish aspirations for greater autonomy.

The Russian Communist Party expected that the Jewish sections would replace the traditional political groups (Bund, *Poale Zion*) and more recent organizations (the *Kombund*, the Bund's successor) that were particularly influential in the Jewish community in the Ukraine, or would become a substitute for the ephemeral Jewish Communist Party of Soviet Russia. The Russian Communist Party supported the Jewish section against these other groups in the hope of wooing troops away and confusing the Jewish masses that were attracted to them. This mission was accomplished by 1922: Jewish parties disappeared or disintegrated into multiple factions, and their followers rallied to the Jewish sections, which attained a near-monopoly of membership among Jews.

The main mission of the Jewish sections, however, was to destroy the traditional Jewish world—something the Russian Communist Party had been unable to do. Beginning in June 1919, the Jewish sections fought Zionism by prohibiting all activities of Zionist organizations. The Jewish sections had a stranglehold on communal organizations in the Jewish community. Religion, their main target, was under constant attack. The *Evsektsiia* urged such ferocious combat against Judaism in the years 1920 to 1922 that even non-Jewish communists were shocked. Maxim Gorky described their attitude as "excessive and tactless." An intensive antireligious campaign continued for two years: meetings, pamphlets, and anti-Jewish parodies presaged the excesses of the general antireligion campaign later waged by the Soviet authorities. But the anti-Jewish campaign became so excessive that the Thirteenth Congress of the Russian Communist Party, which met in 1924, decided to put an end to it.[48]

What, then, were the accomplishments of the *Evsektsiia*? The sections helped sap the strength of a Jewish world, one previously closed to outsiders, without compromising the Russian Communist Party, which remained at a safe distance. Once the Jewish community was considerably weakened, the Jewish sections were no longer useful to the party. The Jewish cadre had much work ahead, and it was up to them to do it. On the remains of the old Jewish order they tried to build a new Jewish Soviet society, integrated into the socialist order. They believed that their task justified the creation of separate Jewish communist organizations. Although in favor of *political assimilation*, they wanted to safeguard their *cultural identity*.

The Russian Communist Party was of a different mind. The continued existence of the Jewish sections was unnecessary, and worrisome to the extent that particularism—which the sections were supposed to eliminate—was being perpetuated. After having served at an early stage as the signpost to assimilation, the sections were not tolerated when they came to symbolize an enduring distinctiveness. Beginning in 1923–24, after a period of temporary concessions to thorny nationality problems, the Russian Communist Party endeavored to reestablish organizational unity, provide a unitary direction for the Soviet federation, and reinforce its centralizing tendencies. Although the Jewish sections survived until 1929, the Russian Communist Party had long since brushed them aside as remnants of an outdated social order.

The Party as an Instrument of Unity

With the adoption of the constitution in 1924, the party's role within the federation became more defined. The direction it was to follow can be gleaned from its structure. In the battle over *autonomization*, Lenin had insisted that all states be equal within the federation. The constitution of 1924 reflected his position, although the organization of the federal party was inspired by Stalin's ideas, not by Lenin's amended versions of these. The Communist Party of the USSR was built on a two-pronged principle, territorial and functional. Its territorial organization was parallel to the country's administrative subdivisions, and its functions included all spheres of activities in which citizens participated. In this regard, two observations must be made. First, whereas each republic had its own national party, the RSFSR did not: the federal party was also its party. What Stalin had advocated for the state organs—overlapping the Russian and the federal levels—was achieved in the case of the party. The justification for the party's privileged status no doubt lay in the size of the RSFSR, the number of its administrative subdivisions, and the fact that a separate RSFSR party, of the same magnitude as the party of the Union, would run the risk of becoming too unwieldy an organization.[49] In any case, the single-party anomaly conferred special status on the RSFSR and its communist organizations, making it "more equal than others."

The second observation is that although the RSFSR's independence appeared to be reinforced by the existence of separate parties in each republic, these were not independent parties at all but halfway between territorial organizations and affiliated parties of the Union. As such, the individual republics' communist parties were not invested with their own powers; like territorial organizations, they were subject to the discipline and authority of a sole central organization, the Communist Party of the Union.

In 1923 the organization and governing principles of the central Communist Party came to supplement and supersede the federal constitution, revealing its true significance. The party's function was to cement national divisions into an ideologically and organizationally centralized state. The sovereignty or national autonomy guaranteed by the state could only be exercised within the given framework of the unitary party.

The leaders of the Russian Communist Party consistently asserted the centralized nature of the party and its role in the unification of Russia. At the Third Party Congress of the Ukraine in 1919 Sverdlov declared: "In all the independent Soviet republics that we have created we must maintain the supremacy of our Communist Party. Everywhere leadership belongs to the Central Committee of the Russian Communist Party."

In 1923 at the Twelfth Congress[50] and again at the enlarged Fourth Conference of the Central Committee of the Russian Communist Party,[51] Stalin defined how nationality groups fit into the party structure. Retreating from Lenin's thesis—that the danger posed to intranational relations by Great Russian chauvinism was infinitely greater than that arising from the particular aspirations of the nations themselves—Stalin accorded both dangers equal importance and perceived local nationalism as a phenomenon of great consequence, not merely a reaction to Russian domination. He concluded that the party had to protect the federation from the divisive effects of this phenomenon; hence, the party had to combat all nationalistic inclinations at the same time as it adapted itself to local realities. Adaptation presupposed party penetration into local masses through the development of national recruitment efforts, as Stalin made clear in his statement before the enlarged Fourth Conference: "In the regions and national republics we must develop communist youth organizations composed of proletarian elements of the local population." Nationality-group communists had to be created not only to fill the ranks of the local parties but also to represent their group of national origin in the USSR's common party organizations.[52]

The local parties had to be familiar with the social reality of their communities in order to be able to represent them at their present status while planning for transformation over the long term. In 1924 Zinoviev asserted it was dangerous to dissociate the party from the masses by turning a blind eye to social realities: "A working-class party in a predominantly peasant society must have in its rank a certain number of peasants."[53] At the same time he stressed that the party should not be overwhelmed by the peasantry or by the propertied classes hidden behind them. What was needed was a working-class party open to the peasants.

These multiple tasks came under the rubric of *Korenizatsiia*, the entrenchment of national parties. From 1923 to 1930, after the purges that rid the local parties of the elements that had used them as a vehicle for nationalist demands, the entrenchment policy led to the equal incorporation of nationality and Soviet components in local parties.

This policy undoubtedly promoted greater nationality-group representation in the Communist Party, to the detriment of the Russian elements (see Table 4).

TABLE 4. Membership in the Party by Nationality, 1922 and 1927

Nationality Group	Percentage of Total Population	Percentage in the Party	
		1922	1927
Great Russian	52.9	72.0	65.0
Ukrainian	21.2	5.9	11.7
Byelorussian	3.2	1.5	3.2
Polish, Baltic peoples	0.7	4.6	2.6
Jews	1.8	5.2	4.3
Minorities of the RSFSR	4.3	2.0	2.3
Peoples of the Caucasus	2.5	3.4	3.6
Peoples of Central Asia	7.0	2.5	3.5
Miscellaneous	8.2	2.9	3.2

Table 4 clarifies certain tendencies of the new nationalities policy that was only partly modified by entrenchment.[54] There remained a wide gap between overrepresentation of Russians and the underrepresentation of nationality groups. The gap was no narrower or less consistent within the non-Russian groups. The Poles and the Baltic peoples, who had no national territory of their own, along with the peoples of the Caucasus, were always overrepresented. Others, such as the Byelorussians, had achieved by 1927 representation in the federation proportional to their numbers. On the other hand, groups such as the Ukrainians and the Moslems of Central Asia were greatly underrepresented, especially the latter, who were the slowest to gain ground. What accounted for such disparity? In the case of the Caucasus, we must remember, there were long-standing, active social-democratic organizations whose members had been recruited from the workers in oil refineries and from among an especially dynamic intelligentsia. It is true that the Caucasian parties were purged when the Sovietization of the republics was taking place, but new members were quickly recruited. The Armenian Communist Party, for example, evolved along similar lines. In November 1921 it had 3,046 members and 5,205 prospective members. The purge excluded 24.5 percent of the first group and 29.9 percent of the second. In 1924, membership in the party was reduced to 4,032 in both categories.[55] A census carried out by the USSR's Communist Party in 1927 revealed that as of 1 January, the Armenian Communist Party had regained its 1921 level, but with the greater imbalance on the side of its active members—4,770 members to 3,436 candidates.[56] Meanwhile, the percentage of members who were workers increased (from 10.5 in 1921 to 27.4 in 1927), the percentage of peasants decreased (from 75.4 in 1921 to 49.7 in 1927), and that of intellectuals rose slightly (from 11.6 in 1921 to 20.5 in 1927). The entrenchment policy had succeeded.

The overrepresentation of Poles and Baltic peoples, and the consistent representation of Byelorussians in the party may be traced to a common characteristic of these groups, beyond their sociological differences—an absence of nationalist conflicts. The former, separated from their communities of origin, were "internationalists" who preferred to be integrated into the Soviet state rather than join non-Soviet entities. In the case of Byelorussia, its sovereign status had not resulted from nationalist demands. In contrast, both the agrarian society in the Ukraine and the strong traditional civilization in Moslem Asia put up sociocultural and political resistance to Sovietization. In these areas the tendency to encourage the local communist parties to express national identity clashed with Moscow's need to exercise tight control.

The backwardness of the educational system was more of an obstacle to the entrenchment policy in Central Asia than elsewhere. Educated natives were generally suspected of nationalist inclinations. The growing working class and the peasantry were uneducated, which forced the Russian Communist Party to call in European elements living in the periphery or to dispatch cadre from the capital.[57] Without question, the policy of incorporating indigenous elements into the party had to work in conjunction with a cultural policy towards nationalities, but even such a policy could not create minority-group communist elites within a few years.

The Russian Communist Party, which in 1925 became the Communist Party of the USSR, was the only institution in the Soviet state that remained unaffected by the Soviet authorities' uncertainty in dealing with nationality problems. Despite disagreements over Lenin's national policy (which gave rise to violent debates in the Eighth Congress), the party began in 1918 to set up regional organizations to transmit messages between the center and a distant periphery that was subject to a plurality of pressures.

At a time of divergent tendencies, the party embodied the unitarian alternative, and in some instances supported and justified the proletariat's experiments in self-determination. Throughout a vast territory, the party adopted solutions that connected states to the whole via a varied array of formal unions and alliances. Although it recognized the sovereignty of national states for a time, the Bolshevik Party kept its sights on future unification and on maintaining authority over communist organizations in the peripheral states. The conflicts that broke out in the early 1920s between Russian Communist Party leaders and local party directors—even where the former came from the Bolshevik Party—illustrate that the party's centralizing role was experienced as a weighty counterforce to the federal system. From 1924 on, the party, through the national organizations established in the formative stages of each republic, had total authority not only over the territorial communist organizations, but also, by virtue of the close superimposition of party organizations and the state, over state institutions. The development of a local "avant-garde" in each republic helped guide the federal system toward unity. Thus the USSR's Communist Party played a double role in the federation. At the time it was an important, though not the exclusive, means to achieve a type of centralization that could coexist with a decentralized federal system. It also looked to the future by keeping alive the idea of the ultimate unity of the Soviet whole.

Part Four

The Cultural
Revolution

CHAPTER 9

A Clean Sweep

"The profound meaning of the revolution is that the people have made a final break with the barbarism of Asia, the seventeenth century, the icons and cant of Holy Russia." Trotsky's remark concerning Russian peasant society was even more applicable to the values of non-Russian society. Diverse minority-group societies were made up of a predominantly peasant population whose cultural universe began and ended with the village or tribe; they were governed by religious faith and clerical authority, bound by a system of family and social relations in which the individual was completely shielded from the influence of the outside world. The Soviet system sought to dismantle the structures of protection and reeducate the individual in isolation, a task made all the more difficult by the ignorance and widespread illiteracy separating local leaders from those under their jurisdiction and obliging the individual to be dependent on traditional stewards of knowledge such as the clergy and the national elites. The first problem was that the Soviet authorities were woefully unfamiliar with the peoples that were part of their political system. Census information from 1897 and 1913, which had revealed the bare outlines of these societies, was rendered useless by war, civil strife, and famine. The Soviet leadership had to identify which aspects of these societies could be changed gradually within the framework of NEP, and which factors impeded integration into the Soviet state, calling for a more radical policy.

Particularistic Sectors in a Heterogeneous Society

In 1922 the central leadership was in a position to evaluate the national composition of the federation,[1] but not until the census of 1926, did it have a breakdown of data comparable to that of 1897.[2] The new census revealed that the Slavic group, representing 77 percent of the population, was the product of a Christian tradition, mainly Orthodox, belonged to a rural civilization, and had a fairly homogeneous level of intellectual development. Within the Russian population 45.9 percent could read and write, as compared to 41.3 percent of Ukrainians and 37.3 percent of Byelorussians. The overall average was 39.6 percent in contrast to the Karaim (84.9 percent), the Finns (76 percent), the Estonians (72.4 percent), and the Jews (72.3 percent).[3] Russians, Ukrainians, and Byelorussians were in the majority in their republics. The highest percentage of foreigners in the Ukraine were Russians, followed by Jews and Poles; in Byelorussia, Jews predominated, followed by Russians and Poles.

Within the RSFSR, non-native peoples, even if they lived for the most part in culturally closed communities, were tied to the Russian economy and had attained the same intellectual progress as the Russians. What distinguished them from the Russians was their attachment to their own languages. The Caucasus presented a different picture: there were few Russians, and ethnic group rivalries persisted even in the postrevolutionary national states. In some cases (for example, Nakhichevan), Soviet division of territory aggravated regional dissension. In addition, the cultural levels of the peoples varied considerably.

Literacy among Georgians (39.5 percent) and Armenians (34.5 percent) was far superior to that of the nearly illiterate mountain peoples such as the Chechens (3 percent) or the Tabasaran (1.6 percent).[4] The peoples of Central Asia (mostly Turkic-speaking Moslems who were not easily assimilated) made up a scant 8 percent of the total population. Some peoples (Kirghiz and Kazakhs) preserved a social organization associated with nomadic traditions. The more sedentary peoples, even those in proximity to Russian colonists, respected Islamic customs and way of life, or held pre-Islamic beliefs. In areas where nomads became sedentary, they clung to the previous social order. Few could read (7.1 percent of the Kazakhs, 3.8 percent of the Uzbeks, and 1.3 percent of the Karakalpaks), with the exception of some urbanized groups. Patriarchy was generally the rule, characterized by respect for elders, tribal or village solidarity, and the sentiment—not unalloyed, but firmer than before the revolution—that they belonged to a Turkic-Moslem world fundamentally different from the Soviet world of the Russians.

Thus it is understandable that the Bolsheviks were concerned more with the closed universe of Central Asia, and to a lesser degree with the Caucasus. Ukrainian national aspirations were expressed as an attachment to language, history, and culture, and the Byelorussians had never displayed nationalist yearnings of any kind. The latter groups were close enough to the Russians for NEP to include them as well as the Russians; and the smaller minority groups dispersed throughout the RSFSR were too narrowly intermingled with the Russians to escape the social transformation the Bolsheviks were working to achieve. But in Central Asia and the bastions of the Caucasus, minority peoples set against the social revolution the strong and ancient traditions that were all of a piece with their faith and their national identity. Endowed with states of their own, why should they willingly accept a new civilization that would deprive them of their national identities? When a social revolution also dissolves nationhood, the problem acquires new dimensions, and popular reaction is of another order. Hence, at a time when the Bolsheviks were pursuing social reconciliation via NEP, which favored radical changes, they followed a different policy in Central Asia, where they aimed at fracturing the singularity of societies in order to bring them into the fold of the rest of Soviet society.

The Revolution in the Law

Of all the ethnic communities of the USSR, the Moslem community was at the furthest remove from the prevailing legal system; its way of life, customs, hierarchies, and social attitudes were tied to Islam, the Mongol heritage, and nomadic traditions. Moslem law specifically prohibited foreign influences. For this reason the Soviet system's first target in the Moslem milieu was the law itself. The idea was to make a clean sweep of the Moslem legal system and the social system surrounding it, especially as regarded the status of families and the place of women and children within the family.

In 1917 a two-tiered legal system still existed in the Moslem territories, based on Koranic law, *Shariat*, and on a type of nonreligious law, *Adat*. Decisions of the Koranic courts were generally accepted throughout the empire, provided they did not contravene imperial law. Koranic law was more deeply rooted among sedentary peoples, whereas nonreligious lawcourts of more limited jurisdiction prevailed in the Kirghiz territories and some areas of the western Caucasus.

On 7 December 1917 the Soviet government abolished the existing judicial system and established in its place elected peoples' courts.[5] The Soviet decree declared null and void any law contrary to "revolutionary legality," but in the absence of new legal codes the courts were to enforce laws in accordance with the new legislation.[6] The justices of the peace, created under Alexander II and empowered to decide misdemeanor cases, were temporarily permitted to carry out their functions. While retaining some elements of the old system, the 7 December decree laid the foundation for a new judicial system applicable to all territories under Soviet authority, although such territories were not clearly defined.

The Bolsheviks in power in Tashkent decided that the decree was applicable to Turkestan, and on 12 December 1917 they abolished the existing legal system[7] (Moslem courts, which resolved disputes related to individuals, marriages, divorces, inheritances; and secular courts of the tsarist government, which had jurisdiction over collective life, criminal matters, and so forth), replacing it with peoples' courts.

Unable to enforce its decisions, the Tashkent government partially retreated on 31 December when it held the new rules in abeyance; however, jurisdiction in political matters was transferred from the existing courts to the local Soviets. A Leninist conception of justice prevailed, in that there was no separation of powers and judicial authority was not divorced from other state institutions. In 1918, in Turkestan, the Soviets did not merely control the judicial system, they monopolized it.[8] Confusion reigned until 1919, when the Soviet system spread to Turkestan.

A federal decree of 21 November 1918, amended on 15 January 1919,[9] defined the composition of the peoples' courts and their relations to other organizations of state authority. These courts consisted of a chief judge and two assessors, who, theoretically, were elected by direct suffrage but in practice were appointed by the local Soviets. Revolutionary courts consisting of a chief judge and six assessors, all appointed, decided political matters and enjoyed great freedom of action.

In theory the regular courts in Turkestan were supposed to enforce Soviet law, but they obtained the right to make reference in their decisions to *Shariat*, Moslem law, or *Adat*, nonreligious law, as long as these did not directly contradict Soviet law. This concession, granted to a population that did not welcome Soviet rule, led to the coexistence of two judicial systems, one for Russians and the other for Moslems, leaving the region ill-prepared for the socioideological integration efforts that began in 1922.

The Soviet legislation promulgated with the constitution of 1918 was officially applicable only to the RSFSR. But at the same time judicial reconciliation began to occur between the RSFSR and the Byelorussian and Ukrainian republics, which, unlike the Islamic regions, accepted Soviet law. In December 1918 independent Byelorussia began to build a judicial system on the RSFSR model, and the structures of "socialist legality" were fully established by 1920. The evolution of the legal system in the Ukraine was only slightly different. The civil legal code adopted on 19 February 1919 differed from the Soviet code only with respect to appellate procedure; other provisions in the law concerning marriage, divorce, sale of real estate, and succession, as well as the criminal code, were identical to those in the Russian system.

In 1922 the Bolsheviks decided to extend their legal system to the republics that were to join the federation. The general principles on which Soviet law was based were the overlapping of powers and party control over the judicial system. Lenin explained these requirements in a note to Stalin on 20 May 1922, "On Double Subordination and the Law."[10] Party authority over the entire judicial system would be ensured by ten people exercising the centralized power of the *Prokuratura* "convened in the center, working under the strictest supervision, and having the most direct contact possible within the three party organs that offer maximum guarantees against local and personal influences: the Bureau of Organization and the Political Bureau of the Central Committee, and the Central Commission of Control."[11]

The conception of the judiciary as centralized in structure and dependent on the party governed the relations among the various judicial systems in the federation. The constitution of 1924 left the drafting of civil and criminal codes to the member republics, within the parameters of the general principles common to the federation as a whole. The Ukrainian Communist Party felt sufficiently competent to direct that Ukrainian jurists begin drafting a civil code in the summer of 1922, before the basic principles were laid down. As John Hazard points out, the Ukrainian code assisted jurists for the federation in defining their ideas.[12] Other republics moved in the same direction. It was not until 1924 that federal jurists published "the basic principles" comprising a common legal vision.[13] While the federation was in the process of formation, considerable laxity reigned in the republics that were establishing their legal systems—conceivable where the social norms were similar from one republic to the next, but not the case on the Turkic-Moslem periphery. After some years of hesitation, in 1922, in the hope of avoiding violence, Moscow instituted a systematic policy aimed at the gradual elimination of Moslem structures. First, the Moslem courts were placed under Soviet control. In May 1922 the local Soviets were put in charge of nominating the *kadis* (judges)—an unpopular measure that did not last long.[14] In August 1922 the election of judges by universal suffrage was abolished by decree, and this power was placed under the aegis of the civil authorities.[15] A "Moslem Section Before the Council of the Peoples' Courts of Turkestan" was created as a forum for appeals and final judgments. A decree promulgated on 23 December 1922[16] further weakened the *kadis'* authority by making them subject to annual reelection and the control of the regional executive committee, which had the right to dismiss them and loosely supervise their activities. Moreover, all persons brought before a Moslem court could at any time have their cases transferred to the peoples' courts.[17] The district peoples' court then became the appeals court for Moslem court rulings, and Moslem court jurisdiction became more and more constricted: Moslem courts lost the authority to order financial restitution in criminal cases, to render decisions in civil inheritance cases, to deal with property disputes, and to rule in matters involving state institutions. With their authority thus curtailed, rigorously controlled by the Soviets, and in constant and unequal competition with the peoples' courts to which any person discontent with their rulings could appeal, the religious courts lost their previous prestige.

Early in 1923, judging that the time for concessions had passed, the Soviet government openly prepared to eliminate Koranic law. The Turkestani Executive Committee decreed that any decision by a religious court could be reviewed by a peoples' court. Any complainant who lost a case (and, in cases of divorce, women, whom the *kadis* generally repudiated) could turn to the peoples' courts, which functioned under guidelines to administer justice "in favor of the workers and peasants."[18]

Economic considerations also discouraged people from appearing before Moslem courts. The state assumed the costs of administering justice until it decreed in 1923 that the cost of any judicial proceeding different from that provided for by Soviet law had to be borne by the party desiring the perpetuation of such a process, that is, the complainants. In addition to the procedural costs, salaries for the *kadi*, his assistant, and his two assessors (required by the new decrees) would have to be paid.[19] In February 1924, criminal or civil cases in which the disputed sum exceeded twenty-five rubles were declared out of the canonic courts' jurisdiction.[20] Finally, the religious courts were directed to cease ruling on the basis of *Shariat* and to adhere to the statutes of the Soviet legal system.

On 16 October 1924 the criminal code of the RSFSR was amended and extended without modification to the Autonomous Soviet Socialist Republic of Turkestan. Certain Islamic practices were expressly prohibited, such as payment of *dija,* compensatory damages to crime victims and their families, and *kalym,* an indemnity for purchasing a dowry in cases of forced marriages and polygamy.[21] Previously, these practices had been adjudicated by the Moslem courts. Once they were eliminated, with nothing to take their place, there was no reason to go before a Moslem court where a costly procedure yielded only immediately revocable decisions.

The rapid expansion of Soviet authority and its legal institutions came later to the popular republics of Bukhara and Khoresm, which managed until the end of their independent existence to stave off the secularization of the judicial apparatus and its codes. In 1925, when all of Central Asia was Sovietized, some reordering became necessary. In the former Republic of Turkestan only ninety-nine religious courts were in existence in 1924, four times less than the number still functioning in 1922,[22] and most were inactive. In contrast, in the independent territories and in Kirghizia in 1924, religious courts were numerous and well-attended. Until 1927 the Soviet leadership tried to eliminate them locally by controlling the elections of the *kadis* and accepting only "progressives" who systematically applied Soviet rather than Moslem law.[23] These measures and the high cost of justice eroded the Koranic courts' *raison d'être* in the independent territories as well.

In mid-1927 there were only seventeen religious courts left in Uzbekistan and eleven in Turkestan; in Kirghiz the last nonreligious court had already disappeared.[24] All that remained was to eliminate the exorbitantly costly nonreligious system by legal means. In its decree of 21 September 1927, the Central Executive Committee of the RSFSR prohibited the creation or reestablishment of any religious or nonreligious court: no decision emanating from these courts had the force of law. Enforcement was relegated to the goodwill of the parties in question. The Moslem judicial system became a thing of the past.

Despite variations in the legal codes of the different republics, the existence of one uniform body of law brought about a uniformity of customs. While NEP was being promoted and Soviet family legislation was lax, the object of having a law common to all was to emancipate women and children, who were considered key players in the struggle for social change. In Moslem territory and the Caucasus, Soviet policy was directed against a patriarchal family structure ruled by elders. The revolution in law between 1924 and 1928 liberated women by criminalizing *bytovye*, or customary, practices such as abduction of a fiancée and payment of ransom. Divorce by mutual consent replaced men's repudiation of women, and, in cases involving disagreements, the peoples' courts tended to rule in favor of women. In order to eliminate polygamy, which was strictly forbidden, men were required to pay alimony. Custody rights redounded to both parents. A separate property system within marriage was established. Women could testify as witnesses, and in public life their rights were equal to men's.

The cohesiveness of the patriarchal family was broken by the prohibition of arranged and forced marriages between adults or involving prepubescent girls (sixteen years old or younger in the Armenian code). Women were given equal rights of succession. The custom of *levirat* (remarriage of a widow to her brother-in-law) disappeared. Child abuse was punished by the loss of parental authority; mistreatment of women was seriously castigated. Finally, the vendetta, widely practiced among Moslems, especially in the Caucasus, was made illegal.

Once women were emancipated and family cohesiveness destroyed, the younger generation had to be reeducated. The Soviet authorities' objective was to eliminate traditional Moslem schooling and implant a Soviet educational system that would act as a barrier between tradition-minded parents and their more malleable children. To accomplish this, it was necessary to do away with all establishments of traditional education in the Moslem and Jewish communities.

Traditional Moslem schooling had taken place in the *mektebs*, where students recited the Koran,[25] and in the *medresseh*, which trained a smaller number of students. Prior to the revolution this system had been weakened by the innovative *Djadids*. A freedom of conscience decree promulgated on 23 January 1918 forbade the inclusion of religious instruction in general education programs[26] and provided for the seizure of assets in the *waqfs* (public or private property in mortmain), the revenues of which were used, among other things, for the upkeep of schools. Between 1922 and 1925 this economic measure gradually undermined institutions of Koranic teaching, which were not suppressed outright until 1930.[27] Despite Soviet interest in weaning youth from Islamic clerical influence, official steps were gradual because of strong popular resistance to secular education.

Education provided for Jewish children in *cheders* was attacked on legal grounds by prohibiting religious education for children under eighteen years of age.[28] In the name of this principle many *cheders* were closed in 1922–23, especially in Byelorussia.[29] Jewish resistance was not great, given that the Jewish sections took charge of education in an attempt to reconcile the need for change and the desire to safeguard Judaism. We shall return to this problem later.

Beyond general matters of family relationships and intergenerational dynamics, Soviet law ruled on individual, social, and moral questions in some regions. Thus, a 1928 addendum to the criminal code of the RSFSR included an article devoted to "crimes related to the vestiges of tribal order," which were quite uncommon in Russia; but the Russian initiative compelled the respective republics to adopt similar provisions in their criminal codes. Although most often the center took the initiative in the struggle against tradition, sometimes legislation in the federated republics inspired federal laws, as was the case with homosexuality. In 1929, when no mention of it existed in federal legal texts, the Uzbek criminal code was the first to outlaw homosexuality involving minors. In 1934 the matter was brought before the federation and the provisions then adopted—defining crimes and their respective sanctions—were incorporated into every republic's criminal code. The only exceptions to the uniformity that existed from 1929 on were the Uzbek and the Tadzhik codes.

While Soviet legal reforms tended to penalize traditional loyalties, they did not make their survival impossible, and some traditions persisted in semi-clandestinity. Where this occurred, the law was reinforced by social pressures from the center.

The "Masses" Against Tradition

From 1926 to 1927 Soviet authority used *mass action* to make reality keep pace with the law. Under this heading, an entire array of popular gatherings were organized, either in the form of spontaneous demonstrations or through specific organizations that combated illegal activities, whether explicit or implied. The focal point of these actions was the female population because social resistance was strongest among women and they had the most direct connection to the future. Dramatic actions were staged: women were forcibly unveiled by crowds outraged at the continuity of vestimentary tradition despite the new laws. Hundreds of such scenes occurred in the streets of Moslem cities from 1926 on.[30] Other apparently "spontaneous" actions of the same kind violated other taboos. "Indignant masses" interrupted wedding ceremonies to prevent the arranged marriages of old men and young girls negotiated by the girls' parents.[31]

The Soviet authorities also established organizations to mobilize women and young people, who were identified as potential agents of change. In order to draw women away from a society that protected itself by placing restrictions on them, in the early 1920s the Communist Party organized *zhenotdel*, or women's sections, in many areas. The very extensive activities of these sections[32] included enrolling women in the party and assisting them in entering government positions or finding employment. In the workplace the *zhenotdel* chose the women most qualified for militant activity and groomed them. The *delegatki*, or chosen female candidates, in whom other women supposedly placed their trust, participated in the *delegatskoe sobranie*, an assembly in which matters pertaining to social mobilization or women's status were discussed. The delegates were also dispatched regionally to a wide variety of places where women's issues arose (for example, abortion or the struggle against prostitution). They helped women obtain alimony payments and acknowledgment of paternity. In Armenia, where the *zhenotdel* went by the name *kinbajin*, the *delegatki* forced their way into traditional homes and inquired about the women who lived there, the relation between husband and wife, father and children, et cetera.[33] In Central Asia the weight of tradition held women back from participating in these activities, but in other regions, above all in urban settings, such actions had a disruptive effect on family relations.[34]

The party was not the only promoter of mobilization activities for women. In 1923 the Soviet state created a special commission for the improvement of women's living conditions with local offices in every republic or region.[35] Like the *zhenotdel*, these commissions were supposed to supervise *in situ*, ensure equality between the sexes in every family, and report any violations of the law to the authorities.[36] They were empowered to intrude at any time into a person's private life. At the same time, because they instructed women in family hygiene and child care, they were sometimes heeded. In cities and occasionally in rural areas these temporary missions were reinforced by permanent women's clubs, which enjoyed some popularity because, even if the ultimate aim was to undermine male authority, they maintained the separation of the sexes that many peoples considered so important.

These institutions survived with uneven results until the late 1920s. The *zhenotdel* disappeared in 1929. Prior to 1926, the commissions for the improvement of women's living conditions were inefficient because they did not have a separate budget; later they were granted substantial financial resources, and their "mass pressure" activities against traditional structures became more widespread.

The mobilization of youth was another part of the policy of "mass pressure." The principal organizing body, Communist Youth (*Komsomol*), was comprised of adolescents from age fourteen to twenty, the most impressionable age. In 1924 Stalin emphasized the importance of this work: "The *Komsomol* forms a reserve of peasants and workers from which the Party can draw its troops. But it is also an instrument in the hands of the Party to ensure Party influence on the young."[37] In order to perform its tasks, the *Komsomol* had to establish itself among the most traditional groups and especially throughout the countryside where old societal structures were most resistant. The mental outlook it encountered varied greatly.

While the youth organizations were developing in the Slavic republics, their growth was slow in Central Asia and the Caucasus, where they were confined to cities and failed utterly to attract the female population. Although there were 310 *Komsomol* organizations and 20,000 members in Central Asia in 1921, the authorities quickly realized that most members were young Russians. Native youth claimed that their lack of Russian-language skills prevented them from joining.[38] Beginning in 1924, when the party called for the creation of local and village organizations and education efforts progressed, the situation began to change. By 1927, the Uzbeks had more than 36,000 *Komsomols*, the Kirghiz 10,000, and the Turkmen 7,000, in both villages and urban areas.[39]

Attempts to recruit adolescents at any price into the *Komsomol* often met with disastrous results. In Armenia, mass recruitment in cities in the early 1920s led to a 1923 purge of "religious fanatics" and drunks. In 1924–25 four-fifths of the recruited youth were of peasant origin, a change which resulted in lower cultural levels: in 1926 half the *Komsomol* membership was illiterate.[40] And despite the pressure of mass action, by the end of the 1920s only 10 percent of the girls in the Caucasus and barely 5 percent in Central Asia had joined, generally the daughters of party leaders. In order to counteract the hostility to *Komsomol* recruitment of girls among the most tenaciously segregationist peoples, *Komsomol* women's organizations were created in rural areas.[41]

Youth mobilization efforts were supplemented by an organization of pioneers, created in 1922, and the Octobrists, created in 1924. But the role of these adjunct organizations was limited, because traditional societies losing sway over adolescents tended to protect their young children from outside influence even more tenaciously.

The *Komsomol* reinforced party pedagogy. They were to disseminate the new laws throughout the USSR, spread antireligious propaganda, and participate in the struggle for the emancipation of women. In villages where the party was not well established, the *Komsomols* took its place and accomplished its tasks. Their most important functions were to trace and report violations of the law, including abuses of marital or parental authority, and to supervise the schools to make sure that teachers were properly defending the new order.

To an even greater degree than the women's organizations, the *Komsomols* promoted public demonstrations against women who wore the veil and against "religious superstitions." In the Ukraine, from 1922 on, the Jewish *Komsomols* figured prominently in the antireligious parodies ridiculing Judaism.[42] The attacks were so virulent that the party had to call them to order. In Central Asia the youth organizations attacked family structures with more than religion, and also participated in the literacy campaign that spread throughout the countryside. In the Christian strongholds of the Caucasus, their main activities revolved around the antireligion campaign.

Revolution in the law is an integral part of the destructive phase through which social change, especially when attempted rapidly, must pass. Pashukanis, the great jurist of this pivotal period, notes that the construction of a socialist society implies the eradication of "the already-expired spirit of bourgeois judicial doctrine." The new laws served two purposes. First they brought down the previous social structures, thus a way of life essential to the definition of the national group's identity; then they incorporated individuals shorn of their particular cultural traits into a uniform system.

Almost from the beginning, the idea of promoting social change on the basis of an egalitarian ideology was met by an unforeseen obstacle. The Soviet judicial model, theoretically applicable to all nationalities, was inspired in many respects— family relations, rapport between generations—by developments occurring in the European part of the USSR. The strained family structures of Russian or Ukrainian peasant society were certainly distinct from those of urban society, but there was definitely a Slavic social model—rural or otherwise—that was essentially inapplicable to many peripheral societies. Thus, the norms held up by the central leadership were the combined product of a European-Slavic tradition and revolution that were completely foreign to peoples who had lived under Islam, Judaism, and other tribal structures or groups united within a culture based on clan.

This explains the two particularities of the cultural revolution of the 1920s: its chronological and its territorial aspects. After the violent social revolution of wartime communism, the Soviet government adopted—in Slavic territory only—a strategy of gradual change. Concurrently, in areas with deeply rooted cultural attachments it had to pursue a policy of rapid social change to close the gap in cultural differences among the different civilizations comprising the Union. Whereas the social revolution of wartime communism stopped in the Slavic countries in 1921, it continued elsewhere until 1929. Thus, in order to understand the development of non-Russian societies, it is important to know that, in the revolution as well, they lagged behind the rest of Russia.

The territorial aspect of the cultural revolution relates to the juxtaposition of very dissimilar local policies in the brief eight-year period from 1921 to 1929. Significantly, the Russian social peace of those years corresponds to the so-called *Khudjum* policy in Central Asia, of all-out war against the social order inherited from the past. The fact that unequal policies coexisted under the flag of an egalitarian ideology substantially weakened the impact of the ideology itself; in the face of inequality, people felt that local reaction to the cultural revolution and pronounced nationalist tendencies were justified.

As a result, some social or nationality groups as a whole rejected and remained detached from the new Soviet order. The revolution in customs, designed to weaken those groups who clung to the old order, caused discontents to mobilize around parties that often had a nationalist orientation. The consequences proved extremely destructive. Instead of toppling the existing social order, the cultural revolution above all sapped the strength of Soviet order. In 1921 Lenin believed that to build a new economic order, mentalities had to be changed. But in 1929 his successors returned to the brutal and "economical" approach of wartime communism: they counted on an economic revolution to change mentalities.

The year 1929 was a turning point for the USSR, all the more sudden because it followed the period of respite provided by NEP. But for the non-Russian peoples who had recently felt the pressures of the cultural revolution, a storm of one kind followed a storm of another kind. These peoples' collective memories hold their own images of history that do not correspond with the general chronology of the Soviet Union. The era of NEP represented a retreat and a pause only for some peoples of the USSR. For others, during those years a dramatic struggle was played out to salvage the political cultures that were the essence of their national identities.

CHAPTER 10

National Culture and Proletarian Culture

All revolutionaries dream of sweeping away the philosophical legacy of their predecessors and creating new forms for the expression of new ideas. In the Russian context, the Bolsheviks' dream was complicated by a need to reconcile a universalist message with the cultural heritage of particular nations. From the outset, two immediate questions had to be decided: what type of status to grant the nations, and what place to give national culture within a Bolshevik universal culture. Concerning questions of status, Stalin had defined his idea of a nation, *natsiia*, as early as 1913. The four criteria he established were the unities of language, territory, economic life, and psychic development. Other factors such as numerical strength and geography would help determine more exactly the political rights associated with groups meeting these criteria. But for various reasons not every ethnic group could acquire status as a nation.

The Soviet system guaranteed cultural recognition only to *narodnost'*, "nationhood"; hence only nations were entitled to recognition of their language and particular institutions. However, national destiny was not identical across the board. In the *Great Soviet Encyclopedia* an analysis of national dynamics concludes: "Not all nationalities are destined to become consolidated into nations. Some, be it because of their backwardness, or because they do not meet certain criteria, cannot constitute a stable territorial and economic community. They are fated gradually to adopt the language of the country to which they are economically and territorially associated and to blend little by little into it."[1]

At first it might appear a simple matter to define the rights of nations in the USSR and their place within the whole. Did not long-established, definite criteria serve as a guarantee that the rights of all people would be respected and that egalitarianism would prevail in all organs? But the theoretical definition did not resolve the difficult question of the parameters of national cultures and their coexistence with a common ideology. It was Stalin who defined how the beliefs of Bolshevism and national rights would become blended in a cultural compromise: "What is national culture? How can it be reconciled with proletarian culture? Aren't the two an irreconcilable contradiction? Obviously, they are not. We are building a proletarian culture. That is perfectly true. But it is equally true that proletarian culture of socialist content takes different forms and uses different modes of expression for different peoples involved in socialist construction, depending on their linguistic diversity, living conditions, et cetera. The culture that is common to all humanity, and toward which socialism moves, is proletarian in content and national in form. Proletarian culture does not abolish national culture; one is contained within the other. And, conversely, national culture does not abolish proletarian culture, but gives it form."[2]

Approaches to the Promotion of National Cultures

If we consider language to be the main aspect of national culture, Stalin was correct in asserting that no contradiction existed between national culture and proletarian culture. But the multiplicity of ethnic groups and languages in the former empire considerably complicated the situation, making it difficult to put Stalin's theory into practice.

Should all languages spoken at the time be considered national languages, or only written languages? What about certain dialects? What about dispersed ethnic groups: should their right to use their own language be recognized (tantamount to the hitherto-rejected idea of extraterritorial cultural autonomy), or should language be linked to territory? What should be done with numerically small groups who used a written language (for example, the Kubashis of Daghestan, who according to the 1926 census numbered only 2,579—they were mainly concentrated in one village and spoke an Ibero-Caucasian language written with Arabic characters)?

The technical problems were compounded by political turmoil. In the linguistic breakup of the empire, a rearrangement of language groups had taken place in the early years of the twentieth century. Some groups grew to considerable size. The Moslems of the tsarist empire communicated mainly in Tatar, their common language.[3] Central Asia had begun to forge political unity in the prerevolutionary years around the Turkic language Jagatai.[4] In the much-partitioned Caucasus, adherents of unity alternately advocated the use of Arabic, Azeri, and Kumyk.[5] In 1919 the Buddhist peoples were still dreaming of Mongol unity, which they tried to build on a common linguistic base.[6] Smaller groups of Finnish origin whose languages came from strictly oral traditions, such as the Mordovin and the Udmurt, showed a decided interest in pan-Finnish unity.

These diverse tendencies were not all equal in importance and of course did not have equal chances of success in achieving their aims. The Soviet leaders had to decide either to foster movements that sought to unify nations around a common cultural heritage or to favor the egalitarian development of every language with a chance of survival. If they recognized the former, they would be responding to the desires of many national groups and encouraging in some cases a developing linguistic consciousness; if the latter approach was adopted, the Soviets would be heeding the consistently declared wishes of formerly consolidated national groups such as Ukrainians, Georgians, and Armenians who considered the use of their language a fundamental political right. These peoples would be alarmed at policies of linguistic amalgamation. In any case, the Soviet government could not pursue more than one cultural policy; there had to be consistency in this domain.

Theory concerning national culture was subject to technical difficulties and political priorities, but the basic choice— recognition of all languages or endorsement of unifying currents—was made by 1920, when the Bolsheviks decided that each nation would have a language of its own and the cultural institutions—schools, publishing houses—to go with it. This option necessarily raised the issue of the peoples whose languages had no written form. Should written systems be devised for their native languages, or should bilingualism be promoted? If the latter, what would the second language be, a common language such as Russian or a written language native to the general territory where the national group resided? It was discovered in the years 1920–29 that not every nationality group—numbering 169 in all—had its own language.[7]

The Consolidation of
Large Nationality Groups

The decision to grant each group the right to use its language satisfied the Ukrainians, Georgians, and Armenians, and, to a lesser extent, the Byelorussians, all of whom lived in fixed areas where national cultures had evolved over time, but other minority groups lived within their borders as well. By September 1920, Ukrainian became mandatory in schools and government offices, and Ukrainian-language publishing developed apace. Armenia, despite the spelling reforms of 1922, which gave rise to two coexisting systems, adopted the same measures.[8] Everywhere words were created to translate political concepts or technical and scientific terms into local languages to avoid dependence on Russian terminology. Administrative and political posts in the republics required that candidates have knowledge of the local language, although this rule was not always followed, especially in the large cities of the Ukraine with sizable Russian and Jewish minority groups.[9] In Byelorussia it was harder to establish a system because no cultural unity existed there. Created in 1921, Byelorussia was enlarged by decree on 3 March 1924 to include nearly three million people in adjacent territories. It had few developed urban centers, and cities such as Minsk and Vitebsk had a large Jewish population (between 45 and 50 percent in 1926). The intelligentsia conceived of Byelorussian identity in opposition to the Russian language and culture, even proposing that its name be changed to Krivichi (name of a Slavic people who had lived there ten centuries before) in order to eliminate the Russian suffix. A language had to be created with terms far different from Russian, often to the detriment of a common vocabulary.[10] The Soviet system had to tolerate this anti-Russian cultural attitude because the nationalist elite of Byelorussia was the only source of national cadre; if the Soviet government condemned Byelorussian cultural nationalism, the implantation policy would be rendered ineffective.

Ultimately, Soviet recognition of the right of nations develop their own cultures led to similar results in three dissimilar situations. Where the essential elements of culture were present—language, folklore, national history—-the Soviet cultural policy resulted in general development of the language and hence an enhancement of nationalist feeling.

Even in Byelorussia, where "Byelorussification" was a rather artificial construct, ethno-linguistic consciousness increased noticeably.

A Language for Every Nation

In 1917 some of the empire's dispersed peoples strove to forge unity on a cultural basis, that is on the basis of a common language. The Moslems of the Volga-Ural region virtually succeeded in this quest; peoples in Central Asia and the Caucasus were looking to identify with a unifying language, and Mongol Buddhists attempted to band together. Whatever degree of success these efforts toward cultural development attained, cultural unification led to political unity founded on a common past and religious—Islamic or Buddhist—community. In 1920 the most advanced unitarian experiment was that of the Tatar-Bashkirs who tried to revive the prestigious Kazan khanate in the *Idel-Ural* state.[11] They based their movement toward unity on the widespread use of Tatar as a cultural and political language. In 1918 the Bolsheviks, in support of self-determination, had accepted a Tatar-Bashkir union, but a scant year later they realized a great Turkish state was in the making. In order to break up developing Turkish unity, Lenin and Stalin decided that each nation should have a language of its own. The Tatars already did, but the Bashkirs had no written language, so the Soviets devised a literary form of the spoken language and through education reduced the use of Tatar, thus fostering a Bashkir nation with its own identity. Tatar influence was also held in check by promoting small groups such as the Kriashen and the Nagaibak (Christianized Turks) to the rank of nationalities; they were given written languages based on dialects that had previously been used in conjunction with Tatar.

The policy inaugurated in the Tatar Republic was applied on a wider scale, and more confidently, in Central Asia, where the situation was more difficult because there was a greater number of ethnic groups than in Tatar-Bashkir territories, and the groups were larger and established on a strategic border. In the early 1920s the peoples of Central Asia had two general aspirations: the dream of Turkestani unity based on the Turkic language Jagatai, and the eventual formation of three political-sociological entities: the nomads of the steppes (Kazakh and Kirghiz); the sedentary peoples of the former emirates of Bukhara, Kiva, and Kokand; and the Turkmenian people.[12]

The Bolsheviks were equally opposed to both aspirations, and established new ethnic and cultural borders in Central Asia to upset existing unity. In 1925 political territories were created—Soviet Socialist Republics (SSRs), Autonomous Soviet Socialist Republics (ASSRs), and Autonomous *Oblasts* (AOs), or Regions, consisting of nations who already possessed a cultural identity, or some groups for whom the Soviet regime created cultural realities.

The Kirghiz people were thus separated administratively from the Kazakhs, to whom they had previously been culturally related. Kirghiz unity gave the Bolsheviks cause for concern because during the war the nomads had strongly resisted conscription.[13] Only the Kazakh people were permitted to use their language. A separate Kirghiz dialect was standardized as a written language in 1922. The definition of the Kirghiz as a nation was noteworthy because in 1925 the Kirghiz population stood at two-thirds of its former strength, many having been annihilated by tsarist repression or having died of starvation after seeking refuge in China in 1917. Despite its cultural and numerical weakness, the Kirghiz nation flourished. In contrast to the Bashkirs, who were slow to establish an identity separate from Tatar culture, the Kirghiz began to build a cultural tradition in 1925 founded on a rich epic folklore.[14]

Likewise, Soviet authorities divided the Uzbeks and Tadzhiks into two separate groups. In one sense this separation was natural—the Tadzhiks spoke Persian, were sedentary, and had emerged from an old civilization, whereas the Uzbeks spoke Turkish and were semi-nomadic, having recently become partly sedentary; but despite their apparent differences, the separation of the two peoples was largely artificial. Until the revolution Tadzhik had been the cultural and political language of the Uzbeks. By promoting Jagatai, the Uzbeks attempted to reconcile their spoken language with the official language and orient it toward a pan-Turkic ideal. But Jagatai spread at a snail's pace. Moreover, many ethnic groups were intermingled in the region, and the creation of homogeneous national republics was not warmly welcomed because it would have involved relocating certain segments of the population.

Nevertheless, the two groups were separated and national subdivisions established to reflect the mixture of other ethnic groups. Jagatai died away in 1923, and a newly formed Uzbek literary language took its place.[15] Uzbek cultural institutions were maintained in Tadzhik territory to safeguard the cultural rights of the Turkic-speaking peoples of the Autonomous Republic.

In 1924 another nation was formed out of bits and pieces. The Karakalpak tribe, nearly identical to the Kazakh and Uzbek tribes in nomadism and traditions, acquired national status as an Autonomous Region established in an enclave of the Kazakh Republic. Later they were incorporated into the RSS of Uzbekistan. Their changing affiliation reflects how difficult it was to define their national identity. Nor was it easy to devise a written language out of the Karakalpak dialect. Unlike the Kirghiz literary language, which quickly gained acceptance, Karakalpak was very slow to spread because it was always in competition with the official language of the republic to which the Karakalpaks were attached.

The history of the Turkmen was more straightforward. A dispersed and unassimilated group until the early nineteenth century, the Turkmen themselves created a common language[16] based on two tribal dialects from which, around 1921, a common written language evolved. During this period, the newly settled population was eager to assert a national identity apart from the Turks and the neighboring tribes of Iran—a desire that coincided with the interests of the Soviet regime.

Soviet cultural policy in Central Asia had two objectives: to inhibit the potential unification of the region around Turkish-Moslem ideals, and to lay the foundation for its future social transformation. The fate of the Turkmen and the Kazakh-Kirghiz peoples illustrates Soviet intentions not only to exert political control over Central Asia but also to draw up a social agenda to make these nomadic peoples adopt a sedentary way of life.

The Soviet regime also paid special attention to the rights of smaller-sized groups with no established territory, such as the Uighur (Turkic people) and the Dolgan (Chinese-speaking Moslems of Arabic-Persian origin), whom they endowed with cultural institutions.[17] On the other hand, although the Arabs appeared in the census as a nation,[18] they did not have their own schools; yet subsequent censuses revealed the survival of the language, at least in its spoken form.

The complexity of the Caucasus places it in a separate category. Notwithstanding its nominal unity, the northern Caucasus was an inextricable web of ethnic groups without national or cultural traditions, ruled by tribal or clanship loyalties. The Bolsheviks wished not to compound the confusion but to simplify the situation by unifying the different groups. In 1919, concerned by secular rivalries in the Caucasus, the Soviets created two republics, each a mosaic of ethnic groups: the Mountaineers' Republic and the Republic of Daghestan. The Mountaineers' Republic splintered almost immediately into eight national groups (Kabardin, Balkar, Chechen, Ingush, Karachay, Adygey, Cherkess, and Ossetian) comprising seven political-territorial formations (the Kabardin and Balkars merged in 1922) attached to the RSFSR. Even this classification was only superficial: in the Adygei autonomous region, the Cherkess people had greater rights; and the Ossetian people was divided between two territories, one of which—Southern Ossetia, was attached to Georgia.[19] The complexity of administrative divisions was matched by the profusion of overlapping languages. Newly created literary languages multiplied, as dialects were ennobled and given written form: Kabardin, Balkar, Chechen, Ingush, Circassian, Karachay, and the two languages of the Ossetian nation, Digor and Iron, were created from dialects spoken more or less in the different administrative regions. Digor disappeared in 1939, and thereafter all Ossetians shared the same language.

In 1925 the Soviet regime was still groping for solutions to the linguistic intricacies of the Caucasus. While Soviet policy was to endow each recognized nationality group with a language, this doctrine was not followed with the Ossetians, who were divided into two linguistic groups; and the Karachay and the Balkars were given two distinct languages to correspond to their territorial separation, despite the fact that they were accustomed to using the same language.

In Daghestan the situation was at once more complex and more simple. Its complexity lay in the fact that it was home to at least thirty-five different groups[20] who belonged to four language groups—Ibero-Caucasian, Turkic, Iranian, Semitic—and were subject to Arabic, Turkic, and Russian influences. The heterogeneity of customs and sociopolitical conditions gave rise to complications. But the language situation was simpler than in other areas because Daghestan had a history of unification movements (Arabic, Azeri, Kumyk) in the late nineteenth century; in all three cases, unity had been sought around a common language. From the outset, the Soviet regime recognized the extreme complexity of the different political tendencies in Daghestan, and accordingly adopted the unusual solution of assigning the republic a geographic name[21] without defining it as a nation. As a result, unlike the Mountaineers' Republic, Daghestan preserved its independence despite its entanglements. The Bolsheviks turned existing prerevolutionary tendencies to their advantage but stopped short of implementing a solution of the Central Asian type, that is, permitting linguistic-cultural but not political diversity. In Daghestan, history and human realities made both unity and diversity dependent on the same language for support.

At an early stage the Soviet regime attempted to unify Daghestan around the Arabic language, a proposal offered by conservative nationalists of the region—the clergy, essentially. In 1920 a simplified

Arabic alphabet was applied to some languages (Avar, Dargin, Lak). In 1923, when Stalin sent a message to the Congress of Moslem clergymen in Kakhib, it was written in Arabic. By then, a Peoples' Commissariat for *Shariat* law—*Narkomshariat*—existed in the republic. However, at the time, the Soviet regime was beginning to combat Islam, and Arabic was considered too closely associated with it, so later in 1923 the use of Arabic was dropped, and the Turkic, Azeri, or Kumyk languages were adopted. In 1917 the first Congress of the Mountaineers of the Caucasus, held in Vladikavkaz, had decided that Kumyk would be the language of secondary education.[22] A few years later, Daghestani leaders, under pressure from Moscow to replace Arabic with a Turkic language, chose Azeri. The reason they chose Azeri over Kumyk, their earlier preference, was that local communists found they were too isolated if they used the languages confined to the Caucasus—Kumyk, among others.[23] Azeri put them in contact with the far vaster universe of Turkic peoples, just as Arabic had done in another context. For Moscow, the virtue of Azeri lay in the elimination of Arabic. However, by 1928 Azeri became the language of pan-Turkic unification tendencies in the Caucasus, a unity that was broken when Moscow declared Daghestan to have eleven official languages rather than one, divided among four major groups: Slavic (Russian), Turkic (Azeri, Kumyk, Nogay), Ibero-Caucasian (Avar, Dargin, Lezgin, Lak, Chechen, Tabasaran), and Iranian (Tati). Chechen, Lezgin, Tabasaran, Nogay, and Tati were exclusively oral languages for which alphabets had to be devised. In some instances literary languages created out of whole cloth came to replace the previously spoken languages, as occurred with the Nogai, who used Nogai locally and Kazan's Tatar in intertribal relations.[24]

The Buddhist peoples—Buryats, Mongols, and Kalmyks—who for a time had cherished the idea of a pan-Mongol entity were the last group to move toward ethnic unification. The Buryats had from the beginning posed a problem to the Soviet regime. Through accidents of history, because they inhabited opposite shores of Lake Baikal, they were caught in the middle of the Japanese invasion just after the revolution. Japanese strategy at the time was to promote the formation of a great Mongol Empire. In 1919 they called a pan-Mongol Congress at Chita, to which many Buryats were attracted. There the Buryats demanded that Russians be expelled from the Baikal region and that the Peace Conference guarantee a great Mongol Empire's right to exist.

Stalin, on the other hand, advocated gathering the Buryats into an autonomous republic, and one was created in 1923 in the hope that the Buryats would thus be diverted from other plans. But far from showing gratitude to the Soviet regime for having given them a national state, the Buryats continued to militate for Mongol unity and looked to the Khalka Mongols of Outer Mongolia. In order to establish closer ties with the Buryats, the intellectuals of the Mongolian republic adapted Buryat vocabulary and syntax to the Khalka-Mongol language, which they planned to convert at a later stage to a common Mongolian language. They also made contacts with the Kalmyks, whose right to an autonomous existence had been recognized by Lenin in June 1919.[25] In 1927 the First Congress of Soviet Buddhists, convened in Moscow, was evidence that a syncretistic Buddhism allied with communism existed in the USSR. The lamasary was preserved in the form of cooperatives where the regular clergy and religious traditions persisted.[26]

But the Soviet leadership, which had tolerated this movement for a short time, broke with Buddhism in 1928 and condemned the vestiges of a religion that "destroyed working-class consciousness."[27] In 1929 the use of a hybrid language—Buryat mixed with Khalka-Mongol— was outlawed, and a western Buryat dialect elevated to a literary language[28] imposed in its place. The Soviet policy of dividing the Mongol group was aided by parallel developments in Outer Mongolia, where Buddhism was under attack and a "de-Mongolization" of the language was taking place via a change of alphabet. In the early 1930s, Latin characters were substituted for vertical Mongol characters. Thus, many signs of Mongol distinctiveness were disappearing simultaneously.

After the dilution of Buryat national culture and the isolation of the Kalmyks by economic changes, Tannu Tuva remained as the last Mongol bastion. It was to be destroyed. Tuva (its Mongol name was Uriankai), with 64,000 inhabitants in 1913 and 70,000 in 1926, had become a Russian protectorate in 1913. In 1921 Chicherin denied that the Soviet state had any pretensions with regard to Tuva territory.[29] The Soviet leadership was disinclined to ensure the continuation of the tsarist empire in Tuva territory because they did not wish to expand their Mongol possessions any further. Culturally, Tuva was part of the Mongol world. Tuva's inhabitants had no literary language or tradition; adherents of Buddhism, they used the Mongol language for religious purposes and for communication. As a first step toward the creation of a greater Mongol state, Tuva's political leaders made overtures to Outer Mongolia. In 1925 the Soviet leadership modified its position, and although not denying Tuva's formal independence, which was to last twenty more years, tried to control Tuva's cultural and political life for the purpose of eradicating Buddhism and the Mongolian language, the constituent elements of Mongol unification. These efforts were assisted by a lama who in 1928 adapted the Roman alphabet to the Tuva dialects. But the attempted innovation conflicted with the religious conscious-ness of the Mongol masses who were attached to Buddhism, the small republic's official religion. Moscow thought that Tuva was setting a bad example for the neighboring nations, and in 1929 the Soviet govern-ment, using the Communist Party it had established and encouraged in Tuva, engineered a coup.

The time was ripe for Tuva to become culturally aligned with the Mongol peoples who were already incorporated into the USSR. As elsewhere in the USSR, the need to consolidate the Tuva nation by giv-ing it a language of its own was the leitmotif of communist policy. The Tuva language replaced Mongolian, and the Roman alphabet the Mon-golian system of writing.[30] The literary Tuva language developed by Russian linguists took root rather quickly. "Ounen," the party journal, which beginning in 1925 had been published in Mongolian, appeared in a bilingual edition for a few months and then was printed exclusively in the Tuva language.

Tuva was an extreme case. The Soviet leadership could not tolerate the survival of a Mongol center in legally independent territory. Only Outer Mongolia, because it was the official Mongol homeland, was per-mitted to use the Mongolian language, but after 1929 it ceased to be a common denominator among peoples who shared the same faith and wished to restore historical continuity.

Nations in Search of Their Cultural Heritage

Unlike the Moslem or Buddhist peoples whose desires for unity were grounded in common religion, historical past, social traditions, and language, the Chuvash people and other groups of Finno-Ugrian ori-gin were much more tenuously related. Yet in the heated political cli-mate of the 1920s, when the affirmation of national rights led to a per-manent quest for national identity, the Chuvash people, too, looked for common ties of historical and cultural kinship. Thus, the Finno-Ugrian peoples living in Soviet territory—especially the most developed, the Mari and Udmurt—turned toward independent Finland, declared themselves Finnish and sought to establish a cultural identity in a pan-Finnish direction. The Maris had the highest degree of national con-sciousness. Mostly Christian, with a small number of Moslems among them, they adopted all religions into a form of syncretism in which pagan rites and sects had considerable importance. Their hostility to

progress was a major impediment to Soviet economic policy. Mari
nationalism of an anti-Russian stripe led Moscow in 1920 to create a
Mari Autonomous Province, gathering together nearly two-thirds of
the Mari people in Russia. The language was not a problem, for although the Maris were divided between two language groups, the language had been written in Cyrillic characters since before the revolution.

The Votiaks, a second Finnish people with a strong national identity,
after 1928 called the Udmurts, were densely concentrated along the
banks of the Kama River (a tributary of the Volga). Before the revolution, their language had also been written in Cyrillic characters. In 1920
they began to look nostalgically to independent Finland. In 1921 an Autonomous Region was created for them on the justification of their high
population density, the existence of a written language, and the Soviet
desire to forestall any movement toward Finnish unity.

The less developed Mordovian and Komi peoples tended to be less
attracted than the Maris and Udmurts by the ideas of pan-Finnish
nationalism. However, for sociological and economic reasons, the
Soviet policy of national consolidation was applied to them as well as to
the other Finnish groups. In 1917 the Mordovians' nationalist sentiments were very diffused, and they were greatly influenced by Russian
culture. Divided into two equally important language groups, they decided at that time to use Russian to communicate among themselves
and with the outside world.[31] Their progressive cultural Russification
caused Moscow to ignore them as a national group until 1928, when the
Mordovians compared their status to peoples of similar origin such as
the Maris, and not understanding why they, too, should not be granted
autonomy, manifested intensely nationalist feelings. Wary that they
might unite with other, politically sophisticated Finnish peoples or that
their discontent might be channeled in the same direction as Mordovian popular religion of the nineteenth century—which predicted a
millennium in which Russians would be excluded and Mordovians
would gain total independence—Moscow decided in 1928 to recognize
the Mordovian nation based on one of their languages.

The Komi and Zyrians, a small group dispersed across a wide territory, claimed to be the heirs of the medieval state of Biarma, which they
sought to revive in the form of a great Komi state, to include their Per-
miak cousins and their neighbors, the Udmurts, and the Nevets if
necessary. They regarded Scandinavia as their cultural and historic
center. Moscow's concern increased as the projected economic importance of Komi territory grew. The Komis claimed ownership of under-

ground natural resources, key to their development, and asserted that Russians had no right of access.[32] In 1929 a survey of the mineral resources of the Pechora region led Moscow to draw up a new ethnographic map of the region in order to isolate the Komis and weaken them politically.

In a similar way, the Chuvash, a Christianized Turkish-speaking people, were isolated from other Turkic peoples of Russia. Their nationalist sentiment inspired them in 1917 to seek to reestablish the ancient empire of the Bulgars, whose descendants they claimed to be. They wanted to be recognized as a Bulgarian, not a Chuvash, people. Moscow took a dim view of their demands, especially because their language had been written in adapted Cyrillic characters before 1917 and Russian was widely used among them.[33] Bulgarian nationalism was a break from this already established tradition. When Moscow recognized the Chuvash nation, it sanctioned the advance of Russification and repudiated identification with a past world.

Turkish peoples of Siberia such as the Kalmyk, belonging to Burkhanism,[34] a messianic and anticolonialist religion, felt nostalgia for the past and wanted to use the rediscovered past as the basis for a modern nation. The religion, which advocated resurrecting the empire of Genghis Khan, encouraged a postrevolutionary Kalmyk national movement and the idea of a great Altai state regrouping the Kalmyk, the Khakass (another Turkic-speaking group in Siberia), the Tuvan peoples, and annexing the Mongolian part of Altai and the then Chinese area of Jungaria. The idea of a great Altai or Karakorum, which was nourished by nostalgia for Genghis Khan, was partly accepted in 1921 by the Commissariat of Nationalities, which contemplated creating a Kalmyk-Khakass region.[35] But one year later, the Soviet leadership, in keeping with its refusal to permit national unification, decided to grant separate recognition to the Kalmyk and Khakass nations. In 1929 Moscow even recognized a third Turkic nation of the region, the Izhor, whose dialect after 1927 was written in Cyrillic. Despite various attempts to regulate it, the language of the Izhor disappeared for lack of use.

The cases of the Finnish Chuvash and the Kalmyk peoples portrayed Moscow's fears and future intent. Nationalist sentiments sought reaffiliation with a prestigious past and a friendly orientation toward other peoples. The Bolsheviks, however, responded by dividing nations, consolidating them around narrow and often artificial bases, even when the groups in question posed no danger of forming large political entities. A great difference existed between a pan-Finnish orientation, or even the resurrection of the Bulgarian kingdom, and actual pan-Turkish unity, but the same policy was imposed on all groups.

The Fabrication of Nations and Cultures

In the Far East and extreme northern regions, a primarily tribal way of life was what united groups or tribes, and with the exception of Yakut, their languages were vernacular tongues used only by the tribe. In these areas the Soviet leadership was most inventive, utterly transforming some tribes into nations with artificially created literary languages, some of which took root.

The sole exception to these fabricated languages was Yakut, a language with an alphabet that had been developed in the nineteenth century by Orthodox missionaries, and, largely due to this fact, the Yakut people in 1917 had a developed national consciousness. From the beginning,[36] the Soviet leadership was mistrustful of Yakut nationalism. Their Turkish origins made them more open to Turkish culture,[37] and they were in a position to play an integrationist role in relation to other tribes. For these reasons an Autonomous Republic was established in 1922, unifying the Yakuts around their language, although the national districts in Yakutia protected the rights of the Paleo-Asiatic minorities (Chukshi and Yukaghir) and the Manchu minority (Even).

The Even peoples were an extreme example of Soviet cultural policy that granted national status and a literary language of their own to tens of thousands of aborigines. Russian linguists and ethnologists were instrumental in promoting the creation in 1922 of institutions to protect, rather than destroy or assimilate, the aborigines of the far north and the Far East.[38] In 1923 a special committee of the *Narkomnats*, divided into two geographic regions and various functional sections, was put in charge of protecting these peoples. Two years later, a specialized institute was established in Leningrad. Scientific curiosity led those who worked for these institutes to promote respect for the identity, ways of life, and structures of the aboriginal groups, a doctrine that won the aborigines a doubly favored treatment: they were promoted to the rank of a nation (from *narod*, or people, they became *natsional'nost*), and allowed to maintain their political tribal institutions, which were not controlled by Soviet common law until the early 1930s. Their languages also had privileged status; until 1931 dialects that were primarily oral or pictorial were conserved and thus escaped the forced consolidation of languages and the sometimes contradictory alphabetization experiments.

This policy was followed in the Far East with regard to tens of thousands of aborigines who belonged to two main groups: Paleo-Asiatic (Allent, Ainu, Eskimo, Kamshadel, Koryak, Nivkh, Chukshi) and the Manchu (Even,[39] Nanay, Tungu, Udegey). In the far north, the two principal peoples were the Evenk-Tungus and the Nents, or Samoyeds. The Evenks, who numbered a few thousand, had developed a national ideology. Their dream of a radiant future when they would rule over their conquerors made them tend not to cooperate with the Soviet leadership, whose downfall they awaited. Institutional independence and the promotion of their folklore to the category of culture only encouraged these tendencies. On the other hand, the Nents were grateful to Moscow for sparing them from being absorbed by the Komis, who claimed kinship with them.

The backwardness, isolation, and dispersion of the peoples living in the Far East and far north certainly did not promote their transformation into intellectually dynamic nationalities. Soviet policy rejected the alternative of Russification, enabling them to preserve their identities and folklore, which would otherwise be fated to disappear in a changing society. The survival of individual peoples with a national consciousness that perpetuated the loyalties of a lost tribal world went beyond mere folklore. By the late 1920s the Soviet cultural experiment was beginning to show results. Uncoerced, small nations harkened spontaneously to Russian culture to complete their own limited local cultures.

The Alphabet Revolution, 1926–1931

From 1925 to 1926 a multiplicity of languages in the USSR and a profusion of writing systems—Cyrillic, Latin, Arabic, Mongolian, Georgian, Armenian, Hebrew, mixed systems—were all in use and impeded the development of a common culture. By 1921 it was clear that the transcription systems of all the different languages in Russia needed to be simplified and unified. An effective literacy campaign could not be waged as long as so many different modes of writing coexisted. New cadre were urgently needed to carry out this work. Russian teachers could not be used in Moslem areas because they did not know the Arabic alphabet, with the result that education was relegated to the (often conservative) local intelligentsia. Ideologically reliable cadre and resources were lacking. Printing educational materials and propaganda in numerous alphabets was costly, complicated, and difficult to control. The system was plagued with problems that slowed intellectual progress and favored different world views rather than a common ideology, thus requiring a revision of the policy of cultural *tabula rasa*.

However, uniform alphabets were adopted at a late date. The central leadership was wary of wounding nationalist sensitivities and disagreed over the appropriate steps to take. Should the Cyrillic alphabet, used prior to 1917 by small nations such as the Tatars of Kazan, be retained?[40] Or was it preferable to promote the Roman alphabet, which had its followers and had been ennobled by the Kemalian revolution in Turkey?

In 1926 the Congress of Turkology in Baku decided in favor of the Roman alphabet, and institutions were established to adapt the writing systems of the Turkic languages. However, some were violently opposed to the Roman alphabet, which was proposed in 1920 and finally imposed in 1929. Moslems felt it deprived them of their means of religious expression. Even nonbelievers rejected an alphabet divorced from Turko-Moslem civilization. By 1930 Latin letters adapted to local languages were widely used in Turkish territories, but the Buryats did not accept them until 1933.

In 1931 a second alphabet battle led to the creation of a unified Roman alphabet tailored to the languages of the north and Far East. Conflicts developed, for some newly created languages had Cyrillic alphabets. The transition from one writing system to another slowed the development of some languages or led directly to the use of Russian. Only the Slavs and nations whose languages had already been Latinized escaped the alphabet revolution—for example, the Finns, or in some instances the Georgians, Armenians, and Jews—the latter partly because of their very high cultural level and their reliance on their own educational structures.

By 1931 sixty-nine languages were made to conform to the Roman alphabet, which contributed to the education effort but did not promote the use of Russian. At the time the lack of a common language retarded the development of relations among the nations of the USSR, a situation rendered all the more critical by the fact that the politically centralized system was ill-equipped to counteract the nations' withdrawal into their own worlds.

The "Third Front" of the Revolution

The USSR's school system was national. In all areas the *Korenizatsiia* saw to it that an indigenous teaching corps was established. Thus in 1925 in Armenia, 80 percent of elementary school teachers and all those who taught in seven-year or secondary schools were Armenian. Armenian students were hastily trained in Moscow to teach in their republic. In the Ukraine, where for a long time the use of Ukrainian had been prohibited in school, the requirement of using the local language led to the rapid development of an "Ukrainized" elite with local institutions and Ukrainian publications. This elite was not proportional to the size of the Ukrainian nation, but represented remarkable progress over the situation that had prevailed in the early 1920s. In Islamic and Jewish communities, education in the local languages was burdened by the fact that in these regions, "Soviet national culture" meant first the displacement of "reactionary" and religious cultures. Indeed, whereas the Ukrainians regarded the use of their language in schools as a victory, the Tatars and Uzbeks viewed the teaching of a Latinized language shorn of religious roots as a deterioration of their prerevolutionary status. Moreover, there was a lack of local cadre who could impart secularized mass education.[41] As late as in 1927–28, the university of Tashkent had only 350 indigenous students out of a total student population of 5,000.

At the Tenth Party Congress, Lunacharsky, the USSR's first commissioner of education, declared, "Education shall be entirely communist; all disciplines shall be imbued with communism."[42] For the Bolsheviks, the communist education of non-Russian peoples was a fierce battle. According to Lunacharsky, it was the "third front" of the revolution. How could local teachers be reconciled to Soviet objectives? A joint commission of the Commissariat of Education and the *Narkomnats* was established to draw up and implement a national-proletarian educational program.[43] Schools, those prime intellectual training-grounds, were supposed to mold the new man, and thus "polytechnic" education was born, stressing all aspects of life, theory, and productive activities. This concept of education was expected to abolish the difference between manual and intellectual labor and at the same time to improve the general intellectual level. The program presupposed a uniform syllabus presenting the same worldview (materialist interpretation of all natural phenomena), the same moral code (introduction of positive historic heroes), and a common ideology (Marxism-Leninism as the fundamental discipline throughout secondary school education).

The second hub of the educational program was the adult literacy campaign, designed both to eliminate illiteracy and to shape adults through *politgramota* (political education). In 1919 it was decreed that all illiterate eighteen-year-olds be taught to read[44]; the Commissariat of Education was ordered to mobilize all literate communists for this task. One year later, the *Likbez*, a special commission for the eradication of illiteracy, was created. At the time, the Soviet leadership conceived of its adult literacy program as uniformly applicable throughout the territories it controlled, regardless of the minority peoples involved. But by 1922 there were obvious differences between literacy efforts in culturally receptive areas (Russia, Ukraine, Christian regions of the Caucasus) and among groups where high illiteracy rates coincided with a need for political education (Moslems) or among peoples belonging to cultures of oral traditions (in the Caucasus and the far north). As a result of these belatedly discovered regional differences, each republic—first the republics with strong national cultures and, after 1929, peoples without a written tradition—was given the task of elaborating and financing its own literacy program. Among the various solutions proposed were night courses in city schools and traveling literacy centers for the countryside.

The educational materials used in the literacy campaign reveal its political nature. According to one Soviet author, the first sentences taught to illiterates were slogans such as "All workers must defend the revolution" or "We will liberate the world." At more advanced levels, adults made their way through Lenin's speeches or similar texts. In many regions of the USSR where women led traditional, isolated lives, problems of the literacy campaign were compounded by the need to provide separate schools for women in which only women would teach. As a result, women's literacy rates lagged behind men's. In 1928 in Armenia, women constituted only 8 percent of the student population in literacy courses.[45]

One of the principal means of disseminating common ideas was through the development of printing in local languages. Despite material difficulties, great progress was made in all regions possessing written languages. In the Ukraine, 54 percent of the books and newspapers published in 1929 were in Ukrainian. In Central Asia, 19 newspapers and 24 magazines were printed in a variety of languages; 11 newspapers put out 36,000 copies in 1923, compared to 107,000 copies in 1927, leading to a greater circulation of ideas. Of course, the development of printing created new problems. The center did not have sufficient control. In 1927 the Russian Communist Party denounced the deviations in the local press in Central Asia,[46] implicitly criticizing all the republics.

Cultural progress in the periphery was slow, held in check by a legacy of backwardness and a lack of resources, but new local elites emerged in 1929 to fill posts in political and cultural institutions. Trained "on the job" and better equipped to handle political slogans than a body of knowledge, this elite certainly imparted the political culture of the institutions with which it was affiliated, if not communist ideas. Education of the youth proceeded along the same lines. Even if education in the outermost regions did not reach all young people, it was a powerful means of socializing children and, through them, of affecting the entire society. Statistics are somewhat deceptive in relation to the total population (in 1927 in Uzbekistan, 128,000 native children attended some 2,000 schools; in Turkmenia, there were 31,997 students in the 499 nonprofessional schools of the republic[47]), but reveal the integration of the younger generation into an educational system heavily slanted toward shared Soviet norms. In addition, the statistics demonstrate a new ideological reality—the right to education, no longer the privilege of a minority, was a right applied to all, without distinction as to national origin. The egalitarian ideology at the foundation of the Soviet system gave proletarian culture, as imparted through education, the best chances of taking root.

A New Vision of History

As the Bolsheviks conceived of it in 1920, proletarian culture rested on general acceptance of the values of Marxism. However, the theoretical denial of differences between nations did not eliminate these differences in practice, especially not in a multi-ethnic society in which one group had dominated others for a prolonged period. Marxist egalitarianism explicitly rejected domination of this sort. But history played an essential role, for the peoples of the USSR had a long history in common, and before they were united by Marxism and revolution they had been united by force. Their future had to be built on criticism and rejection of the past, the pillars of proletarian culture.

Lenin admitted that for the empire's dominated peoples, the terms "Russian" and "oppressor" were synonymous.[48] In order to do away with Great Russian chauvinism and inspire confidence, in the 1920s the Soviet leaders and their historians began to define the characteristics of past interrelationships among nations from a rigid doctrinal perspective. The first characteristic they pointed to was the perversity of the tsarist system of domination, as a manifestation of capitalism that oppressed social classes and nationalities alike. Stalin developed this point of view in some detail at the Party's Tenth Congress.[49] In their analysis of the tsarist system of domination, Russian historians and especially Pokrovsky, who after the revolution refashioned a school of history in the light of a triumphant ideology, did more than simply denounce capitalism; they condemned the tsarist system of domination as totally negative. A second characteristic of empire, as Pokrovsky saw it, was that Russian colonial policy from the time of the Grand Duchy of Moscow had been to seek continuous expansion by aggressive and violent means,[50] with incomparable postconquest cruelty that ignored the desires of the dominated peoples. According to this interpretation, the empire's expansionism had been in the interests of a military caste who saw expansion as the means to impose their will to power or their death wish (Pokrovsky cites General Kaufman, who dreamed of nothing but massacres in Central Asia[51] and the methodical pillaging of the conquered territories for his own personal benefit).

The defects of empire, it was further argued, were deepened by the flaws of a ruling class who had gained control over the conquered territories in reward for loyalty to the tsar. Pokrovsky's analysis of the colonial system led him to condemn the tsarist system of government and the manner in which it had ensured authority over its army and administration. What the non-Russian peoples had experienced was described as a variant of serfdom. Generally, Soviet historians of the 1920s described in lurid detail the systematic brutality of colonization, or genocide, as some called it. Thus the *Great Soviet Encyclopedia* described the destiny of the Kirghiz,[52] Galuzo the destiny of Turkestan,[53] and Asfendiarov the extermination of aborigines such as the Ostiaks in Siberia.[54] Tsarist colonialism was held to have been so cruel that its horrors surpassed those of all other colonial systems, which appeared benign in comparison. In describing Russian colonialism as diabolical to an extreme, Pokrovsky repudiated the idea that Russian domination had sometimes spared the conquered peoples a greater evil. His analysis rejected outright the possible arguments that some peoples (those of Georgia, for example) had been threatened by worse dangers, or that the horrors of colonization had sometimes been partly compensated by civilizing factors. He saw no sign of civilizing tendencies in Russian colonization; it had simply been an indefensible outrage that could not be justified by subsequent developments. In his view, and that of his colleagues, the fact that colonized peoples had taken part in a revolution that decolonized them in no way righted the harm done to them in the past.[55]

This unalloyed condemnation of the past and painstaking analysis of the Russian empire's debt to the conquered peoples was combined with total glorification of resistance to the conquerors. If the Russian past was absolute evil, then any form of struggle by the dominated peoples should be revered and enshrined in their culture and their heritage. Thus, examining Russian diplomacy, Pokrovsky underlined the important historical role played by the Imam Shamil of the Caucasus, whom he portrayed as a man of progress despite his religious fanaticism and the dictatorial nature of his reign.[56] His insistence on Shamil's personal role is all the more remarkable considering that his general conception of history ennobled social groups and denied the importance of individuals.

The monumental work of Mikhail Hrushevsky, published in Kiev in the late 1920s, presented the thesis that the history of non-Russian societies was the history of struggles against Russian domination.[57] Hrushevsky discussed the historic personality of the Ukraine, as distinguished from Russia, and, like Pokrovsky, rejected the notion of a community of Slavic peoples. Each nation had to reclaim its own history, from which Russia was necessarily excluded.

Russians and non-Russians had had nothing in common but violence, until revolution brought about decisive change, starting with the eradication of capitalism and its faults, and ending with the liberation of peoples and of humanity. Soviet historiography of the 1920s held that Great Russian chauvinism should not be taken for granted; it had to be roundly and repeatedly condemned everywhere.

The revolutionary interpretation of the nations' past emphasized Russian intransigence and the tragedy of conquered peoples. But the intention was not to nourish national feeling or add to the research of regional histories: on the contrary, this version of history was meant to contribute to proletarian culture and help create a collective memory among the USSR's nations, one based on the conviction of their equality. Historical revisionism was part of the clean-slate policy whereby the Bolshevik leadership hoped to replace the ancient political culture of the empire's nations with a new political culture accepted by all. Yet this destruction of the past is the greatest and most chronic debt the Russian people have incurred.

Russian avowal of "past crimes" against nations had two consequences. First, it deprived Russians of their history, just as minority peoples had been deprived of their cultures or had been unable to develop one. By divesting themselves of their past, Russians had to embrace a common culture, which consisted first and foremost of rewritten history. Second, Russian recognition of past horrors also affected the future, for Russians backed away from playing a leading role in the Union. According to Bolshevist revisionist history, Russians could demand nothing but to do their duty, assist in the development of those nations whose destiny they shared, and help make up for the time lost during the colonial era. Proletarian culture was to be the essence of all national cultures and of Russian culture as well.

Questions of culture and political self-determination were finally resolved by the Bolsheviks in a general way. Culture was considered the birthright of the nation as a whole rather than of a single political class. At the Tenth Party Congress, Georgi Safarov stated that cultural self-determination on the local level should concern workers only insofar as it jeopardized socialist doctrine: it was important to maintain the distinction between the "culture of the exploited" and the "culture of the exploiters."[58] Lenin and Stalin hammered home the thesis of the harmonious combination of the two. In this area, Stalin's contribution was perhaps the more decisive: although in matters of political jurisdiction he had long favored restricting working-class exercise of the right to self-determination, at the same time he was convinced of the importance of ethno-linguistic cultural rights. In 1922, Stalin saw self-determination as a compromise between political control by the center and the free development of national cultures. Of course, such development was far from limitless, and, moreover, culture's proletarian content and its national form were not considered equal in importance. The dynamic of culture was tied to that of political institutions and economic structures.

National cultures were accepted as a transitional phenomenon, a step toward a uniform, common culture that would express the values of the working class and the Party. Bolshevik promotion of national cultures and languages was conceived as a necessary stage in the attainment of a universalist culture that, it was hoped, would triumph over time.

CHAPTER 11

The Roads to
Economic Equality

For the nascent Soviet state, the national question was often intertwined with the problem of the peasantry. The national territories that acquired definitive independent status in 1921 were in economic terms the most developed states, where a working class existed and the cultural level of the masses was highest, whereas the territories that remained within the Soviet orbit were essentially peasant or nomadic societies where industry was virtually nonexistent or limited to the simple transformation of raw materials.

In comparison to the periphery, peasant Russia seemed to be a proletarian state. Thus, de facto social and political inequalities existed when the USSR was created. Russia, the center of power, was more advanced than the other areas; despite the damage and destruction of the war, it had industry, a proletariat, cadre. How, then, to proceed with the necessary development of the Soviet state? A decision had to be made whether to focus attention on already existing resources (the simplest and least costly solution), or to set the economies in the different regions on equal footing, which implied a radical transformation of the economic structures in the periphery. Despite extreme shortages

195

and the urgent need for reconstruction, the Soviet leadership chose the second approach—to eliminate the economic inequalities among the different nations. This option required treating the economic problems of the center differently from those of the periphery. The gradual application of NEP was designed to transform the Russian economy, not the economies of the non-Russian nations who lagged far behind in economic development. NEP represented a respite for Russia, but elsewhere economic structures had to be transformed rapidly so as to reduce the disparities between the center and the periphery and phase out economic relations of the colonial type.

Although the Soviet leadership searched for egalitarian solutions to economic problems, they discovered that some problems required dissimilar solutions. Maurice Dobb has studied the extent to which the Russian economy was paralyzed when deprived of its imperial "rear."[1] Without the Ukraine, the Donbass, and the Caucasus, Russia had only 10 percent of its energy resources, 50 percent of its grain, and 10 percent of the sugar-beet fields. Without Dometz, the Urals, and Poland, there was no metallurgy or steel industry. Without Turkestan and Transcaucasia, the textile industry in Vladimir and Ivanovo-Voznessensk was worthless. The supply of raw materials for Russian industry and the livelihood of the Russian working class depended on the peripheral areas. And after the Bolsheviks recovered the peripheral territories rich in raw materials, they faced a second problem.

Prior to the revolution, the division of labor between the industrial center and the periphery, supplier of raw materials, ensured the continued growth of Russian industry. A more egalitarian approach to economic development required a new division of labor, but any such measures would weaken the center and demand considerable resources to spur on development in the periphery—not a politically or economically rational solution. Thus, the Soviet leadership tried to devise a policy that would reconcile the government's economic needs—reconstruction of the Russian economy and consistency in the division of labor—with their political needs, which included economic equality, a prerequisite for future unity.

In 1921 there was much work to be done in the periphery in the economic sphere. NEP had to be extended to these areas, and an economy in ruin rebuilt and consolidated in order to create the conditions for the "leap forward" into the future. Specific policy had to address three objectives: the rapid development of the national economies, the creation of proletarian consciousness, and the reduction of political differences among nations to equalize their standard of living,

that is, their material existence. "The economic development of a country, a nation, or a territory is a complex operation in which various factors, some of them economic, come into play, [factors] that presuppose
the existence of various economic, social, cultural, and political conditions. Economic development is not a matter of a few individuals or of
smaller or larger extended groups. . . . In a developing economy, it is
the permanent edification of man by man that constitutes true development."[2]

The decisive participation of the "multitude" in the development
process[3] caused particular problems in the USSR because development
was joined to the national question: the goal of development was to
make nations economic equals in order to eliminate any sense of difference among them, and thus to resolve altogether the problem of separate national identities.

However, the great economic "leap forward" in the periphery, the
corollary of NEP in the years 1921–29, was not a general policy. The
Soviet leadership diversified its approach according to the problems encountered and the interests at stake.

Urban Development and the
"Indigenization" of the Periphery

There was scant information available on the cities at the time. In
1897, 12,969,000 people lived in cities,[4] and 1914 estimates put the
urban population at 24,000,000.[5] The number of city-dwellers in 1920
was not known, but was probably closer to the 1897 than to the 1914
levels, to judge by the 1926 census results in Moscow and Leningrad.[6]
A more important factor was where the cities were located. The 1897
census, demographic studies,[7] and subsequent census figures[8] all reveal a certain pattern: the empire's most inhabited cities were largely in
one of three regions. There were fifteen cities in the northwest (Baltic
states, Byelorussia, the northwest and central regions of what was later
to become the RSFSR); thirteen in the Ukraine and Moldavia; and thirteen well in the eastern part of European Russia. In contrast, the Asiatic
regions of Russia had only three large cities (Orenburg, Tomsk, and Ir-
kutsk), and in Transcaucasia, Central Asia, and Kazakhstan together
there were only six sizable cities (Kokand, Namangan, Samarkand, Tiflis, Tashkent, and Baku).

In the Caucasian and Central Asian peripheries, urbanization had to
precede economic transformation; in the Ukraine, where urban de-

velopment kept pace with the rate of industrialization up to the dawn of the twentieth century, the cities' national composition was the true problem. According to the 1896 census, Russians in the Ukraine made up only 8 percent of the general population, but were essentially urban and proletarian, and more active in Ukrainian political life than their numbers suggest. In the 1920s, cities in the Ukraine were populated by two or more nations, with the Ukrainian nation in the minority. Beginning in 1926, Soviet efforts to make the cities more Ukrainian were having visible results. In Kiev, Ukrainians represented 25.4 percent of the population, with 36.2 percent Russian, 32.1 percent Jewish, and 3 percent Polish.[9] In the early 1930s, the population of Kharkov was 48 percent Ukrainian, 30 percent Russian, and 17 percent Jewish. In the area around Odessa, Ukrainians counted for 41 percent of the population, which fell to 17 percent in the city itself as compared to 38 percent for (Russians) and 36 percent for Jews. In 1926 in Dnepropetrovsk, the Ukrainian segment of the population was slowly beginning to outnumber the Russian segment. The Ukrainian urban population grew as a result of the planned "Ukrainization" of the working class. Before 1914, Ukrainians in industry were a minority; on the eve of the first five-year plan, Ukrainians nearly equaled the Russians (41 to 42 percent, respectively).[10] "Ukrainization" also created frustrations, especially among the Jewish population, whose economic role decreased.

In 1926 Jews made up 5.4 percent of the population and 22 percent of the urban population, but only 8.7 percent of the working class in the Ukraine.[11] They resented the "Ukrainization" slogan. At the Third Congress of Soviets of the USSR in 1925, Yuri Larin declared that Ukrainization worked against Jews, Russians, and Poles. He concluded, "This policy—correct in principle—bullies those isolated minorities of the republics just as these great groups of the periphery were previously bullied by tsarist policy."

Although successful in the Ukraine where economic conditions favored migration from the countryside to the cities, the indigenization of the urban population did not work in Byelorussia, which was industrially weak and lacking in natural resources. Only two cities in Byelorussia (Vitebsk and Minsk) figured on the list of the fifty largest cities in the empire's 1897 census. Even as late as 1939, Byelorussia had only five cities with more than 50,000 inhabitants, out of a total of 174 in the entire USSR.[12] The stagnation of city life accounted for a weak nationalist element in the cities, which were mostly dominated by the Jewish community.

In 1926 8.2 percent of the population of Byelorussia was Jewish, but they constituted 40.2 percent of the urban population of the republic and one-fifth of the proletariat. The Jewish population outstripped that of the Byelorussians in Minsk (43.6 to 40 percent), Vitebsk (45 to 30 percent), and Gomel (40 to 22 percent). Mogilev was the only city where Jews were not in the majority. National-social conflicts broke out in Byelorussia between Byelorussian peasants and Jewish workers.[13] Byelorussian nationalist sentiment was suffused by anti-Semitism, for economic stagnation prevented Byelorussia from being able to carry out an indigenization policy.

Although generally the Soviet leadership encouraged nations to take charge of their urban development, in some instances, they depended on urban growth to dampen nationalist sentiment, especially among medium-sized nations who lived in strategically important regions. For example, a highly concentrated and demographically dynamic people with a strong national identity lived on the banks of the Kama River, in the heart of a region where the steel and metallurgical industries had flourished well before the revolution. The Soviet leadership wanted to develop urban life in Udmurtia but was wary of arousing nationalist feeling in a region that was economically important to the USSR. In the end, the Udmurts, classified as a nation, were given a political and administrative center not in Glazov (a city of 5,000 inhabitants where Udmurts had historical ties), but in Izhevsk an industrial center dominated by the Russian proletariat and considered a foreign enclave by the Udmurts. The Soviets held up the development of Izhevsk, which by 1930 had more than 10,000 inhabitants, as a symbol a economic progress for a nation that had remained attached to its traditions and peasant origins.[14]

Soviet desire to promote urbanization and curb nationalist tendencies, together with considerations of a highly political nature, determined the destiny of the Germans of the Volga region. Until 1920 it was believed that Germany would be the focal point of world revolution. The Soviet leaders treated the Germans of the Volga as the vanguard of the dreamed-of revolution. For symbolic reasons they first regrouped them as a Workers' Commune[15] and in 1924 granted them status as an Autonomous Republic. Although the population of the republic was predominantly German (66 percent, as compared to 20 percent Russian and 12 percent Ukrainian[16]) and essentially rural, the Soviets encouraged urbanization but dislocated urban life by changing the capital city from Marxstadt, a center of German population and culture, to Pokrovsk, a Russian city. By so doing, the Soviets tried to weaken the dynamism of German cultural life. Pokrovsk, which became Engels in

1930, had a population that was 44 percent Russian and 42 percent Ukrainian; it grew from 33,000 inhabitants in 1926 to over 50,000 in 1930. Yet although the German population in Pokrovsk-Engels remained stagnant, the city rapidly became a veritable center of Germanic culture.

Whereas in the Ukraine, the urbanization and "Ukrainization" of the proletariat was carried out by Ukrainians; with other nations, the Soviet leadership searched for a middle ground between urbanization and the indigenization of cities. In the colonial periphery, it promoted the urbanization of nations together with the creation of national industries. In Turkestan, a leftover colonial appendage of empire that the Soviets had inherited, important businesses belonged to Russians and were used to process raw materials for industry in Russia, but the labor force was 75 percent indigenous. Russians held specialized posts and worked in training and supervision.[17] In 1921 the Soviet leadership, now master of the situation, declared its desire to break up economic colonialism in Central Asia,[18] notably "by transferring industry to the east, to get maximum yield from the factories producing energy resources and raw materials." In practice, this meant reviving the businesses that had suspended operations during the war and rebuilding a nearly destroyed industrial potential. By 1927 this goal was largely accomplished[19] and new factories were build in the Fergana valley (two oil refineries, textile and shoe factories) and in Samarkand, Margelan, and Bukhara (silk weaving). The major cities were supplied with hydroelectric stations which in 1928 produced 46 million kilowatt hours. In Kazakhstan, where a special development policy was pursued, economic development proceeded according to the Central Asia model. After 1923 efforts got under way to revitalize industry that produced important already identified natural resources. In 1928 oil production in the fields along the Emba River, which had been operating at 50 percent in 1920, was double the 1913 production levels.[20] On the other hand, mineral production, the industrial life-blood of Ekibastuz, remained inactive until 1929. As late as in 1928, food industries still comprised the most important sector of the Kazakh economy.

These development efforts hardly affected the ethnic composition of cities. According to the 1926 census, industry in Central Asia (excluding Kazakhstan) employed 98,237 people, 49,500 of whom were natives of the region.[21] Indigenous workers were weakly represented in key sectors (energy, textiles) and in railway communications. In order to build a qualified indigenous labor force from unskilled laborers, the Soviets established professional schools, which in 1926 attracted 13,500 trainees, half of whom were natives.[22] However, restricted to subordinate posts and victims of employment changes (beginning in 1926, unemployment rose everywhere in the USSR), the indigenous population distrusted industry and hesitated to settle in cities where they felt culturally alienated. The 1926 census confirms this trend. Central Asia and Kazakhstan remained rural regions with a weak indigenous proletariat. Rather than focus on the cities, the Soviet leadership was then obliged to look to the countryside to carry out their campaign for the proletarianization of the masses.

Toward a Proletarian Countryside

While the Bolsheviks were keenly aware of the importance of the rural problem in Russia, they were unfamiliar with the particular problems in the non-Russian countryside until after the revolution. At least in the cases of the Ukraine and Byelorussia, they did not err in believing that their program to transform the rural landscape could be applied to other nations. But for non-Slavic peoples and the Moslems in particular, the agrarian problem was closely intertwined with the national question, thus making it unlikely that a program for the Russian peasantry could be easily transferred to the Moslem periphery. There was no class struggle in the countryside except in the sense that the class enemy of the poor peasant or nomad was the Russian colonist who in the past had monopolized the best plots of land. Indigenous property owners, or *bays*, certainly existed,[23] but they were dispersed throughout the countryside and tied to the poorer of their coreligionists by a community of faith and a similar way of life. Thus, in comparison to other natives of the region, they had only slightly different income levels; compared to the Russian colonists, the disparity was much greater. Economic differences were mainly traceable to national origin. The class struggle was far removed from a nomadic population united by tribal solidarity: the only economic differences were those separating one tribe from another, for social divisions within the tribe were not perceived as inequalities.[24]

It is hardly surprising then that the revolution of 1917 did not disrupt the Moslem countryside in the same way as it did the Russian rural areas. Because the Bolsheviks believed that economic equality among nations was the cornerstone of true equality, the living conditions of peasants had to be made uniform; change had to be rooted in the disintegration of an existing social solidarity and in the creation of a more proletarianized peasantry. Although concessions were made to the peasantry throughout Soviet territory in the years 1921 to 1926, these same years in Moslem regions represented a total agrarian revolution. This revolution had several simultaneous goals: to liquidate colonial opposition, which masked social contradictions; to do away with "feudal" relations[25] by introducing a class structure to the countryside; to make the nomadic population more sedentary; and to create an indigenous peasant proletariat.

The suppression of colonial relations seemed at first a simple task. On 4 March 1920 the government of Turkestan decreed that lands previously confiscated by Russians were to be returned to the indigenous population.[26] However, little action followed, causing an indignant Lenin to insist on 13 June 1920 on the need "to take away from the colonists settled in Kirghiz regions the lands they appropriated . . . and to gather them into a land fund that will be distributed to collectives, artels,* and individual Kirghiz." In the margin of the text, Lenin wrote "What to do with the kulak colonists? Destroy them?" And subsequently, when he recommended that "former tsarist functionaries be sent to Russian concentration camps," he added in the margin, "What percentage of kulaks, one in ten?"[27] On 29 June the Party passed a resolution putting the governmental decisions into immediate effect.[28]

A few months later the results could be evaluated. Nearly 285,000 hectares were distributed to 13,000 families.[29] But out of prudence and for fear of arousing national reaction in the countryside, the Bolsheviks did not introduce with these land measures any changes in social relations among the native population. When the Fifth Party Congress of Turkestan met in 1920 and decided to make landholdings of uniform size,[30] property was transferred directly to the chiefs of the tribes whose lands had been appropriated in the past, and these chiefs were given the liberty of organizing land distribution.[31] This reform—which was implemented at the expense of the Russians—combined with the fact that the central leadership imposed no other measures on the indigenous peoples, had a positive political effect in the periphery. The indigenous peasantry who lived in colonized areas and had been violently anti-Russian now had no target for their frustration. The Soviet regime proved that its desire for equality prevailed over the defense of Russian interests. A radical change of opinion certainly did not take place among the peasantry, but, however ill-informed, they were very impressed by this political turning point, which for a time weakened support for the Basmashi guerrillas in the countryside.

Although the confiscation of land from Russian colonists was successful in lessening national rancor, it did not encourage nomads to

---

Artels are cooperatives sharing land, draft animals, seeds, and tools, while the house and a plot of land remained as private property.

adopt a sedentary existence. Even with the increased number of sedentary peasants among the Turkmen, the nomadic population of Central Asia was sizable in the early 1920s. Of 100 Turkmen households 75 were sedentary; but in Kazakh territory on the eve of the reform measures, of 100 households, 6 were sedentary, 76 were nomadic or semi-nomadic, and 18 were Russian; and among the Kirghiz, 28 were sedentary, 51 nomadic, and 21 Russian.[32] Contrary to the authorities' hopes, the nomads were not inspired by landownership to settle; at most, they became only partially sedentary. Some tribes leased their lands to peasants; some spent the winter on the land and in the spring left their arable fields and returned to their wandering ways. The operation was an economic disaster and did not change ways of life.

In 1924 the Soviet regime decided that the problem of nomadism had to be resolved in a comprehensive and compulsory manner. As a first step, nomadic movement was regularized by limiting and controlling nomadic zones. This burden was then shifted to the sedentary population, a more easily reached and confined group, among which the Soviets tried to create a consciousness of class conflict.

The first phase of the program was to gather a manageable mass of poor peasants into organizations acting as trade unions and cooperatives, the *Koshchis* and *Rabzemles*. The first Union of Poor Peasants was formed in September 1920, consisting of landless peasants, peasants crippled by debts, sharecroppers, and village craftsmen who eked out a meager living. The union's reason for existence was "to organize the class struggle in the countryside."[33] In fact, it replaced the nearly-nonexistent Communist Party that held no meetings in rural areas. The *Koshchis* penetrated the rural milieu, carried out indoctrination campaigns, and called for reforms. The leadership made an effort to lend them legitimacy by integrating rural figures of political authority into the Soviets and making provisions for a representative of the peasant organization to sit on all the administrative bodies associated with the countryside, such as the *Sovnarkoms*, the republics' Council on National Economy, and the Commissariat of Agriculture.[34] In the regions its members acted as representatives of state power and of the Party, which in fact closely controlled the *Koshchis*. The organization had a decided class character. At first it welcomed all who wished to join but after 1923 its rules excluded the wealthy (landowners, businessmen, moneylenders, Moslem religious figures and their relatives). For several years—the *Koshchis* continued to act until 1933 but became weaker after 1926—the Union of Poor Peasants, drawing on its familiarity with the milieu, became powerful and exercised a near-total terror campaign throughout the countryside. In 1926 the Soviet leadership accused the

Koshchis of confusing itself with the state and the Party, encroaching on their jurisdiction and trying to function autonomously to the benefit of the nonproletarian elements that had infiltrated the organization. Thereafter, the *Koshchis* was gradually replaced by its rival, the Union of Workers of the Land and Forests, or *Rabzemles*.

The status of the *Rabzemles* was more clearly defined. Developed mostly after 1924, when it had 15,000 members,[35] it was a union of poor peasants whose ambitions—to organize agricultural workers exclusively—were more limited than those of its rival and whose powers were more restricted, for it claimed no role in state management. The *Rabzemles* seemed an unlikely competitor for the powerful union of the *Koshchis*, which for the same period claimed more than 260,000 members. The real figures were much more modest. Membership rolls of the *Kosachis* existed only on paper[36] and however poor the peasants of Central Asia were, they were disinclined to oppose the traditional village authorities. However, even if the *Koshchis* had fewer members than it maintained, it grew steadily until 1929 and wielded more influence than even the figures suggest.

The peasants who belonged to these unions, having an authority structure, controlling power, and economic means apart from the village, fatally undermined the traditional authority figures of the village, clan chiefs, elders, or any property owners who were more fortunate than others. Until 1924 the authority imposed on the countryside was Russian, hence foreign, in the face of which the local peasantry continued to respect the traditional authorities. But with the organization of the poor peasantry into pressure groups that acted as intermediaries between the government and the local peasantry, the role played by the old figures of authority was reduced.[37] The agrarian reform of 1925 demonstrated the potential of poor peasants' organizations in Central Asia. It focused on three areas: management of water usage, land distribution, and development of cooperatives.

Although there are no exact figures on the situation just prior to the revolution, water posed a major impediment to the region's development.[38] We know that Bolsheviks must have taken note of the ruined state of the irrigation system (two-thirds of the system was not in use) in 1920,[39] of the survival of a water distribution system in which traditional village authorities played a leading role.[40] For this reason, at the same time as the Soviets worked on rebuilding an irrigation network (completed in 1924), they tried to set up a system of equal water distribution. In August of 1922, the water supply was declared state property, a five-year plan was drawn up by the Central Asian Bureau on

Irrigation Problems, and a specialized department was established on a regional scale with local offices.[41] In May 1924 temporary rules were devised for water usage and distribution as a prelude to the promulgation of specialized codes. The hallmark of the new legislation was the relationship between labor and water rights. Water usage, limited to those who personally worked the land, was denied to large property owners and to lands that were part of *waqfs*.[42] Financial aid was given to small peasants to reestablish their own irrigation systems linking them to the general system. The associations of poor peasants were in charge of supervising the enforcement of the new measures. Thus, water became a decisive element in the breakup of old property rules and the class war in the countryside, deriving from the powers of the peasantry enrolled in the *Koshchis* and *Rabzemles*.

Land distribution, no less decisive in the gradual class differentiation of rural society, and the necessary foundation for the establishment of socialist relations, was considered a pressing problem by the Bolsheviks. Specific and drastic solutions were needed to counteract the great disparity between the Soviet countryside, "where the tasks of the bourgeois revolution have been accomplished," and the Central Asian countryside, at the stage of semi-feudal or clan relations. Reform was indispensable but a delicate matter, for the central leadership was wary of meeting opposition that could be exacerbate nationalist rancor and revive the Basmashi movement that had only recently been contained.[43] In this regard, the poor peasants' organizations became most useful; where the central leadership was hesitant to impose reforms, the peasant avant-garde, the most disadvantaged elements of the peasantry, demanded them. This was clearly revealed by the *Koshchis'* role. In 1924 they actively recruited new members and flooded the government of the republic with innumerable demands for land to be distributed to those who worked it. On site they surveyed the lands subject to confiscation. Because in the 1920s there were no written deeds certifying landownership in the Moslem countryside, only those participating in the campaign were in a position to evaluate the condition of the properties. The *Koshchis* finally enforced land reform because mass actions carried out throughout the year 1924 had completely disorganized rural life. They began expropriations in the overpopulated lands of Fergana, and gradually the practice spread to all of Central Asia. Threatened landowners reacted to the expropriations by organizing and arming themselves.[44] Thus social hostilities began to be expressed in a region where previous opposition had fallen along national lines. But reaction was not uniform. In recently sedentarized regions or areas of semisedentary settlements, traditional authority figures still had strong influence on the population. In these areas the peasantry sent their traditional leaders to the local Soviets, that is the party organs, where they were on equal footing with the poor peasants.

Faced with a complex regional situation, the Soviet leaders remained hesitant for a long time about fomenting revolution in the Central Asian countryside while encouraging cooperation with the peasantry throughout the rest of the Union. Later, even if they still advocated revolution, they hesitated over the form it would take. Several of Stalin's statements suggest that the form of agrarian revolution he championed in principle in 1925 was the kind that spread in 1929 throughout the USSR:—revolution from above, carried out by state organs, directed against medium and large landowners, and supported by the associations of poor peasants. The goal was not to collectivize but to expropriate lands from the kulaks (the official numbers of kulaks in Central Asia were as unrealistic as the later federal figures during collectivization) and give them to the landless peasants and small landowners. Reforms adopted in the Turkmen Soviet Socialist Republic in September 1925 and in Uzbekistan the following month[45] involved the nationalization of all arable lands, forests, and hydraulic resources. In its first stage the reform targeted three regions—Fergana, Tashkent, and Samarkand—where the Soviet regime judged the rural class struggle advanced enough and the traditional authority figures sufficiently weakened to forestall an insurrection in response to the measures. Merv and Poltorask, two regions of Turkmenistan, were also included. Property holdings were confiscated in their entirety from large landowners, from *waqfs*, and in part from other peasants who owned more than the established norm. The reform of 1925 was above all pragmatic. Permissible property was defined by mode of irrigation and yield.

Confiscations were carried out in three stages. The first stage consisted of seizing "large properties" (50 hectares or more) from their owners, together with agricultural equipment and other assets. A few months later all rental properties of more than 4.6 hectares, as well as lands with absentee owners or owners who lived in the city, became subject to confiscation. The final stage singled out any directly exploited land of a size in excess of the norm (9 to 14 hectares, depending on the region[46]). By staggering the seizures over a six-month period, the regime was able to carry out its plan without provoking unrest. Peasants who were threatened or isolated by the *Koshchis'* action reacted by attempting to hide their possessions through fictitious property sales, rent stoppage, or sales of agricultural equipment at a low price, although in early 1925 the republic forbade all land transactions. These actions, often carried out with the complicity of the local Soviets, sometimes reduced the scale of the expropriations. In Uzbekistan the reform resulted in the total or partial dispossession of 25,000 households, to the benefit of 66,000 deprived households (with an additional 13,000 beneficiaries in 1929). In all, 317,400 hectares changed hands between 1924 and 1929. In Turkmenistan, partial or total land confiscation in accordance with the reform affected 18,000 households and benefited 33,000 landless peasants or small landowners.[47] The redistributed property represented an average of 3 to 5.5 hectares, depending on the region and local conditions.

In practice, pressured by poor peasants and in the absence of a general land redistribution plan, the Soviet regime sometimes created inequalities and unfavorable conditions for peasants. Although the agrarian codes of the various Central Asian republics basically reproduced the RSFSR agrarian code of 1922[48] forbidding land sales, the peasants often tried to circumvent these provisions in order to enlarge their landholdings. Although the number of agricultural workers and rented lands diminished, the number of properties that were too small to be profitable remained very high (about 80 percent of the households).[49] But the beneficiaries of the distribution had an advantage because along with lands they received equipment, seed, animals, and credits.

Soviet policy benefited the poorest. We must understand the 1925 reform in the light of its real objectives, which were not so much to change the economic facts of rural life as to bring the social revolution into a milieu that for the most part had been overlooked. In this respect, the reform showed significant results. Above all, modes of ownership that were foreign to the Soviet order were eliminated. The *waqfs*, which in 1918 had unleashed such a severe political crisis that in 1920 the Soviets rolled back a nationalization scheme, disappeared when land and water reforms were instituted. In 1925, *waqfs* were no longer attacked as property associated with Moslem law but as a form of social inequality. The Bolsheviks did not attack the *waqfs* as a vestige of a socioreligious order; rather, they mobilized Moslem peasants to their side and, in the name of the social justice underlying Moslem ideology, justified the eradication of the *waqfs*.[50] In Turkmenia the reform did away with the *karanda*, another form of landownership based on common tribal property.[51] Lands were purposely redistributed to individuals, and property rights were conditioned on development of the land.

Thus the solidarity of the tribal structure, which rested on the distribution of assets and tasks, was weakened among the semi-sedentarized population.

Indeed, it was more difficult to carry out reforms in areas where tribal property rules persisted. Land redistribution was a much more delicate matter among groups than among isolated households. Moreover, the existence of tribal communal property prevented perceptions of inequality and united the entire tribe against the power-structure as well as against other tribes. Nevertheless, the reform created the aspiration for private property while at the same time undermining community life. From 1927 on, the pace of agrarian reform in tribal regions accelerated.[52] While certain forms of private property were eliminated in Central Asia, agrarian reform brought other symptoms to the surface.

Social antagonism in the countryside grew more acute as rural communities became polarized into hostile groups. Not only did the Unions of Poor Peasants play a destabilizing role, but the Soviet leadership tried to draw into the reform efforts peasants who were not allied to communist organizations. Ad hoc commissions were formed for this purpose, called "Committees for Peasant Assistance" in the Uzbek regions and "Reform Commissions" in Turkmenian areas. Both were closely modeled on the *Kombedys* (Committees of Indigents) of the war period. Whereas the *Koshchis* produced propaganda to promote reforms, the local *Kombedys* participated in expropriations and denounced to the authorities secret transactions, hidden assets, or extensive wealth.[53] Although their activities were generally directed against property owners, their primary task in places where tribal community structures persisted was to cause friction between peasant landowners and the tribe. The central government also sought to weaken tribal structures by transferring land from one tribe to another; on the pretext of redistributing land to individuals, it strengthened certain tribes and pitted some against others. When unsuccessful in causing rifts among members of the same group,[54] the government set about exacerbating intertribal conflicts. These diverse approaches aimed at destroying old authority hierarchies—the links of solidarity that ensured the cohesion of rural society in Central Asia. However, because the reform measures were conceived by a leadership unfamiliar with rural societies and suspicious of peasants, social needs were not taken into account. Instead, an urban proletariat brutally interfered in a foreign milieu where reforms were systematically applied despite local opposition. When the Soviet government decided to effect a retreat (NEP) throughout the territory under its control, opposition by the majority of the Central Asian peasantry in 1925–27 to the transformation imposed from above in no way altered the course of governmental policy. The "style" of collectivization measures remained the massive use of urban elements to carry out reforms. Prepared by a special commission created through the republics' *Sovnarkoms*, reforms were applied in the field by local commissions appointed by the Party and consisting of urban Party members. These commissions certainly called on the *Koshchis* and *Kombedys* for assistance but retained complete control over expropriations and land distribution. To the peasants, they symbolized urban interference in rural affairs and provoked profound hostility comparable to real class hatred.[55] In 1929 such sentiments were everywhere on the rise, even in the region around Tashkent, where the borderline between city- and country-dwellers had always been hard to define.

The third aspect of the rural revolution was the attempt to foster cooperative entities, especially among sedentary peoples and nomadic nations, in order to supplant tribal loyalties by weaving a much more intricate web of solidarity. Soviet accomplishments in this regard were generally inconclusive.

Opinions differed in the 1920s about exactly what type of cooperation to foster, and Central Asia was ridden with problems. A choice had to be made between consumer cooperatives and credit cooperatives. Given the importance of cotton cultivation in the regional economy and the need for credit to finance the crop, it is not surprising that credit operations were offered as the basis for cooperation. The development of credit cooperatives in Central Asia began in 1914. In 1926[56] an official study of the region revealed little progress in this domain. Obstacles to success were the differences between the sedentary and semi-nomadic nations and the nomadic nations, which impeded the development of consistent policy; and the strength of traditional structures, for example, the social importance of the bazaar—a universe in which consumer cooperatives had little place.[57] Thus it was understandable that in cotton-producing areas credit cooperatives were essentially the only type of cooperative in existence; their numbers (approximately 1,000) hardly changed from the prewar years.[58] Cooperatives were formed in nomadic regions, mainly for marketing livestock and milk products. After 1925 villages were encouraged to establish consumer cooperatives. Their numbers rose from 80 to 216 in 1926. Timid local attempts to organize craft cooperatives were curbed by the central government, which distrusted forms of trade unlisted in the census and not easily monitored. By 1929 it was clear that the Soviet policy of establishing cooperatives had failed in Central Asia. But social relations in the countryside were transformed by other means. The reforms of the 1920s were tantamount to a radical revolution of structures and mentalities that changed the face of Central Asia during a period when social peace reigned throughout the rest of the USSR.

Jewish Colonization:
An Experiment in Socioeconomic Integration

Soviet national policy in the 1920s worked toward diminishing the differences between city and country by proletarianizing the rural regions. The Jewish community was an exception: it was a particular type of national community, not settled in a defined territory but concentrated in certain states among other nationality groups, primarily in cities and urban areas, with only 10 percent of its members, for the most part craftsmen, living in villages.[59] The difference between Jews and other nations was most apparent in the professional sector of the community. According to the 1926 census, 14 percent of Jews were workers and 9 percent peasants; the rest were engaged in commercial, handicraft, or administrative activities. Soviet ideology in the 1920s emphasized workers and egalitarianism, concepts not readily adaptable to the Jewish milieu. In order to prevent Jews from being isolated from the rest of society as they had been before the revolution, it was necessary to integrate the Jewish community into the workers' world.[60]

Jewish leaders—cadre of *Evsektsiia*—had two concerns. First, they wanted to separate Jews from their intellectual world and associate them with workers and peasants. But at the same time they did not want such integration to affect their national identity, for the Jewish group was weaker than other nations because it lacked a territorial base. Jewish cadre were afraid that integration into the workers' milieu, although logical by virtue of the Jews' cultural level and professional qualifications, might result in dispersion. For this reason it was considered preferable to transform Jews into peasants. When the Central Committee of the Russian Communist Party decided in 1924 to encourage Jewish colonization, it was less an economic experiment than an attempt to integrate them socially as a national group. *Komzem*, a committee established for the integration of Jews in rural areas, contemplated a first phase of relocating 100,000 Jewish families to the countryside.

Aided by governmental land grants and credit for the purchase of equipment, tax exemptions for the start-up period, and foreign aid (the

Joint Distribution Committee supported colonization), Jews began an exodus to the countryside. By 1928 more than 200,000 Jews lived among the rural population.[61] Colonists organized themselves into artels or communes (in which everything was put at the disposal of the community), although by 1926 there were traces of a trend toward de-collectivization. As a result of its resettlement in the countryside and integration into the economic activities promoted by the Soviet system, the Jewish community argued for their group to be recognized as a *nation*.

Kalinin, the Soviet head of state, supported them: to ensure their existence as a nation, Jews needed to obtain a fixed territory. After exploring several possibilities for settlement in the Crimea or Siberia—as Kalinin suggested—or in Kazakhstan, the central leadership decided to send Jewish colonists to Birobidzhan, where they began to settle in early 1928.[62]

The two goals that the Soviet government systematically pursued in the case of the Jewish community were to weaken the peasantry and weaken the nations. Why else seek to transform a people who had little contact with the land into peasants? Why encourage national aspirations to take root by providing rural settlements? There were several justifications for departing significantly from general policy in the case of the Jews. First, according to the egalitarianism that guided Soviet policy in the 1920s, the economic and social status of the Jewish community should be comparable to that of other nations. Once Jews became rooted in the world of manual labor, the Bolsheviks thought, they would no longer have exceptional status, and thus there would be no basis for anti-Semitic feeling such as existed in the Ukraine and Byelorussia. The Soviet leaders—Kalinin's positions in evidence—and the leaders of the Jewish community agreed that the social integration of Jews was desirable. Past and present experience justified granting Jews separate status by giving them a national territory; thus, despite their earlier declarations, the Bolsheviks recognized them as a nation.

The previous colonization period, which took place in areas where Jews traditionally lived among other nations, had shown that the mere settlement of Jews in the countryside did not lead to their integration into society. In the Ukraine, peasants were hostile toward them and anti-Semitic demonstrations multiplied.[63] At the Tenth Congress of Soviets of the Ukraine, Shubar, president of the republic's *Sovnarkom*, was compelled to declare solemnly, in order to ease tensions, that Jewish peasants did not enjoy special privileges and were not poised to take over the countryside.[64] The Jewish colonists faced a difficult situation. They had no cultural institutions, and the property-owning population of the republic—once again, this tendency was most marked in the Ukraine—opposed the establishment of Jewish schools in the countryside, which would have given farms firmer roots and made Jewish colonization more definitive. Jewish colonists were disheartened by their cultural isolation, which led them either to leave the land or to dream of settling in Palestine, where Jewish colonization was developing.

The difficulty of integrating Jews among other nations, the desire to quell Zionist urges, and, perhaps most important, the concern for resolving national problems equitably explain Soviet willingness to establish Jewish peasants in a territory of their own. Stalin was said to have declared: "The tsar did not give land to the Jews. Kerensky didn't, either. On the other hand, we did."[65]

In Birobidzhan, seemingly sincere gestures toward equality coincided precisely with the interests of the Soviet state, which wanted rapidly to populate a vulnerable area threatened by Chinese expansionism. Many Jews who had been attracted to the idea of settlement in the Crimea[66] did not want to go to Birobidzhan because its climate was unpropitious to agriculture and its geographical remove would render too difficult the development of a normal cultural life. But, despite criticisms, the Soviets proceeded with their project for strategic reasons and for fear of fueling anti-Jewish sentiment in already-settled areas like the Crimea. In actuality, the project sounded the death knell of both Jewish colonization and the idea of creating a Jewish homeland in the USSR. Yet, despite the project's failure, the Soviet attempt to settle Jews in the countryside remains significant.

Nations Forgotten by Progress

The Moslems and the Jews were not easily integrated into the new socioeconomic world, but they were not alone. Aborigines in the outermost areas were also strangers to a society that was interested in a radical transformation of structures and attitudes. The problems of these peoples, however, were unique. They constituted small, dispersed nations generally untouched by colonization. At first, their dispersion, isolation, and widely varying customs made them appear less threatening to the center than close-knit, compact nations united by tradition and attached to important civilizations. The aboriginal peoples led an essentially tribal life organized around discrete systems of authority, and in the areas not penetrated by Christian missionaries, often influenced by shamans, who mediated between the spirit world and the tribe.[67]

In the early years, the Bolsheviks followed a policy of nonintervention in the political and economic life of peoples who lived in the northern and far eastern territories, refraining from introducing economic changes on the theory that cultural progress ought to precede any attempt at reform. The government recognized tribal institutions and promoted tribal assemblies to the rank of local Soviets. During this period the government's only contact with aboriginal groups was in providing health or veterinary services. In the north, the establishment of medical centers marked the first phase of Russian penetration in the region.[68]

In 1926 the government's attitude changed subtly. The concept of class struggle was gingerly introduced, and a modicum of control of aboriginal economic life was attempted. Government representatives were hostile toward the shamans, whom they accused of having a negative influence on the aborigines and of impeding progress. Yet, in the early 1920s, the population ignored governmental health policies and refused to go to the newly created "medical points." Rightly or wrongly, the Soviets accused the shamans of encouraging defiance and "anti-economic" superstitious practices (such as prohibiting the sale of live reindeer or fishing under certain conditions, or catching walruses). At this time a campaign was begun to undermine aboriginal beliefs and practices. Shamans were branded as kulaks who exploited and lived off the aborigines' credulity. However, the facts belied these charges—shamans frequently belonged to the poorest sector of the population—and the shamans' status in the community remained unaffected. In the late 1920s shamans continued to be respected by the aborigines and used their authority to wage a bitter struggle against collectivization.[69] In response to the Soviet authorities' first foray into the daily life of the aborigines, figures of moral authority in these isolated regions mobilized against any outside initiative. The Soviets repeatedly tried to organize and develop reindeer-raising—the Soviet flock grew from 175,000 in 1923 to 2,200,000 in 1926[70]—but the animal was revered by the aborigines, and they reacted violently to these attempts. In 1926 several attempts to trade reindeer met with such opposition that the governmental authorities retreated altogether.

From that time on the government decided to integrate aborigines through general change, not specific policies of difficult application. A few years of respite followed, during which the government concluded that the aboriginal peoples were impossible to assimilate. Soviet prudence with regard to unique nations at different evolutionary stages probably saved the aborigines from destruction. Professor Tan Bogoraz, the first to define Soviet policy toward the aborigines, advocated a strict "hands-off" policy, stressing that any introduction of progress might very well lead to the extinction of these nations.

The policy that set out to equalize living conditions among non-Russian nations was only modestly successful yet exceedingly important. From 1920 to 1921, for practical purposes if not explicitly, the Soviets divided nations into three groups. The first consisted of those who shared similar living conditions and were subject to general policy such as NEP. This category included the Slavic republics of the Ukraine and Byelorussia, as well as the Transcaucasian republics and other nations attached to the RSFSR. The Soviet leadership judged granting these peoples political and cultural equality to be an adequate response to their national aspirations, and although the economy was a common problem throughout the Union, it was hoped that NEP would help build up the cities and spur economic reconstruction. Of course, the Georgian revolt of 1924 demonstrated that the political recognition of nations did not succeed in assuaging nationalistic feeling. Georgian nationalism was nurtured when the central government introduced agrarian specialization in Georgia—tea and citrus fruit production—which made the republic closely dependent on the federation and seemed to re-create a system of domination, despite Soviet assurances of equality. But the Soviets interpreted the Georgian revolt of 1924 as a vestige of the independent republic's nationalism and did not revise agricultural policy.

The second group included those nations whose socioeconomic structures reflected national character and impeded future integration into the USSR's economy. Central Asia was a case in point. Subject to colonial domination, even after the changes of 1917 it preserved a way of life and certain structures linked with the colonial world, structures that made it an unequal member of the Soviet universe. A radical change was needed there, not only because Soviet national policy required it, but also in order to prevent the institutionalization of colonial relations. The agrarian revolution in Central Asia in the 1920s was the true revolution (far more significant than the Bolsheviks' ascendance to power) that wrested the different nations of the region away from their individual universes and made them equal to the European peoples of the federation. No doubt, the Soviets' concern for equality in the region was allied to their desire to maintain Central Asia in its traditional role as a cotton-producing region. As in Georgia, they wanted the region to adopt economic specialization. In the 1920s the socialist division of labor and plans for specialization were still in their infancy—the work of reconstruction had first to take place—but the ultimate vision remained: equal, reconciled nations, and specialized economies designed to adjust to regional capacities rather than foster the domination of one region (not one nation) over another.

The final category consisted of nations not easily classified into either of the first two. At opposite ends of the spectrum were the Jews and the aborigines. For reasons of equity, the Soviet leadership granted national status to both, but did not know how to reconcile their status with reality. Despite their great differences, the idea was to define them as nations and then adapt them to an economic model that would make them similar to other nations. The Soviets approached the problem of socioeconomic inequality from various perspectives, but always in tireless pursuit of the same aim, to eliminate differences in the lives of groups and fit them all into the same mold.

In this connection, Stalin's definition of the two components of culture comes to mind. Standardization of the economic conditions of nations on the basis of their social structures would give rise to a new, uniform social type; thus, all nations would uniformly approach socialist standards. This was the proletarian content of "national cultures" as they were most broadly envisioned.

CONCLUSION

Variation on an Old Theme, or a New World?

How, then, are we to evaluate the Bolsheviks' national policy? Was it, as they claimed, revolutionary in concept and form, or was it just another variation on the "imprisonment of peoples" theme that has been played throughout Russian history?

Beginning in 1920 the political system that emerged from the revolution was based on the state, as it had been under the empire. But the imperial state had been a *nation-state*; its government had progressively tightened the Russian nation's political and economic stranglehold on the conquered peoples. Surely the Russian leaders did not set out to destroy the nations. Still, they were convinced that all dominated nations naturally and inevitably must follow the same path in order to become more thoroughly integrated into the empire. The task of keeping ethnic diversity in check gradually evolved into the task of forging links of political unity, which led to the cultural Russification of ethnic minorities, at least for the weakest among them.

The Soviet state, then, chose an approach opposite to the empire's approach. In 1921 the Bolsheviks were building not a nation-state but a *sociological* state. Their purpose was to bring society and its political structures into harmony on the basis of a new culture: the culture of the previously dominated classes, not that of a single dominant national group. Just as their socialist predecessors believed in the unifying virtues of working-class consciousness, the Bolsheviks believed that a transformed society endowed with socialist economic structures would resolve the national question. This is why they emphasized, on the one hand, the role of socioeconomic factors in paving the way for a socialist society, and cultural egalitarianism, on the other.

Certainly the utopian vision was not carried to an extreme. The Bolsheviks' policy toward national groups was motivated both by the ideology of egalitarianism and by the objective of unification. Thus the policy had to accomplish two contradictory ends: to maintain equality among the nations and to strengthen the Soviet state, that is, Soviet control over the nations. Theoretically, a balance could be struck between the egalitarian ideology and the need for control, given that the egalitarian ideology lay at the foundation of the entire system. However, in practice, other needs came to dominate national policy, which destroyed the fragile equilibrium the Bolsheviks had striven to attain. The scarcity of leadership and resources, coupled with the urgency of the problems they faced, led the Bolsheviks to develop the capacity for state intervention, one that would issue from the state itself, which quickly became Leviathan. The Bolsheviks inherited certain traits from the *military culture* of war communism—traits that were indispensable in times of danger—yet they also inherited characteristics of the tsarist empire that have been underscored by the great historian Kliuchevskii[1]: a militarized state structure, a highly authoritarian government, and unlimited license to intervene in the name of a supreme authority with unlimited powers. These were all features previously imprinted on the course of Russian history; they constituted a political tradition that had molded Russian minds and thus were part of the cultural heritage of the Bolsheviks. Before the revolution, when developing their ideology within European society, the Bolsheviks had adopted European ideas; after 1921, however, confronted with reality—backwardness, insularity, foreign hostility—how could they have prevented certain past political traditions from emerging? It would be overly simplistic to link Russian political tradition to Bolshevik ideology without qualification, but it is equally erroneous to think that the Bolsheviks' desire, which prevailed in 1917, to wipe the slate clean of all previous political tradition, remained impervious to change in the years that followed. The Bolsheviks, too, had to respond to the national reality confronting them, and they did not draw exclusively from the legacy of Russian political tradition.

The problem of the diversity of national groups, which played a pivotal role in the revolution and counted for much in the political choices made after 1917, also had an impact on plans for modernization. Modernization, Europeanization, Westernization, industrialization—or whatever name it went by—was a current running throughout Russian history. It was also a basic element of the dream that the Bolsheviks pursued in different forms over time. Modernization comprised three fundamental tasks: political revolution, agrarian reform to assure the rational use of agricultural resources in the great transformation of the economy, and the creation or consolidation of a national state. The national problem in Russia, and the egalitarian ideology presented in 1921 as a solution to that problem, affected the entire modernization effort, and for this reason Soviet history cannot be viewed as the history of a monolithic, uniform society.

We must recall that the political revolution occurred on two levels, as a domestic and as a foreign phenomenon. The Russian revolution was a domestic revolution carried out by a national elite that dealt a decisive blow in wartime to an already severely shaken political system. The values this elite offered to society were not altogether foreign. The ideals of change, of material and cultural progress, had been put before the Russian masses in the past by groups that eventually either seized or were ousted from positions of power. Peter the Great himself had attempted to Westernize Russia, to liberate it from *aziatshchina*, or Asian backwardness.[2] But in the national periphery the political revolution was of a completely different character. At the time both the nationality elites and the masses were struggling for independence and for the full expression of their national identities, an effort that presupposed political sovereignty and the development of each national culture (language, customs, individual rights, and so forth). In 1921 the imposition of the Soviet system on the non-Russian nations represented a foreign revolution and implied the suppression of local elites and traditional values, to the benefit of Soviet elites and values. Clearly, the perpetuation of tradition did not suit the aims of modernization. Yet ideological conflict not only spread among the nations that were at the furthest remove from the Russian cultural model, but affected all national groups. Before 1917 the Ukrainian and Georgian nations had been moving in essentially the same direction as Russian society: they were ripe for socialist revolution. Still, the adoption of the Soviet model in 1921 was for them synonymous with the loss of their national independence. The foreign nature of the revolutionary process for nearly one-half of Soviet society was to have serious and lasting future consequences, witness the current concerns expressed by Mr. Gorbachev.

Agrarian reform was marked by the same duality that characterized the political revolution, even though the nations that had to submit twice to agrarian reform were few. The main distinction to be drawn is not between Russians and non-Russians but between the more advanced societies of the Soviet state and the traditional societies in which modes of ownership, means of production, and religious traditions—or even a tendency to superstition—were uniquely combined.

Yet it was during the construction of the national state that the ambiguity of Soviet aspirations became most evident. The Soviet state in 1921 was a combination of three things. It was heir to the legacy of an anciently constituted national state, Russia, whose territory was well-defined and whose frontiers simply needed to be secured. It was also a federation of older or newer historic states (Georgia, Armenia, and others) for whom revolution and modernization were synonymous with existence as a nation. And, finally, it was potentially a new state searching for an original solution that would combine authority, centralization, a shared system of values and the national renaissance desired by the nations belonging to it. Philosophically, the Soviet state could not follow in the footsteps of its predecessor and reconstruct a nation-state. It had to invent an unprecedented national structure in which nations would join together to form a new whole: the Soviet community.

We may now ask: Has it succeeded in this aim?

Despite opposition from the nations, the central leadership for a long time has been calling the innovative approach a success; however, the skeptical statements of Mr. Gorbachev would suggest that in the end the climate of doubt in the periphery is permeating the center. It is now admitted that the link Lenin envisioned between cultural progress, material betterment, and the weakening of national consciousness has yet to be borne out by history. Does the blame lie solely with Stalin for his brutality and the "Russification" approach to the national problem, which in the 1930s and to a greater extent in the postwar years came to replace Lenin's egalitarian ideals? It is indisputable that Stalinism, with its open hostility toward nations and the officially endorsed supremacy of the Russian people (giving rise to the myth of the Russian "big brother" in relation to the USSR's minority groups), contributed considerably to cementing national loyalties. However, beyond the vicissitudes of Stalinism, one cannot help but notice that contrary to Karl Deutsch's belief—that modernization would lead to the erosion of nationalism—the experience of developing societies, and not only the USSR, has shown instead that modernization brings about a deepening of national sentiment; and far from being a transitory phenomenon, it bears every sign of enduring over time.[3] While the Soviet state is not merely the empire in another guise, three-quarters of a century after the state replaced the empire, the state has had to struggle on the horns of the same dilemma that bedeviled the empire: consciousness of a common destiny, on the one hand, and national aspirations, on the other.

Notes

Introduction

1. Report to the Plenum on 27 January 1987, in *Pravda*, 28 January 1987, and the article by academician Y. Bromlei in *Kommunist*, no. 8 (1986): 78–86.
2. See *Literaturnaia gazeta*, articles by A. Guliaga, 7 May 1986, and academician D. Likhachev, 4 July 1986, on the necessity of republishing these historians.
3. Text in *Mir Islama* 2, no. 4 (1913): 260–64.

Chapter 1
Nation, Culture, and Revolution

1. On the works of Marx and Engels, see S. Bloom, *The World of Nationalisms* (New York: Columbia University Press, 1941); Demetrio Boersner, *The Bolsheviks and the National and Colonial Question* (Geneva and Paris, 1957); H. B. Davis, *Nationalism and Socialism: Marxist and Labor Theories of Nationalism to 1917* (New York and London, 1967); G. Haupt, M. Lowy, and C. Weill, *Les Marxistes et la question nationale, 1848–1914* (Paris, 1974); and G.

Haupt and C. Weill, "Marx et Engels devant le problème des nations," *Economies et sociétés* 8, no. 10 (October 1974): 1461–69.

2. Before Marx, Robespierre had developed this second idea: "In aristocratic states, the word fatherland has no meaning except for the patrician families who have seized sovereignty for themselves." Maximilien Robespierre, *Discours et rapports* (Paris and Velay, 1908), p. 308.

3. "The Congress declares it is wholly in favor of full autonomy for all nations." The Internationale's lack of precision on the national question is obvious in the text that refers to it. The English-language text uses the term "autonomy" (see *International Workers and Trade Union Congress*, London, 1896).

4. Haupt et al., *Les Marxistes*, p. 25.

5. K. Kautsky, "Die moderne Nationalität, " *Neue Zeit* 5 (1887): 392, 405, and 442–551; in Russian, K. Kautsky, *Nationalizm nashego vremeni* (St. Petersburg, 1905).

6. K. Kautsky, in Haupt et al., *Les Marxistes*, pp. 121–22.

7. Synopticus, *Staat und Nation* (Vienna, 1899).

8. Excerpt from the French translation of *Staat und Nation* in Haupt et al., *Les Marxistes*, p. 215.

9. Ibid., p. 222.

10. R. Springer, *Der Kampf der österreichischen Nationen um den Staat* (Vienna, 1902), p. iv.

11. O. Bauer, *Die Nationalitätenfrage und die Sozialdemokratie* (Vienna, 1907).

12. On Otto Bauer, see Y. Bourdet's study, *Otto Bauer et la révolution* (Paris, 1968).

13. Bauer, *Die Nationalitätenfrage*, p. 109. K. Deutsch in *Nationalism and Social Communication* (Cambridge, 1966), p. 20, has stressed some inconsistencies in Bauer's concept.

14. Haupt et al., *Les Marxistes*, p. 40.

15. Translation by Haupt et al. of *Die Nationalitätenfrage*, pp. 270–71.

16. R. Schlesinger, *Federalism in Central and Eastern Europe* (London, 1970), pp. 210–12.

17. Haupt et al., *Les Marxistes*.

18. Ibid., p. 271.

19. J. Ladreit de Lacharrière, *L'idée fédérale en Russie de Riourik à Staline* (Paris, 1945), p. 30.

20 M. Bakunin, *Confessions* (1857) (Paris, 1932), pp. 302–3; A. Herzen, *Izbrannye filosofskie proizvedeniia* (Moscow, 1948), 2: 2, p. 139.

21. T. Anderson, *Russian Political Thought: An Introduction* (New York, 1967), pp. 159–70.

22. Hrushevsky, *Histoire de l'Ukraine*, p. 183.

23. R. Portal, *Russes et Ukrainiens* (Paris, 1970), p. 42; Hrushevsky, *Histoire de l'Ukraine*, p. 184.

24. P. Sydoruk, *The Ideology of the Cyrillo-Methodians and Its Origins* (Winnipeg, 1951), pp. 11–19.

25. K. Kostomarov, "Mysl' o federativnom nachale v drevnei Rusi," *Osnova* 1, no. 1 (1861): 72.

26. N. M. Karamzin, *Istoriia gosudarstva Rossii* (St. Petersburg, 1892), vol. 5, pp. 230–35.

27. Letter to Herzen, 15 January 1860, cited in *Le Monde slave* 2 (1918): 550.

28. M. J. Dragomanov, *Essai d'un programme politique et social ukrainien* (Geneva, 1884), p. 18; L. Wasilewski, *Kwestia Ukrainska jako Zagadnienie międzynarodowe* (Warsaw, 1934), p. 76; A. Sein, "Die ukrainische Frage," *Die Neue Zeit* 26 (1916): 807.

29. Ladreit de Lacharrière, *L'Idée fédérale* p. 96.

30. Ibid.

31. A. Iashchenko, *Chto takoe federativnaia respublika i zhelatel'na li ona dlia Rossii* (Moscow, 1917), p. 18; Wasilewski, *Kwestia Ukrainska jako Zagadnienie międzynarodowe*, p. 26.

32. J. Feldman, *Geschichte der politischen Ideen in Polen seit dessen Teilungen, 1795–1914* (Munich, 1917), pp. 310–55.

33. L. Wasilewski, *Polityka narodów osciowa Rosji* (Krakow, 1916), p. 32.

34. G. Uratadze, *Vospominaniia gruzinskogo Sotsial-Demokrata* (Stanford, 1968), p. 15.

35. Ibid., pp. 96–99.

36. Ibid., p. 224.

37. O. Bauer, *National'nyi vopros i sotsial-demokratiia* (St. Petersburg, 1909), 59; R. Springer, *Gosudarstvo i natsiia* (Odessa, 1908); *Natsional'naia problema* (St. Petersburg, 1909), 25. See Uratadze, *Vospominaniia*, p. 98. On the discussions in the Caucasus, see N. Zhordania, *Moia zhizn'* (Stanford, 1968), and Haimson's introduction to Uratadze, *Vospominaniia*, p. viii.

38. M. Matossian, "Two Marxist Approaches to Nationalism," *American Slavic and East European Review* (April 1957): 489–500, and A. Ter-Minassian, "Le Mouvement révolutionnaire armenien," *Cahiers du monde russe et soviétique* (April 1973): 536–63.

Chapter 2
Lenin: Organization and Strategy

1. V. I. Lenin, *Polnoe sobranie sochinenii* (5th ed., 55 vols., Moscow, 1958–65) (hereafter *Pss*), vol. 30, p. 107.

2. G. Plekhanov, *Sochineniia* (Moscow, 1923), vol. 12, p. 239.

3. B. D. Brutskus, *Statistika evreiskogo naseleniia* (St. Petersburg, 1909), vol. 3, pp. 3 and 8.

4. Ibid., Table 1.

5. *Sbornik materialov ob ekonimicheskom polozhenii evreiskogo naseleniia* (St. Petersburg, 1904), vol. 1, p. 198; A. Patkin, *The Origin of the Russian Jewish Labor Movement* (Melbourne, 1947), pp. 130–32.

6. Ibid., and I. Gezler, *Martov: A Political Biography of a Russian Social*

Democrat (Cambridge, 1967), pp. 29–29; on Martov's attitude toward Judaism and assimilation, see also L. Haimson, *The Russian Marxists and the Origins of Bolshevism* (Cambridge, 1955), p. 64.

7. A. Kremer was one of the founders of the Bund. See Z. Gitelman, *Jewish Nationality and Soviet Politics* (Princeton, N.J., 1972), p. 24.

8. *Encyclopaedia Judaica* (Berlin, 1928), vol. 4, col. 1, p. 208.

9. Ibid.

10. V. Medem, *Sotsial-demokratiia i natsional'nyi vopros* (St. Petersburg, 1906).

11. Plekhanov, *Sochineniia*, vol. 13, pp. 161–68.

12. S. Schwartz, *The Jews in the Soviet Union*, p. 25.

13. R. Pipes, *The Formation of the Soviet Union* (Cambridge, Mass., 1954), p. 34; T. Burmistrova states: "The Mensheviks of the Central Committee office of the RSDLP abroad sold [*torgovali*] the principles of internationalism" (*Natsional'nyi vopros i rabochee dvizhenie v Rossii*, Moscow, 1969), p. 87.

14. G. Uratadze, *Vospominaniia gruzinskogo sotsial-demokrata* (Stanford, 1968); p. 152.

15. Plekhanov, *Sochineniia*, vol. 19, p. 525.

16. Uratadze, *Vospominaniia*, p. 97.

17. Lenin, *Pss*, vol. 1, p. 129–346.

18. Ibid., vol. 7, p. 240; vol. 2, p. 433.

19. Ibid.

20. Ibid., vol. 7, p. 233.

21. Ibid., vol. 7, p. 103.

22. Ibid., vol. 7, p. 300.

23. Ibid., vol. 24, pp. 174–78.

24. A. Kaihanidi, *Leninskaia teoriia i programma po natsional'nomu voprosu* (Minsk, 1962); Lenin, *Pss*, vol. 24, p. 129.

25. Lenin, *Pss*, vol. 24, p. 130; see also vol. 23, p. 318.

26. Ibid., vol. 24, pp. 118 and 130.

27. Uratadze, *Vospominaniia*, p. 213.

28. S. M. G. Shaumian, *Izbrannye proizvedeniia* (2 vols., Moscow 1948–75), vol. 1, pp. 132–61, and "O natsional'no-kul'turnoi avtonomii" (Tiflis, 1914), in Shaumian, *Izbrannye proizvedeniia*, vol. 1, p. 457.

29. *Protokoly pervogo s'ezda partii sotsialistov revoliutsionerov* (St. Petersburg, 1906), pp. 361–62 and 168–73.

30. B. Savin, "Natsional'nyi vopros i partiia SR," *Sotsialist-revoliutsioner* 3 (1911): 95–146.

31. V. Chernov, "Edinoobrazie ili Shablon," *Sotsialist-revoliutsioner* (1911) 147–60.

32. Uratadze, *Vospominaniia*, p. 251, and Lenin's reaction in *Pss*, vol. 15, p. 368.

33. Pipes, *Formation of the Soviet Union*, p. 37, and Burmistrova, *Natsional'nyi vopros*, vol. 3, pp. 60–64.

34. *Leninskii sbornik*: 30, p. 52.

35. Burmistrova, *Natsional'nyi vopros*.

36. R. Arsenidze, "Iz vospominanii o Staline," *Novyi zhurnal* 72 (June 1963): 218–36.

37. Lenin, *Pss,* vol. 48., pp. 160–63.

38. G. Haupt, *Le Congres manqué* (Paris, 1965), p. 103.

39. Stalin, "Marksizm i natsional'nyi vopros," *Sochineniia* (Moscow, 1946–51); vol. 2, pp. 295–367.

40. Ibid., p. 315.

41. Ibid., p. 317.

42. Ibid., p. 312.

43. Ibid., p. 314.

44. Ibid.

45. Burmistrova, *Natsional'nyi vopros*, p. 137, speaks about this without even referring to Stalin's work, except p. 99, when she mentions it among other articles; see also Lenin, *Pss*, vol. 48, p. 162.

46. Without quoting Stalin, Burmistrova, *Natsional'nyi vopros*, pp. 137–38, refers to the identical opinion.

47. Stalin, *Sochineniia*, vol. 2, 338.

48. Ibid., vol. 2, p. 286.

49. M. Djilas in *Conversations with Stalin* (New York, 1962), p. 157, says that Stalin assured him that in this work he was merely interpreting Lenin's ideas.

50. Lenin, Pss, vol. 24, pp. 57–59.

51. Ibid., vol. 25, pp. 255–320.

52. Ibid., vol. 25, pp. 275.

53. Ibid., vol. 24.

54. Ibid., vol. 23, p. 318.

55. Ibid., vol. 24, p. 123.

56. Ibid., vol. 7, pp. 117–22.

57. Ibid., vol. 25, pp. 308–10.

58. Ibid., vol. 48, p. 233.

59. Ibid., vol. 48, p. 235.

Chapter 3
The Nations "Manipulated"

1. T. Burmistrova, *Natsional'nyi vopros i rabochee dvizhenie v Rossii* (Moscow, 1969), p. 165.

2. *Alfavitnyi ukazatel' k sobraniiu uzakonenii i rasporiazhenii pravitel'stva za pervoe polugodie 1907 goda* (St. Petersburg, 1907), pp. 1301–4.

3. J. Gabrys, *Vers L'indépendence lituanienne* (Lausanne, 1920), p. 85.

4. A. Dallin, "The Future of Poland," *Russian Diplomacy and Eastern Europe 1914–1917*, (New York, 1963), p. 177.

5. A. Senn, *The Russian Revolution in Switzerland* (Madison, Wis., 1971), pp. 48–49. See Dmowski's contribution in P. Miliukov and P. Struve, *Russian Realities and Problems* (Cambridge, 1917).

6. H. Neuboch, "Das Polen-Museum in Rapperswill," *Zeitschrift für Ostforschung* 13 (1964): 721–28.

7. M. Leczyk, *Komitet Narodowy Polski a Ententa i strany Zjednoczone, 1917–1919* (Warsaw, 1926), pp. 29–30.

8. Senn, *The Russian Revolution*, p. 56.

9. *Golos*, 21, 24, and 25 November 1914.

10. Lenin, *Pss*, vol. 49, p. 50.

11. Quoted by Senn, *The Russian Revolution*, p. 59.

12. R. Dmowski, *Polityka polska i odbudowanie państwa* (Warsaw, 1926), p. 169.

13. Ibid., p. 165.

14. Zalewski called Dmowski a "Polish counterrevolutionary." *Naše Slovo*, 2 February 1916.

15. The census of 1910 identified 4,607 Russian-language speakers of the 8,458 persons who came from Russian Europe. *Die Ergebnisse der eidgenössischen Volkszählung vom 1 Dezember 1910* (2 vols., Bern, 1915), vol. 1, p. 65.

16. Senn, *The Russian Revolution*, pp. 60–74.

17. Lenin, *Pss*, vol. 27, pp. 48–51; Z. A. Zeman, *Germany and the Revolution in Russia, 1915–1918* (London, 1958), p. 6.

18. W. Stefanowski published a small book in England before the war, *The Russian Plot to Seize Galicia*. During the war he occupied an ambiguous position between the Allied powers, which he claimed to support, and the Central Powers, on which he was financially dependent.

19. J. Gabrys had settled in Paris in 1907; he established there the Union of Nationalities, along with its organ, the *Annales des nationalités*. With the financial aid of the Catholic Lithuanian community in the United States, he created a Lithuanian Bureau in Paris.

20. See J. Gabrys, *Vers L'independence lituanienne and Le problème des nationalités et la paix durable* (Lausanne, 1917).

21. 21 September 1915.

22. On Parvus, see Z. A. Zeman and W. Scharlau, *The Merchant of Revolution* (London, 1965), pp. 145–50, and Solzhenitsyn, *Lenin in Zurich* (Paris, 1976), pp. 102 and 107.

23. Zeman and Scharlau, *The Merchant of Revolution*, pp. 157–58.

24. Gabrys, *Vers L'indépendence lituanienne*, p. 203.

25. Ethnographic map of Europe (Lausanne, 1918), with twenty-one pages of text.

26. Gabrys, *Vers L'indépendence lituanienne*, p. 67.

27. P. N. Miliukov, "Dnevnik Miliukova," *Krasnyi arkhiv* 54–55 (1932): 3–48.

28. *Manchester Guardian*, 3 June 1916.

29. Miliukov, "Dnevnik Miliukova," p. 45.

30. *Annales des nationalités*, fasc. 4, June–August 1916, and *Annales des*

nationalites, third conference on nationalities, preliminary documents (Lausanne, 1916).

31. Dallin, "The Future of Poland," p. 60.

32. S. Filasiewicz, *La Question polonaise pendant la guerre* (Paris, 1928), p. 358.

33. Gabrys, *Vers L'indépendence lituanienne*, p. 302.

34. Dmowski, *Polityka polska*.

35. Ibid., p. 242.

36. Commentary referred to in *Berner Tagewacht*, 29 December 1916.

37. Quoted by Senn, *The Russian Revolution*, p. 196.

38. M. Ferro, *La révolution de 1917* (Paris, 1967), p. 41.

39. Filasiewicz, *La Question polonaise*, p. 277.

40. Dallin, "The Future of Poland," *Russian Diplomacy and Eastern Europe, 1914–1917* (New York, 1963), p. 68.

41. *Bulletin des nationalités de Russie*, no. 1 (1917).

42. Gabrys, *Vers l'indépendence lituanienne*, p. 296, and *Le problème des nationalités*, p. 142, and M.-C. Rivas, *La Lituanie sous le joug allemand, 1915–1918* (Lausanne, 1918).

43. P. Renouvin and J.-B. Duroselle, *Introduction à l'histoire des rélations internationales*, 3d ed. (Paris, 1970), p. 187.

44. Ibid., pp. 178–79 and 187.

Chapter 4
Nationalities: Yeast for the Revolution

1. G. Haupt, "Guerre et révolution chez Lénine," *Revue française de science politique*, 2 April 1971, pp. 256–81; and Lenin, *Pss*, vol. 26, pp. 13–23.

2. Lenin, *Sochineniia*, 3d ed., vol. 16, p. 378.

3. N. Krupskaya, *Memories of Lenin* (London, 1942), p. 213.

4. Lenin, *Pss*, vol. 26, p. 6.

5. Olga Hess Gankin and H. H. Fischer, *The Bolsheviks and the World War* (Stanford, 1940), p. 133.

6. Lenin, *Pss*, vol. 26, pp. 201–5, 209, 265, and 195–200.

7. Ibid., vol. 26, pp. 13–23.

8. Ibid., vol. 26, pp. 282, 285, and 383–85.

9. Ibid., vol. 26, pp. 106–10, and Gankin and Fischer, *The Bolsheviks*, p. 394.

10. V. K. Ignateva, comp., *Partiia bol'shevikov v gody mirovoi voiny: Sverzhenie monarchii v Rossii* (Moscow, 1963), p. 158.

11. The Bundist A. Litvak, who wrote *In Zurich and in Geneva during the First World War: Reminiscences* (New York, 1945), notes on page 246 that he asked Lenin at that time if he realized that he was proposing that Russia be cut off from all its vital economic routes.

12. Lenin, *Pss*, vol. 26, pp. 106–16.

13. Texts in Gankin and Fischer, *The Bolsheviks*, pp. 211–15, 219–21, and 223–39.

14. Ibid., p. 221.

15. Texts ibid., p. 507.

16. Ibid., p. 511.

17. Ibid., p. 513.

18. Lenin, *Pss*, vol. 27, pp. 252–66.

19. Ibid., pp. 260–61.

20. Ibid., vol. 23, pp. 314–22 and 444–48.

21. Ibid., vol. 24, pp. 57–59 and 11–13.

22. Ibid., pp. 223–29.

23. Ibid., p. 58.

24, Ibid., vol. 48, p. 233.

25. Ibid., vol. 7, pp. 233–34.

26. Ibid., vol. 24, p. 143.

27. "Pis'mo k Shaumianu," Lenin, *Pss*, vol. 48, p. 233.

28. Lenin, *Pss*, vol. 24, p. 123.

29. Ibid., p. 145.

30. Ibid., vol. 27, p. 260.

Chapter 5
Self-Determination

1. R. Pipes, *The Formation of the Soviet Union* (Cambridge, Mass., 1954) pp. 50–240.

2. E. H. Carr, *The Bolshevik Revolution* (3 vols., London, 1951), vol. 1, p. 292.

3. *Dekrety Sovetskoi vlasti* (Moscow, 1964), vol. 3, pp. 257–260. The absence of Bolshevik initiative in Poland can be clearly seen in Manu et al., *Lenin i Pol'sha: Problemy, kontakty, otkliki* (Moscow, 1970).

4. *Sobranie Uzakonenii, 1917–1918*, decree of 29 August 1918.

5. *Dekrety Sovetskoi vlasti* (Moscow, 1968), vol. 4, pp. 15–18 (VCIK resolution of 13 November 1918).

6. *Dokumenty vneshnei politiki SSSR* (Moscow, 1957), vol. 1, p. 7.

7. Lenin, *Pss*, vol. 35, p. 304.

8. Ibid., pp. 286–290.

9. Ibid., vol. 36, p. 22.

10. O. V. Kuusinen, *Revoliutsiia v Finlandii* (Petrograd, 1919), p. 12; S. D. Katala, *Terror burzhuazii v Finlandii* (Petrograd, 1919), chap. 1.

11. Stalin, *Sochineniia*, vol. 4, p. 178.

12. *Dekrety Sovetskoi vlasti* (Moscow, 1968), vol. 4, pp. 157–158.

13. Ibid, (articles 2, 3, and 4 of the *Sovnarkom* decree) and the Soviet of the Republic, which appealed to "all the workers," *Zhizn' natsional' nostei*, 8 December 1918.

14. *Zhizn' natsional'nostei,* 22 December 1918.

15. *Dekrety Sovetskoi vlasti* (Moscow, 1968), vol. 4, p. 242. See also A. Drizul, *V. I. Lenin i revoliutsionnaia Latvia* (Riga, 1970), and V. Sosnov, *Lenin i latyshskaia revoliutsionnaia sotsial' demokratiia* (Riga, 1970).

16. Carr, *The Bolshevik Revolution,* p. 318.

17. Ibid.

18. Trotsky, *Ma Vie* (Paris, 1930), vol. 3, p. 169–70.

19. Lenin, *Pss* vol. 51, p. 238; L. O. Frossard, *De Juarès a Lénine: Souvenirs d'un militant* (Paris, 1930), p. 130.

20. B. Vaitkiavichius et al., *Bor'ba za sovetskuiu vlast' v Litve v 1918–1920 gg: Sbornik dokumentov* (Vilnius, 1967), pp. 48–53.

21. *Dekrety Sovetskoi vlasti,* vol. 4, pp. 243–45.

22. Ibid., pp. 335–36. In the VCIK resolution of 31 January 1919 on the independence of Byelorussia, the union of Byelorussia with Lithuania was mentioned.

23. *S'ezdy Sovetov v dokumentakh, 1917–1936* (Moscow, 1960), vol. 2, pp. 232–33.

24. Notably, at the conference of April 1917; see Lenin, *Pss,* vol. 31, pp. 432–38.

25. Ibid., vol. 35, pp. 268–90.

26. S. Dimanshtein, *Revoliutsiia i natsional'nyi vopros* (Moscow, 1927), vol. 3, pp. 196–97.

27. R. Portal, *Russes et Ukrainiens* (Paris, 1970), p. 106.

28. Resolution of the Congress of Soviets of the Ukraine on self-determination: *S'ezdy Sovetov v dokumentakh, 1917–1936* (Moscow, 1960), vol. 3, p. 17.

29. *Obrazovanie SSR: Sbornik dokumentov, 1917–1924* (Moscow, Leningrad, 1949), pp. 74–75.

30. J. Reshetar, Jr., *The Ukrainian Revolution, 1917–1920* (Princeton, N. J. 1952), p. 115; and V. M. Kuritsyn, *Gosudarstvennoe Sotrudnichestvo mezhdu Ukrainskoi SSR i RSFSR v 1917–1922 gg* (Moscow, 1957), pp. 38–39.

31. Portal, *Russes et Ukrainiens,* p. 106.

32. Reshetar, *The Ukrainian Revolution,* pp. 170–74.

33. Vinichenko has maintained that General d' Anslem was very well disposed to this appeal, but the French archives in the Ministry of Foreign Affairs suggest the contrary, that the French leadership was reticent. See Dossiers Z–619–11, and Z–617–1.

34. Regarding all of Rakovsky's activities, see the thesis by F. Conte, *Christian Rakovski, 1872–1941,* (Lille, Paris, 1975). On this particular point, see vol. 1 pp. 207–8, and Iu. Borys, *The Russian Communist Party and the Sovietization of the Ukraine* (Stockholm, 1960), p. 40.

35. Popov, *Ocherki istorii kommunisticheskoi partii Ukrainy* (Simferopol, 1929), p. 174.

36. Ibid., pp. 9–11; Borys, *The Russian Communist Party,* pp. 146–49; and Kuritsyn, *Gosudarstvennoe sotrudnichestvo,* p. 37.

37. M. Ravich-Cherkasski, *Istoriia kommunisticheskoi partii Ukrainy* (Kharkov, 1923), pp. 57–62, and Kuritsyn, *Gosudarstvennoe sotrudnichestvo*, p. 37.

38. V. A. Antonov-Ovseenko, *Zapiski o grazhdanskoi revoliutsii* (Moscow, 1912–22), vol. 3.

39. Popov, *Ocherki istorii kommunisticheskoi partii Ukrainy*, p. 180.

40. Stalin, *Sochineniia*, vol. 4, p. 175.

41. Ibid., p. 180.

42. Quoted by Carr, *The Bolshevik Revolution*, vol. 1, p. 306.

43. Regarding the constitution of the republic of 10 March 1919, see *S'ezdy Sovetov v dokumentakh*, vol. 2, pp. 52–58; F. Conte, *Christian Rakovski*, p. 221; and especially Borys, *The Russian Communist Party*, pp. 206–11, for the most detailed study of this episode.

44. *Protokoly VIII Konferentsii RKP* (Moscow, 1919), p. 95. On Lenin's attitude, see *Pravda*, 26 January 1919; regarding the takeover of Orenburg, Lenin wrote, "Now we will get enough and even more wheat from the Ukraine." In an editorial in *Pravda*, 1 February 1919, entitled "Wheat and Coal," he took up the same theme.

45. Lenin, *Pss*, vol. 38, pp. 182–84.

46. Ibid., p. 162.

47. *KPss v resoliutsiiakh* (Moscow, 1971), vol. 2, pp. 73–74.

48. Lenin, *Pss*, vol. 38, pp. 400–1.

49. *Dekrety Sovetskoi vlasti* (Moscow, 1970), vol. 5, pp. 73–74.

50. Popov, *Ocherki istorii*, p. 240.

51. N. Vakar, *Bielorussia* (Cambridge, Mass: Harvard University Press, 1956), p. 75. N. Vakar has published a most useful bibliography on Byelorussia, *A Bibliographic Guide to Bielorussia* (Cambridge, Mass: Harvard University Press, 1956), p. xiv. See also Meshkov, *Ocherki istorii kommunisticheskoi partii Belorussii* (Minsk, 1968), and S. Agurskii, *Ocherki po istorii revoliutsionogo dvizheniia v Belorussii* (Minsk, 1928).

52. Regarding these subdivisions, see A. Sobolevski, "Belorusskoe narechiie," *Zhurnal ministerstva narodnogo prosveshcheniia* 5–6 (1887): 137–47.

53. V. G. Knorin, *Zametki k istorii diktatury proletariata v Belorussii* (Minsk, 1934), pp. 30–34.

54. Dimanshtein, *Revoliutsiia i natsional'nyi vopros*, pp. 271–76.

55. Vakar, *Bielorussia*, p. 109.

56. *Dekrety Sovetskoi vlasti*, vol. 4, pp. 335–36.

57. *S'ezdy sovetov v dokumentakh, 1917–1936* (Moscow, 1960), vol. 2, p. 232.

58. Ibid., pp. 233–37.

59. *Obrazovanie SSSR: Sbornik dokumentov, 1917–1924* (Moscow, Leningrad, 1949), p. 125.

60. *S'ezdy sovetov v dokumentakh*, vol. 2, pp. 248–53.

61. I. Ananov, *Sud'ba Armenii* (Moscow, 1918), p. 5. Regarding the dispersion of the Armenian people, see Pipes, *The Formation of the Soviet Union*, pp. 15–16, on the general situation in the Caucasus, and *Narody*

Dagestana (Moscow, 1955) for the particular situation in Daghestan and Terek. Regarding the Bolsheviks' assessment of the situation in the Caucasus, see Dimanshtein and Jordania, *Za dva goda* (Tiflis, 1920), pp. 111–19.

62. Pipes, *The Formation of the Soviet Union*, p. 103; see Stalin, *Sochineniia*, vol. 4, p. 53.

63. *Obrazovanie zakavkazkogo pravitel'stva*, and *Dokumenty i materialy po vneshnei politiki Zakavkazii i Gruzii* (Tiflis, 1919).

64. Ibid., pp. 8–10.

65. S. Shaumian, *Izbrannye proizvedeniia* (Moscow, 1958), vol. 2 (1917–18), pp. 153–55; G. K. Zhvaniia, *Velikii oktiabr'i bor'ba bol'shevikov Zakavkazii za sovetskuiu vlast'* (Tbilisi, 1967), p. 150; F. Kazemzadeh, *The Struggle for Transcaucasia, 1917–1921* (New York: Oxford, 1951), p. 65.

66. *Dokumenty i materialy po vneshnei politiki Zakavkaziia*, pp. 339–42.

67. Pipes, *The Formation of the Soviet Union*, p. 219, emphasizes that Lenin was so late in recognizing Georgia that in November 1918 it was not yet acknowledged.

68. Noah Jordania, who headed the government from June 1918, always minimized the choice that Georgia had made, arguing that it had had no other alternative.

69. Various documents assembled in folder Z–619–11 of the French Ministry of Foreign Affairs speak to this point. They demonstrate a clear divergence between the British and French positions (see especially Chardigny's report of 17 June 1919 and the telegram sent by Nabokov, Russian *chargé d'affaires* in London, to Sazonov on 27 February 1919, which states that as far as England is concerned, the fate of the Caucasus will be decided at the Peace Conference); reports by Lt.-Col. de Chardigny (17 June 1919); report by Col. (10 July 1919); letter by the French Consul in Tiflis, M. Nicolas, to Minister Pichon (3 July 1919), which illustrate the French hostility toward Georgia.

70. Dossier AE–Z–619–11 on the conference at the Georgian Ministry of Foreign Affairs on 23 May 1919 attended by General Briggs, Gegeshkori, and Ramishvili. Briggs said: "Stop being proud. . . . Hold your hand out to Denikin and tell him, 'We are with you for a great Russia.' " In addition, see the document of 25 May 1919 (telegram from Britforce of Transcaucasia to Britforce of Constantinople).

71. Kazemzadeh, *The Struggle for Transcaucasia*, p. 202.

72. Dossier Z–619–11. Telegram from Pichon to Miller and Denikin. Clemenceau demands that they press Admiral Kolchak to define clearly the future he contemplates for the nations, and for him to recognize definitively the independence of Finland and Poland.

73. Dossier AE–Z–619–11.

74. Kazemzadeh, *The Struggle for Transcaucasia*, p. 212.

75. Stalin, *Sochineniia*, vol. 4, p. 408.

76. *Izvestiia*, 29 April 1920, and Lenin's response, *Pss*, vol. 41, p. 119.

77. Lenin, *Pss*, vol. 41, pp. 161–68.

78. *Dokumenty vneshnei politiki SSSR* (Moscow, 1959), vol. 3, pp. 346–49; *Zhizn' natsional'nostei*, 8 December 1920; and Lenin, *Pss*, vol. 41, p. 119.

79. Kazemzadeh, *The Struggle for Transcaucasia*, p. 204. *Traité conclu le 7 mai 1920 entre la République démocratique de Georgie et la République socialiste fédérative russe* (Paris, 1922).

80. *S'ezdy Sovetov v dokumentakh* (Moscow, 1959), vol. 1, pp. 30–31 (see Article 6 of the 15 January 1918 resolution).

81. M. A. Saidacheva, *Lenin i soialisticheskoe stroitel'stvo v Tatarii, 1918–1923* (Moscow, 1969), p. 328.

82. Lenin, *Pss*, vol. 38, pp. 156–62.

83. Pipes, *The Formation of the Soviet Union*, p. 167.

84. *Zhizn' natsional'nostei*, 18 June 1919.

85. Z. V. Togan, *Bugünkü Türkili (Turkistan) Ve Yakin Tarihi* (Istanbul, 1942–47), p. 408.

86. Ibid., pp. 412–14.

87. G. I. Safarov, *Kolonial'naia revoliutsiia: Opyt Turkestana* (Moscow, 1921); *Bol'shaia sovetskaia entsiklopediia*, (1927), vol. 4, p. 35, and Lenin's commentary about it in 1921, *Leninskii sbornik*, (Moscow, 1959), vol. 36, pp. 320–21.

88. Safarov, *Kolonial'naia revoliutsiia*, p. 10.

89. B. Hayit, *Die nationalen Regierungen von Kokand und Alash Orda* (Münster, 1950).

90. Steinberg, *Ocherki po istorii Turkmenii* (Moscow, 1934), p. 154.

91. H. Carrère D'Encausse, *Réforme et révolution chez les musulmans de l'Empire russe* (Paris, 1966), pp. 233–39, and *Voina v peskakh* (Leningrad, 1955), p. 255.

92. Muraveiskii, "Sentiabr'skii dni v Tashkente," *Proletarskaia revoliutsiia* 10 (1924): 138–61.

93. *Zhizn' natsional'nostei*, 1 June 1919.

94. R. Abdushukurov, *Oktiabr'skaia revoliutsiia, rastsvet uzbekskoi sotsialisticheskoi natsii i sblizhenie ee s natsiami SSSR* (Tashkent, 1962), pp. 146–47.

95. T. Ryskulov, *Revoliutsiia i korennoe naselenie Turkestana: Sbornik statei, dokladov, rechei* (Tashkent, 1925), p. 22.

96. *M. V. Frunze na frontakh grazhdanskoi voiny* (Moscow, 1941), pp. 119–20.

97. Akademia nauk Uzbekskoi SSR, *Istoriia Uzbekskoi SSR* (Tashkent, 1956), vol. 2, pp. 110–11.

98. *Pervyi s'ezd narodov vostoka* (Petrograd, 1920), pp. 31–179.

99. Togan, *Bungünkü Turkili (Turkestan) Ve Yakin Tarihi*, pp. 370–71 and 398–402.

100. Lenin, *Pss*, vol. 41, 433–36.

101. Ibid., p. 436.

Chapter 6
A Parliament for Nationalities

1. *Spravochnik narodnogo komissariata po delam natsional'nostei* (Moscow, 1921), p. 5.

2. M. Ironikov, *Sozdanie sovetskogo tsentral'nogo gosudarstvennogo apparata: Sovet narodnykh komissarov i narodnye komissariaty* (Moscow, 1966), pp. 237–39; E. Gorodetskii, *Rozhdenie sovetskogo gosudarstva* (Moscow, 1964), p. 158; A. Denisov, "Narodnyi Komissariat po delam natsional'nostei," *Bolshaia sovetskaia entsiklopediia* (Moscow, 1931), pp. 213–14.

3. E. Pesikina, *Narodnyi Komissariat po delam natsional'nostei* (Moscow, 1950), p. 63.

4. *Narodnyi komissariat po delam natsional'nostei, Politika sovetskoi vlasti po natsional'nym delam za tri goda* (Moscow, 1920), p. 24.

5. *Zhizn' natsional'nostei*, nos. 1 and 9 (November 1918).

6. S. Pestkovskii, "Vospominaniia o rabote v Narkomnatse," *Proletarskaia revoliutsiia* (June 1930), pp. 129–30.

7. Regarding the creation of the commissariat for Jewish affairs, *Evkom*, see *Evreiskii rabochii*, 20 July 1918 and 31 July 1918; Pestkovskii, "Vospominaniia," p. 130.

8. *Politika sovetskoi vlasti po natsional'nym delam*, p. 79, and the note written by the lieutenant on the vessel *Rollin*, dated 8 July 1919, French archives, Dossier Z 619–11 (IX).

9. *Shest' let natsional'noi politiki sovetskoi vlasti i narkomnats* (Moscow, 1924), p. 18.

10. Pesikina, *Narodnyi Komissariat*, p. 66.

11. Regarding Stalin's activities, see Pestkovskii, "Vospominaniia," p. 128; Leon Trotsky, *Stalin: An Appraisal of the Man and His Influence* (London, 1947), p. 245; and S. Dimanshtein, *Revoliutsiia i natsional'nyi vopros* (Moscow, 1927), p. 34.

12. Pesikina, *Narodnyi Komissariat*, p. 67.

13. On 15 June 1919 *Zhizn' natsional'nostei* published an article by Peskovskii in support of Rosa Luxemburg's theses.

14. Pestkovskii, "Vospominaniia," p. 124; Pesikina, *Narodnyi Komissariat*, p. 89; and *Shest' let natsional'noi politiki*, p. 218.

15. Pesikina, *Narodnyi Komissariat*, p. 67.

16. M. Mukhariamov, *Oktiabr' i natsional'nyi vopros v Tatarii* (Kazan, 1958), pp. 187–95.

17. R. Nafigov, "Deiatel'nost' tsentral'nogo musul'manskogo Komissariata po delam natsional'nostei v 1918 godu," *Sovetskoe vostokovedenie* 5 (1958), 116–20, especially 116.

18. *Politika sovetskoi vlasti po natsional'nym delam*, p. 81.

19. *Zhizn' natsional'nostei*, 23 May 1920.

20. I. Lozovskii and I. Bibin, *Sovetskaia politika za 10 let po natsional'nomu voprosu v RSFSR* (Moscow, 1928), p. 114.

21. *Zhizn' natsional'nostei*, 7 November 1920.

22. Ibid., 31 December, 1920.

23. *Politika sovetskoi vlasti po natsional'nym delam*, p. 150.

24. *Shest' let natsional'noi politiki*, p. 52.

25. *Politika sovetskoi vlasti po natsional'nym delam*, p. 150

26. *Zhizn' natsional'nostei*, 13 January 1921.

27. *Zhizn' natsional'nostei* 16 (15) (1922): 1. (At this time, the regularity of the organ changed from the date of the introductory issue.) B. El'baum, "Rol' narkomnatsa v nalazhivanii pomoshchi tsentral'nykh raionov strany narodam Srednei Azii," *Trudy Instituta Istorii partii pri TSK Turkmenistana* (Ashkhabad, 1971), p. 190.

28. *Zhizn' natsional'nostei*, 13 January 1921.

29. *Shest' let natsional'noi politiki*, p. 63.

30. Landa, *Sozdanie narodnogo komissariata po natsional'nym delam Turkestanskoi ASSR* (Tashkent, 1956), p. 43. A. Ishanov, "K voprosu o pomoshchi RSFSR v ukreplenii sovetskoi gosudarstvennosti v Srednei Azii," *Trudy Sagu* (Tashkent, 1960), p. 3.

31. *Shest' let natsional'noi politiki*, pp. 23–24.

32. C. Urazaev, V. I. *Lenin i stroitel'stvo sovetskoi gosudarstvennosti v Turkestane* (Tashkent, 1967), p. 250.

33. Landa, *Sozdanie narodnogo komissariata*, p. 99.

34. *Shest' let natsional'noi politiki*, p. 53.

35. Ibid., p. 54.

36. V. Ignat'ev, *Sovet natsional'nostei tsentral'nogo ispolnitel'nogo komiteta SSSR* (Moscow, 1926), p. 10, deals with this reform; *Zhizn' natsional'nostei* 16 (15)(1922): 1.

37. *Shest' let natsional'noi politiki*, pp. 148–50.

38. Ibid., p. 150.

Chapter 7
Diversity: The Federal State

1. Lenin, *Pss*, vol. 33, pp. 123–307.

2. Ibid., vol. 33, 1–120.

3. F. Engels, *L'origine de la famille, de la propriété privée et de l'Etat* (Paris, 1946), p. 229, and letter to Bebel, 18 March 1875, in *Critique des programmes de Gotha et d'Erfurt* (Paris, 1950), pp. 43–51.

4. Marginal annotations by Marx, to Engels, *Critique des programmes de Gotha et d'Erfurts*, pp. 16–39.

5. Lenin, *Pss*, vol. 33, p. 151.

6. Ibid.

7. *Dekrety Sovetskoi vlasti* (Moscow, 1957), vol. 1, pp. 12–16.

8. J. Y. Calvez, *Droit international et souverainete en Urss* (Paris, 1953), pp. 53–54.

9. Lenin, *Sochineniia*, 3d ed., vol. 9, p. 60.

10. *Sobranie uzakonenii* (text in Annex I), no. 2 (1917): 18.

11. Lenin, *Pss*, vol. 33.

12. Quoted by J. Laloy, *Le socialisme de Lenine* (Paris, 1967), p. 104.

13. *Dekrety Sovetskoi vlasti* (Moscow, 1957), vol. 1, pp. 341–43.

14. Ibid. (title IV, s 3), p. 343.

15. Lenin, *Pss*, vol. 35, pp. 286–90.

16 Ibid., p. 287.

17. Ibid., vol. 34, pp. 304–5.

18. Ibid., vol. 36, p. 76.

19. Ibid., p. 15.

20. G. S. Gurvich, *Istoriia sovetskoi konstitutsii* (Moscow, 1923), pp. 146–48.

21. *S'ezdy sovetov . . . v dokumentakh, 1917–1936* (Moscow, 1959), vol. 1, pp. 70–84.

22. E. H. Carr, *The Bolshevik Revolution*, (London, 1951) vol. 1, p. 148.

23. R. Pipes, *The Formation of the Soviet Union*, p. 246.

24. S. Atnagulov, *Bashkiria* (Moscow, 1925), pp. 71–72, and *Politika sovetskoi vlasti po natsional'nomu voprosu* (Moscow, 1920), p. 19.

25. *Sobranie uzakonenii* (1920), no. 45, art. 203; no. 51, art. 222; and no. 59, art. 262.

26. B. Hayit, *Die nationale Regierungen von Kokand und Alash Orda* (Münster, 1950), p. 42.

27. *Dekrety Sovetskoi vlasti* (Moscow, 1971), vol. 5, pp. 398–400.

28. Ibid., p. 399.

29. T. Borisov, *Kalmykiia* (Moscow, 1926), p. 63.

30. Stalin, *Sochineniia*, vol. 4, pp. 394–97.

31. Ibid., pp. 402–3.

32. *Sobranie uzakonenii* (1921), 5, no. 39, and 6, no. 41.

33. D. N. Magerovski, *Soiuz sovetskikh sotsialisticheskikh respublik* (Moscow, 1923), and *Piat' let vlasti sovetov* (Moscow, 1922), p. 227.

34. Stalin, *Sochineniia*, vol. 4, p. 360.

35. *Zhizn' natsional'nostei*, 15 February 1920, announces the establishment of a commission devoted to the preparation of these treaties.

36. *Sobranie uzakonenii* (1920): no. 85, 426.

37. Ibid.

38. Ibid. (1921), no. 1, 13.

39. F. Conte, *Christian Rakovski* (Bordeaux, 1969), particularly pp. 139, 142, and 150.

40. V. Markus, *L'Ukraine soviétique dans les relations internationales, 1917–1923* (Paris, 1959), p. 51; Iu.-Borys, *The Russian Communist Party and the Sovietization of the Ukraine* (Stockholm, 1960), p. 293–95.

41. T. Bell, *Pioneering Days* (London, 1941), pp. 149–50, on this confusion of tasks, and M. Roy, *Memoirs* (Bombay, 1964), p. 200.

42. M. Body, *Contribution à l'histoire du Komintern* (Geneva, 1965), p. 52.

43. *Soviet Documents on Foreign Policy,* vol. 1, 1917–24 (London, 1951), p. 258. Litvinov's letter on the difference between the Soviet government and the Comintern (September 1921).

44. *Izvestiia,* 6 April 1921. The treaty was signed on 16 January 1921.

45. *Sobranie uzakonenii* no. 1 (1921): 13.

46. *RSFSR: Sbornik deistvuiushchikh dogovorov* 2, no. 41 (1921): 7.

47. F. Kazemzadeh, *The Struggle for Transcaucasia, 1917–1921* (New York: Oxford, 1951), p. 198; on the elections of 1919, see p. 186.

48. "Traité conclu le 7 mai 1920 entre la République démocratique de Georgie et la République socialiste fédérative russe" (Paris, 1922).

49. N. Racine, "Le parti socialiste SFIO devant le bolshevisme," RFSP, no. 2 (April 1971): 281–96.

50. Kazemzadeh, *The Struggle for Transcaucasia,* p. 200.

51. Stalin, *Sochineniia,* vol. 4, p. 383.

52. Ibid., p. 408.

53. Zhvania, V. I. *Lenin: TSK partii bol'sheviki Zakavkaziia* (Tbilisi, 1969), pp. 260–61.

54. Article by Zhvania in *Zaria vostoka,* 21 April 1961.

55. Ibid., and in Zhvania, V. I. *Lenin,* pp. 261–67.

56. Text in Lenin, *Pss,* vol. 52, p. 71.

57. N. Jordania, *Moia zhizn',* pp. 110–12, and David M. Lang, *A Modern History of Soviet Georgia* (New York, 1969), p. 235.

58. Pipes, *The Formation of the Soviet Union,* p. 236; I. Tseretelli, *Promethée,* June 1928, p. 11; *Promethée,* June 1930, pp. 12–14.

59. Zhvania, V. I. *Lenin,* pp. 262–68.

60. Lenin, *Pss,* vol. 41, p. 22. X. Zheukoff Eudin and R. North, *Soviet Russia and the East, 1920–1927* (Stanford, 1957), pp. 186–88. Letter from Chicherin to Mustafa Kemal of 2 June 1920, and Kemal's response of November 1920.

61. On Trotsky's position, see Jordania, *Moia zhizn',* p. 110; Leon Trotsky, *Stalin: An Appraisal of the Man and His Influence* (New York, 1946), p. 268.

62. *The Trotsky Papers, 1917–1922* (The Hague, 1971), vol. 2, p. 385.

63. Lenin, *Pss,* vol. 52, p. 71.

64. Telegram of 16 February 1921, *Dokumenty vneshnei politiki SSSR* (Moscow, 1959), vol. 3, pp. 526–27, and telegram of 18 February 1921, ibid., pp. 527–28.

65. Lenin, *Pss,* vol. 42, p. 367.

66. *Sobranie uzakonenii* no. 29 (1921): 161, and no. 35 (1921): 187.

67. Ibid., no. 73 (1921): 595 and 596.

68. Statement by Yakovlev, assistant commissar of foreign affairs of the SSR of Ukraine, quoted by F. Conte, *Rakovski,* p. 145.

69. Iu. V. Kliuchnikov and A. V. Sabanin, *Mezhdunarodnaia politika* (Moscow, 1928), vol. 3, p. 139.

70. *Kommunisticheskaia partiia—vdokhnovitel' i organizator ob'edinitel'nogo dvizheniia Ukrainskogo naroda za obrazovanie SSSR* (Kiev, 1962), p. 247.

71. *Dokumenty vneshnei politiki SSSR* (Moscow, 1961) vol. 5, pp. 110–11.

72. Ibid., pp. 111–12; regarding the invitation to the nations of the former empire, see "Millerand papers" in archives of Foreign Affairs, 14 (dossier Vignon). Two notes on the "Cannes conference" numbers 6 and 8, 10 January 1922.

73. A. Bennigsen and C. L. Quelquejay, *Le Sultangaliévisme au Tatartsan* (Paris, 1960), pp. 176–82.

74. Harmandarian, *Lenin i stanovlenie zakavkazskoi federatsii* (Yerevan, 1969), p. 214.

75. Letter to the communists of the three republics of the Caucasus, 14 April 1921, in Lenin, *Pss*, vol. 43, pp. 198–200.

76. Azerbaijan (19 May 1921), Armenia (4 February 1922), Georgia (2 March 1922); *S'ezdy sovetov v dokumentakh*, vol. 2, pp. 326–39, 373–84, and 415–32.

77. Article 8 of Title I, ibid., pp. 373–84.

78. Article 4 of Title I, ibid., pp. 415–32; and see Resolution of the Soviet of Baku, 11 April 1921, in *Obrazovanie SSSR: Sbornik dokumentov, 1917–1924* (Moscow, Leningrad, 1949), p. 270.

79. Stalin, *Sochineniia*, vol. 5, pp. 227–28.

80. Lenin, *Pss*, vol. 44, p. 689.

81. Quoted by Harmandarian, *Lenin i postanovlenie*, p. 205.

82. Ibid., p. 217.

83. G. K. Ordzhonikidze, *Stat'i i rechi* (Moscow, 1956), vol. 1, p. 228.

84. *Obrazovanie SSSR: Sbornik dokumentov, 1917–1924*, pp. 288–89.

85. Ordzhonikidze, *Stat'i i rechi*, vol. 1, p. 275.

86. F. Makharadze, *Sovety i bor'ba za sovetskuiu vlast' v Gruzii, 1917–1921* (Tbilisi, 1928), shows the increase in divergences beginning in the spring of 1922.

87. Lenin, *Pss*, vol. 41, p. 164.

88. Ibid., p. 438.

89. Ibid., vol. 45, p. 330.

90. M. Kulichenko, "V. I. Lenin o federatsii i ee roli v stroitel'stve sovetskogo mnogonatsional'nogo gosudarstva," *Voprosy istorii KPSS*, p. 67.

91. Lenin, *Pss*, vol. 45, p. 211 (letter to Kamenev).

92. Ibid., pp. 211–13.

93. Published letter by Stalin, but quoted in Lenin, *Pss*, vol. 45, p. 558, and Leon Trotsky, *La Révolution trahie* (Paris, 1937), pp. 160–61.

94. Lenin, *Pss*, vol. 45, p. 559; and see M. Lewin, *Le dernier combat de Lénine* (Paris, 1967), p. 64.

95. Lenin, *Pss*, vol. 45, p. 214.

96. *KPSS v rezoliutsiiakh* (Moscow, 1970), vol. 2, pp. 401–2.

97. Published in *Zaria vostoka*, 2 November 1922.

98. A. F. Miasnikov, *Izbrannye proizvedeniia* (Yerevan, 1965), pp. 423–24.

99. *XII s'ezd RKP (b)*, pp. 536–37; Stalin, *Sochineniia*, vol. 5, p. 526.

100. Lenin, *Pss*, vol. 54, pp. 299–300.

101. Lenin was concerned about its composition and abstained when the time came to vote. *Pss*, vol. 45, p. 702.

102. V. Kirilov and A. Sverdlov, *Ordzhonikidze: Biografiia* (Moscow, 1962), p. 175.

103. Lenin, *Pss*, vol. 45, pp. 356–62.

104. Lewin, *Le dernier combat de Lenine*, pp. 97–108.

105. Lenin, *Pss*, vol. 45, p. 356.

106. Ibid., vol. 54, p. 330.

107. *S'ezdy sovetov v dokumentakh, 1917–1936* (Moscow, 1960), vol. 2, p. 148, 151–52, and 152–55.

108. Ibid., pp. 478–79, 482, and 483–91.

109. Ibid., pp. 302–3, 304–5, and 305–7.

110. Ibid. (Moscow, 1960), vol. 3, pp. 16–17 and 18–22, and *Izvestiia*, 30 December 1929.

Chapter 8
Unity: The Communist Party

1. G. Safarov, *Kolonial'naia revoliutsiia: Opyt Turkestana* (Moscow, 1921), pp. 119–27; P. G. Antropov, *Kommunisticheskaia partiia Turkestana, pervyi kongres* (Tashkent, 1934).

2. T. Guba, *Bor'ba bol'shevikov Kazakhstana za pobedu Oktiabr'skoi revoliutsii* (Alma Ata, 1957), pp. 107–8 and 110.

3. Ibid., p. 111.

4. *Nasha gazeta*, 22 December 1918.

5. Antropov, *Kommunisticheskaia partiia*, p. 41.

6. M. Veksel'man, *Dokumental'nye istochniki po istorii ustanovleniia sovetskoi vlasti v Uzbekistane* (Moscow, 1964), p. 17.

7. A. Bennigsen and C. L. Quelquejay, *Le Sultangaliévisme au Tatarstan* (Paris, 1960) pp. 114–18; see Stalin's criticisms in *Zhizn' natsional'nostei*, 17 November 1918.

8. Ibid., 22 December 1918.

9. *Musburo RKP (b) v Turkestane* (Tashkent, 1922), p. 13.

10. *Rezoliutsii i postanovleniia s'ezdov kommunisticheskoi partii Turkestana* (Tashkent, 1934), p. 35.

11. Safarov, *Kolonial'naia revoliutsiia*, p. 96; *Musburo RKP (b) v Turkestane*, p. 33.

12. S. Muraveiskii, *Ocherki po istorii revoliutsionnogo dviezheniia v Srednei Azii* (Tashkent, 1926), pp. 25–26.

13. *Musburo RKP (b) v Turkestane*, p. 31.

14. *Trudy 3–go s'ezda kommunisticheskoi partii Turkestana* (Tashkent, 1919), p. 71.

15. R. Kh. Abdushukurov, *Oktiabr'skaia revoliutsiia* (Tashkent, 1962), pp. 144–45.

16. *Pravda*, 12 July 1922.

17. T. Ryskulov, *Revoliutsiia i korennoe naselenie Turkestana* (Tashkent, 1922), p. 76.

18. Peters, "Stranitsa predatel'stva," *Pravda vostoka*, 16 and 18 December 1922.

19. A. M. Bogoutdinov et al., *Istoriia kommunisticheskikh organizatsii Srednei Azii* (Tashkent, 1967), p. 380.

20. Ibid., p. 388.

21. *Zhizn' natsional'nostei*, no. 3 (132), 26 January 1922.

22. *Vserossiiskaia perepis' chlenov RKP (b) 1922 g.* (Moscow, 1923), vol. 4, p. 39.

23. Table established on the basis of the combined data from *Istoriia kommunisticheskikh organizatsii Srednei Azii*, p. 570, and *Vserossiiskaia perepis' Chlenov (b) 1922 g.*, as well as the report of the Seventh Congress of the CPT.

24. *Leninskii sbornik*, vol. 24, p. 156.

25. Lenin, *Pss*, vol. 53, p. 105.

26. *Istoriia kommunisticheskikh organizatsii Srednei Azii*, p. 563.

27. G. Zhvania, *Velikii oktiabr'i bor'ba bol'shevikov za Sovetskuiu vlast'* (Tbilisi, 1967), p. 276.

28. Harmandarian, *Lenin i stanvolenie zakavkazskoi federatsii*, p. 30.

29. Lenin, *Pss*, vol. 52, pp. 35–36; vol. 53, p. 276.

30. Ibid., vol. 44, p. 689.

31. M. Ahmedov, "V. I. Lenin i obrazovanie SSSR," *Voprosy istorii KPSS 6* (1962): 27.

32. *II s'ezd kommunisticheskikh organizatsii zakavkazii stenootchet*, p. 38.

33. Declaration of 12 March 1922, *Obrazovanie SSSR: Sbornik dokumentov* (Moscow, Leningrad, 1949), pp. 288–89.

34. Constitution of 13 December 1922, *S'ezdy sovetov v dokumentakh* (Moscow, 1960), vol. 2, pp. 483–91.

35. M. Lewin *Le dernier combat de Lénine* (Paris, 1967), pp. 101–4.

36. Lenin, *Pss*, vol. 45, pp. 606–7, and vol. 54, p. 330.

37. Ibid., vol. 54, p. 214.

38. Ibid., p. 329.

39. *Bor'ba za uprochenie sovetskoi vlasti v Gruzii: Sbornik dokumentov*, pp. 145–46.

40. *Pravda*, 5 April 1923.

41. *XII s'ezd RKP (b)*, pp. 158-61.

42. Ibid., pp. 183–186.

43. Stalin, *Sochineniia*, vol. 5, pp. 227–28.

44. J. Sharapov, *Natsional'nye sektsii RKP (b)*(Kazan, 1978), p. 239.

45. Z. Gitelman, *Jewish Nationality and Soviet Politics* (Princeton, N. J., 1972), p. 106.

46. Dimanshtein, *Revoliutsiia i natsional'nyi vopros* (Moscow, 1930), vol. 3, p. 34.

47. Sharapov, *Natsional'nye sektsii RKP (b)*, p. 75.

48. *Izvestiia*, 3 June 1924.

49. M. Lesgae, *Les régimes politiques de l'URSS et de l'Europe de l'est* (Paris, 1971), p. 207.

50. *XII s'ezd RKP (b)*, pp. 443-44.

51. Stalin, *Sochineniia*, vol. 5, pp. 301–3 (Stalin's speech at the conference).

52. Ibid., pp. 297 and 307.

53. L. B. Kamenev, J. V. Stalin, and G. E. Zinoviev, *Leninism or Trotskyism* (Chicago, 1925), p. 21.

54. H. Righby, *Communist Party Membership in the USSR, 1917–1967* (Princeton, N. J., 1968), p. 366.

55. M. K. Matossian, *The Impact of Soviet Policies in Armenia* (Leiden, 1962), p. 45.

56. *Sotsial'nyi i natsional'nyi sostav VKP (b)* (Moscow, Leningrad, 1928), pp. 140–42.

57. Ryskulov, *Revoliutsiia i korennoe naseleniie Turkestana*, p. 81.

Chapter 9
A Clean Sweep

1. *Itogo vsesoiuznoi gorodskoi perepisi 1922 gg* (Moscow, 1923). *Itogi perepisi naseleniia 1920 g* (Moscow, 1928); F. Lorimer, *The Population of the Soviet Union* (Geneva, 1946), p. 289.

2. N. A. Vorob'ev, *Vsesoiuznaia perepis' naseleniia 1926 g* (Moscow, 1927); *Kommunisticheskaia Akademiia, komissiia po izucheniiu natsional'nogo voprosa* (Moscow, 1930).

3. Lorimer, *Population of the Soviet Union*, pp. 67–70, and *Kommunisticheskaia Akademiia*, p. 122.

4. Astemirov, "Itogi Kul'tstroitel'stva Dagestana, 15-letiiu oktiabria," *Revoliutsiia i natsional'nosti*, nos. 11–12 (1932): 100.

5. *Sobranie Uzakonenii i rasporiazhenii rabochego i krest'ianskogo pravitel'stva RSFSR* (1917), no. 4, art. 50.

6. A. S. Trainin, *Deklaratsiia prav trudiashchegosia i ekspluatiruemogo naroda* (Moscow, 1938), p. 21.

7. Suleimanova, "Istoricheskii ocherk o sozdanii sovetskikh sudov v Uzbekistane," *Sovetskoe gosudarstvo i pravo* 3 (1949): 62.

8. Suleimanova, "Zarozhdenie sovetskogo ugolovnogo prava v Uzbekistane," 10 (1948): 67.

9. Suleimanova, "Istoricheskii ocherk," pp. 64–65.

10. Lenin, *Pss*, vol. 45, pp. 197–201 and 427–28.

11. Ibid.

12. This opinion was based on N. Avdeenko and I. Kabakova, "Grazhdanskoe protsessual'noe pravo," *40 let Sovetskogo prava* (Moscow, Leningrad, 1957), p. 653.

13. *Sobranie Zakonov SSSR,* vol. 1, p. 203.

14. Shokhor, "Religiozno-bytovye sudy v RSFSR," *Sovetskoe stroitel'stvo,* nos. 8–9 (13–14) (1927): 108.

15. *Izvestiia,* 1 September 1922.

16. N. Fioletov, "Sudoproizvodstvo v mussul'manskikh sudakh Srednei Azii," *Novyi vostok,* nos. 23–24 (1928): 218.

17. Suleimanova, "Istoricheskii ocherk," p. 68.

18. Vinokurov, *Tsk vtorogo sozyva, vtoraia sessiia* (Moscow, 1924), p. 212.

19. Suleimanova, "Istoricheskii ocherk," p. 69.

20. Fioletov, "Sudy Kaziev v Sredne-Aziatskikh respublikakh," *Sovetskoe pravo* 1, no. 25 (1927): 144, and Suleimanova, "Istoricheskii ocherk," p. 69.

21. Fioletov, *Osnovnye voprosy sovetskogo brachnogo prava* (Tashkent, 1929).

22. Il. Lozovski and I. Bibin, *Sovetskaia politika za 10 let po natsional'nomu voprosu* (Moscow, 1928), pp. 316–18.

23. Fioletov, in *Novyi vostok,* p. 214.

24. Shokhor, "Religiozno-bytovye sudy," p. 109.

25. Ostroumov, in *Mir Islama* (1913): 305, and Carrère D'Encausse, "La Politique culturelle du pouvoir tsariste au Turkestan," *Cahiers du monde russe et soviétique* 3 (July–September 1962): 376–78.

26. E. Iaroslavski, *Religion in the USSR* (London, 1932, translated from the Russian), pp. 19–20.

27. *Zhizn' natsional'nostei* 1 (1923): 246.

28. G. Massell, "Law as an Instrument of Revolutionary Change in a Traditional Milieu: The Case of Soviet Central Asia," *Law and Society Review* 2 (1968): 179.

29. N. Vakar, *Bielorussia* (Cambridge, Mass.: Harvard University Press, 1956), p. 60.

30. G. Massell, *The Surrogate Proletariat: Moslem Women and Revolutionary Strategies in Soviet Central Asia, 1919–1929* (Princeton, N. J., 1974) pp. 186–191.

31. For an account of these events by a witness, see E. Maillart, *Turkestan Solo* (London, 1938).

32. "Zhenskoe kommunisticheskoe dvizhenie v SSSR," *Bol'shaia sovetskaia Entsiklopediia,* 1st ed., vol. 25, p. 139.

33. M. Matossian, *The Impact of Soviet Policies* (Leiden, 1962), p. 65.

34. See Massell, on the effects, and M. Shaginia, *Puteshestvie po Sovetskoi Armenii* (Moscow, 1951), p. 82.

35. "Zhenskoe kommunisticheskoe dvizhenie v SSSR."

36. Pachukanis, "Predislovie," *Obshchaia teoriia prava i marksizm* (Moscow, 1927), 3d ed., not paginated; and Matossian, *The Impact of Soviet Policies,* p. 67.

37. Stalin, *Sochineniia,* vol. 6, pp. 65–66.

38. J. Castagne, "Le Turkestan depuis la révolution russe," *Revue du monde musulman* (June 1922), p. 69; *Kommunisticheskaia Akademiia,* p. 159; Y. Mushpert and E. Fainberg, *Komsomol i molodezh natsional'nykh menshinstv* (Moscow, 1926), p. 17.

39. Mushpert and Fainberg, *Komsomol i molodezh natsional'nykh,* p. 25.

40. *Kommunisticheskaia Akademiia,* p. 163, n. 71.

41. Matossian, *The Impact of Soviet Policies,* p. 74.

42. Z. Gitelman, *Jewish Nationality and Soviet Politics* (Princeton, N. J., 1972), p. 312.

Chapter 10
National Culture and Proletarian Culture

1. *Bol'shaia Sovetskaia entsiklopediia,* article "narodnost' " (Moscow, 1954), vol. 24, p. 159.

2. J. V. Stalin, *Marksizm i natsional'nyi vopros,* p. 198.

3. "Pan-Islamizm i pan-Turkizm," *Mir Islama* 2 (1913): 559–62.

4. Ibid.

5. A. Bennigsen and H. Carrère D'Encausse, *Une république soviétique musulmane: Le Daghestan* (Paris, 1956), p. 10.

6. I. Zarubina, *Spisok narodnostei SSSR* (Leningrad, 1927), p. 12.

7. *Komissii po izucheniiu plemennogo sostava naseleniia Rossii, 1917–1927,* vol. 1.3.15.

8. M. Matossian, *The Impact of Soviet Policies in Armenia* (Leiden, 1962), p. 198.

9. *Evreiskoe naselenie Rossii po dannym perepisi 1897 g. i po noveishym istochnikam* (Petrograd, 1917); *Goroda i poseleniia v uezdakh imeiushchikh 2000 i bolee zhitelei* (St. Petersburg, 1905); *Itogi vserossiiskoi gorodskoi perepisi 1923 g.*

10. N. Vakar, *Bielorussia* (Cambridge, Mass.: Harvard University Press, 1956), pp. 139–140.

11. H. Gabidullin, *Tatarstan za sem' let* (Kazan, 1927), p. 20.

12. L. P. Nemchenko, *Natsional'noe razmezhevanie Srednei Azii* (Moscow, 1925).

13. D. Sokol, *The Revolt of 1916 in Central Asia* (Baltimore, Md., 1954), and especially Brodio, "Materialy k istorii vosstaniia Kirgiz," *Novyi vostok* 6 (1924): 407–35.

14. *Kratkaia literaturnaia entsiklopediia* (Moscow), vol. 4, 1967, article "Manas"; and T. Ryskulov, *Kirgizstan* (Moscow, 1935).

15. Sarev, *Sovetskaia literatura na novom etape* (Moscow, 1933), p. 122.

16. A. Potseluevskii, "Iazikostroitel' stvo Turkmenii i ego osnovnye problemy," *Revoliutsiia i natsional'nosti* 67 (September 1935): 42–50.

17. S. P. Tolstov et al., eds., *Narody Srednei Azii i Kazakhstana* (Moscow, 1963), p. 488.

18. *Itogi vsesoiuznoi perepisi naseleniia 1959 g,* 16 vols. (Moscow, 1962, 1963).

19. *Revoliutsiia i natsional'nosti* 35 (February 1933): 59–60.

20. Bennigsen and Carrère d'Encausse, *Le Daghestan*.

21. Walter Kolarz, *Russia and Her Colonies* (London, 1952), p. 196. Daghestan: country of mountains ("dagh" is "mountain" in Turkish, and "stan" is "country" in Persian). The conservation of a Turkish-Persian name is illustrative of the Soviet predicament.

22. Astemirov, "Itogi kul'tstroitel'stva Dagestana k 15-letiiu oktiabria," *Revoliutsiia i natsional'nosti*, 10 November 1932, p. 100.

23. N. Samurskii, *Dagestan* (Moscow, Leningrad, 1925), p. 118; and Taho-Godi, *Revoliutsiia i kontr-revoliutsiia v Dagestane* (Moscow, 1927), pp. 115–63.

24. Samurskii, *Dagestan*, p. 116.

25. *Dekrety Sovetskoi vlasti* (Moscow, 1971), vol. 5, pp. 398–400.

26. K. Gerasimova, *Obnovlencheskoe dvizhenie buriatskogo lamaistskogo dukhovenstva, 1917–1930* (Ulan-Ude, 1964).

27. *Antirelioznik* 7 (1930), quoted by Kolarz, p. 153.

28. *Za industrializatsiiu sovetskogo vostoka* (Moscow, 1933), no. 3, pp. 218–19.

29. S. Shodzhelov, *La R. P. Tuva* (Moscow, 1930), p. 80.

30. *Rossiia, polnoe geograficheskoe opisanie nashego otechestva* (St. Petersburg, 1914), vol. 5, p. 206.

31. Gurvish Dolgikh, *Preobrazovanie v khoziaistve i kul'ture i etnicheskie protsessy u narodov Severa* (Moscow, 1970).

32. *Revoliutsiia i natsional'nosti* 27 (June 1932): 86.

33. *Revoliutsiia i natsional'nosti* 67 (September 1935); 58–59.

34. *Zhizn' natsional'nostei*, 14–12 (1921).

35. *Zhizn' natsional'nostei*, 25 February 1922.

36. *Zhizn' natsional'nostei*, 13 August 1921.

37. *Revoliutsionnoi vostok* 27 (1934): 205–6.

38. *Zhizn' natsional'nostei*, 10 January 1922; R. Dolgikh, *Ocherki po etnicheskoi istorii Nentsev i Entsev* (Moscow, 1970); and V. Boiko, *Sotsial'naia struktura naseleniia Sibiri* (Novosibirsk, 1970); and N. Onishchuk, *Sovetskoe stroitel'stvo u malykh narodov Severa* (Tomsk, 1973).

39. G. Vasilevich, *Evenki-Istoriko-etnograficheskie ocherki* (Leningrad, 1969).

40. The missionary Il'minskii had already attempted to disseminate the Cyrillic alphabet in Kazan in the nineteenth century. See *Zhurnal ministerstva narodnogo prosveshcheniia SP b, 1907*, nos. 9–10, p. 130, and *Samouchitel' russkoi gramoty dlia Kirgizov*, composed by Il'minskii (SL.ND.), p. 142.

41. G. Ulianov, "K voprosu o podgotovke uchitel'stva natsional'nykh menshchinstv," *Narodnoe prosveshchenie*, 11–12, 1924, p. 79.

42. *Desiatyi s'ezd RKP (b)*, p. 157.

43. *Zhizn' natsional'nostei* (6), 15 December 1918, and (7) 2 March 1919. *Vysshee obrazovanie v SSSR: statisticheskii sbornik* (Moscow, 1961) gives precise indications of the state of teaching in 1913, pp. 79 and 237.

44. A. Ivanova, *Chto delala sovetskaia vlast' po likvidatsii negramotnosti sredi vzroslykh* (Moscow, 1949), p. 30.

45. Matossian, *The Impact of Soviet Policies*, p. 89. In Central Asia the social resistance was so strong that even this policy of separate education could not be carried out.

46. The instrument for these denunciations was the Srednazburo. *Rezoliutsii XII plenuma* (Tashkent, 1927), p. 20.

47. Steinberg, *Ocherki po istorii Turkmenistana*, p. 193.

48. Lenin, *Pss*, vol. 38, p. 183.

49. Stalin, *Sochineniia*, vol. 5, p. 19.

50. Pokrovskii, *Russkaia istoriia s drevneishikh vremen* (Moscow, 1933), vol. 1, p. 249.

51. M. N. Pokrovskii, *Diplomatiia i voiny tsarskoi Rossii v XIX stoletii* (Moscow, 1923), p. 331.

52. *Bol'shaia sovetskaia entsiklopediia*, 1st ed., vol. 32, p. 377.

53. P. Galuzo, *Turkestan: Koloniia* (Tashkent, 1935), pp. 38–41.

54. *Istoriia Kazakhstana* (Alma Ata, 1935), vol. 2, p. 110.

55. Pokrovskii, *Diplomatiia i voiny*, vol. 1, p. 250, n. 50.

56. Ibid., pp. 211–30.

57. On the problems that Hrushevsky encountered, see L. Tillet, *The Great Friendship* (University of North Carolina Press, 1969), pp. 37–40.

58. *Desiatyi s'ezd RKP (b)*, p. 204.

Chapter 11
The Roads to Economic Equality

1. M. Dobb, *Soviet Economic Development since 1917* (New York, 1948), p. 97.

2. H. Chambre, *Union soviétique et développement économique* (Paris, 1967), pp. 47–48.

3. According to F. Perroux, "L 'Econ'omie du XXe siècle," quoted by H. Chambre, *Union soviétique*, p. 47.

4. F. Lorimer, *The Population of the Soviet Union* (Geneva, 1946), p. 31.

5. Ibid., p. 32. In addition, see *Goroda i poselenie v uezdakh imeiushchi 2000 i bolee zhitelei* (St. Petersburg, 1905), and *Vsesoiuznaia gorodskaia perepis' 1923 g* (Moscow, 1925), vol. 17, 20 and Itogi. . . . , vol. 4.

6. Moscow: 1,800,000 inhabitants in 1917; 1,120,000 in 1920. Petrograd: 2,300,000 inhabitants in 1917; 740,000 in 1920. See Prokopovich, *Dinamika russkogo naseleniia SSSR*, quoted by Lorimer.

7. *Goroda i poselenie* (note 5); *Turkestan: tsentral'noe statisticheskoe upravlenie otdel promyshlennoi statistiki* (Tashkent, 1923), 2 vols.

8. Notably, the census of 1970 enabled scholars to reestablish the cities classified in order of importance in 1897. See J. Newith, *The 1970 Census*, a conference paper presented at the annual meeting of NASEES, 1973, pp. 6–7.

9. Quoted by Walter Kolarz, *Russia and Her Colonies* (London, 1952), p.

127. Also see on this point J. Armstrong, *Ukrainian Nationalism* (Columbia University Press, 1963), p. 361.

10. R. Portal, *Russes et Ukrainiens* (Paris, 1970), p. 80.

11. Z. Gitelman, *Jewish Nationality and Soviet Politics* (Princeton, N. J. 1972), p. 401.

12. Alec Nove and J. A. Newith, *The Soviet Middle East: A Model for Development* (London, 1967), pp. 6–7.

13. Ibid., and N. Vakar, *Bielorussia* (Cambridge, Mass., 1956), p. 206.

14. *Revoliutsionnyi vostok* 19–20 (1922): 250; A. J. Bobrova and A. S. Korobeinikova, *Kul'turnoe stroitel'stvo v Udmurtii* (Izhevsk, 1970).

15. *Revoliutsiia i natsional'nosti* (4 April 1931), p. 19.

16. Regarding the republic's evolution, see Foreign Affairs archives, Dossier Z. 617, 1 and 2, telegram of 10 July 1928 (no. 510); *Bol'shaia sovetskaia entsiklopediia*, 2d ed. (1951), vol. 8, ignores the Germans of the Volga region, and vol. 49 (1957), p. 55, does not mention the name of the city of Engels. The first edition, vol. 41, p. 596, contains important entries on this national group.

17. *Turkestan: tsentral'noe statisticheskoe upravlenie, otdel promyshlennoi statistiki* (material pertaining to the data for 1920), and *Vsia Sredniaia Aziia* (Tashkent, 1926), p. 159.

18. Stalin, *Sochineniia*, vol. 5, p. 39; Lenin, *Pss*, vol. 21, p. 330, and vol. 30, p. 35.

19. A. F. Khavin, *Sotsialisticheskaia industrializatsiia natsional'nykh respublik* (Moscow, 1933), p. 80.

20. Ibid.

21. *Vsia Sredniaia Aziia*, p. 327.

22. A. Valiev, *Formirovanie i razvitie sovetskoi natsional'noi intelligentsii* (Tashkent, 1966), pp. 77–82.

23. Lenin, *Pss*, vol. 30, p. 35, and O. Vaganov, "Zemel'naia politika tsarskogo pravitel'stva v Kazakhstane," *Istoricheskie zapiski* 31 (1950): 75–78, and Galuzo, *Turkestan: Koloniia*, p. 15.

24. Semenov, Tian Shanskii, ed., *Rossiia, i polnoe geograficheskoe opisanie nashego otechestva*, vol. 19, *Turkestanskii krai* (St. Petersburg, 1913), pp. 417–19.

25. H. Drikker, "Iz istorii bor'by za preodolenie feodal'no-baiskikh perezhitkov v sel'skom khoziaistve Tadzhikistana," *Sovetskoe vostokovedenie* 6 (1956): 80.

26. Alkin, *Sredniaia Aziia* (Moscow, 1931), vol. 1, pp. 357–58.

27. Lenin, *Pss*, vol. 41, pp. 433–36.

28. Safarov, *Kolonial'naia revoliutsiia*, p. 137.

29. *Sotsialisticheskoe pereustroistvo sel'skogo khoziaistva v Uzbekistane, 1917–1926* (Tashkent, 1962) discusses the reform in detail; Zel'kina, "Zemel'naia reforma v Srednei Azii," *Revoliutsionnyi vostok* 3 (1927): 133–67; A. Gurevich, "Zemel'no-vodnaia reforma v Uzbekskoi SSR," *Voprosy istorii* 11 (1948): 55–56.

30. Zhalilov, *Vozniknovenie i razvitie sovestskogo zemel'nogo prava v Uzbekistane* (Tashkent, 1970), p. 272, especially the first chapter.

31. Zel'kina, "Zemel'naia reforma," p. 140.

32. Ibid., p. 152.

33. *Zhizn' natsional'nostei* 2 (1923): 37; and Sanyshev, "O soiuzakh koshchi," *Sovetskoe stroitel'stvo* 4–5 (1926): 124 ff.; *Vsia Sredniaia Aziia*, p. 327.

34. Park, *Bolshevism in Turkestan*, has studied this problem in depth. See also Sanyshev (No. 46), p. 126.

35. *Vsa Sredniaia Aziia*, p. 327.

36. *Zhizn' natsional'nostei* 2 (1923): 37.

37. B. Hayit, *Turkestan im XX Jahrhundert* (Darmstadt, 1956), pp. 256–59.

38. Semenov, Tian Shanskiiu, *Rossiia*, p. 428, and A. M. Aminov, *Ekonomicheskoe razvitie Srednei Azii* (kolonial'nyi period) (Tashkent, 1959), p. 234.

39. O. Zhamalov, ed., *Istoriia narodnogo khoziaistva Uzbekistana* (Tashkent, 1962), vol. 1, pp. 83–84.

40. E. Schuyler, *Turkistan: Notes of a Journey in Russian Turkistan* (New York, 1887), vol. 1, pp. 297–303, describes the system of water distribution, which remained unchanged until 1917.

41. N. Arkhipov, *SSSR po raionam: Sredne-aziatskie respubliki* (Moscow, 1928), pp. 48–50.

42. J. Castagane, "La réforme agraire au Turkestane," *Revue des Etudes islamiques* 2 (1928): 396–97.

43. R. Kh. Aminova, *Agrarnye preobrazovaniia v Uzbekistane* (Tashkent, 1965), p. 105; and Alekseenkov, *Krest'ianskoe vosstanie v Fergane* (Tashkent, 1927), p. 158.

44. Ibid., and Dembo, *Zemel'nyi stroi vostoka* (Leningrad, 1927), pp. 100–102.

45. Kraskin, *Zemel'no-vodnaia reforma v Srednei Azii: Sbornik dokumentov* (Moscow, 1927), pp. 170–71.

46. Ibid., p. 55.

47. *Ocherki istorii Turkmenii*, p. 118.

48. Kraskin (no. 69), p. 169.

49. Castagne, "La réforme agraire," p. 395.

50. Kraskin, *Zemel no-vodnaia reforma*, p. 170.

51. The "Karanda" lands were properties belonging to families or villages; the revenue from these lands was earmarked for communal needs. Schuyler, *Turkistan*, pp. 297–393.

52. Steinberg, *Ocherki istorii Turkmenistana*, p. 138.

53. Kraskin, *Zemel'no-vodnaia reforma*, pp. 55–56.

54. Solidarity against the Russians can be seen in the accounts of the anti-Basmashi struggle. See M. Shokaev, "The Basmaji Movement," *The Asiatic Review* (April 1928): 283.

55. A. Nurimov, "Pervyi s'ezd kolkhoznikov udarnikov Uzbekistana,"

Nauchnye trudy aspirantov (Tashkent, 1962), pp. 219–29, shows the psychological evolution of this time.

56. *Vsia Sredniaia Aziia*, pp. 266–68.

57. A thesis was devoted to this subject in Leningrad in 1969; S. Ahadov, *Deiatel'nost' KP Uzbekistana po razvitiiu potrebitel'skoi kooperatsii v respublike.* Regarding the Moslem Caucasus, see also A. Kuprava, *Istoriia kooperatsii Abkhazskoi ASSR, 1921–1929* (Tbilisi, 1968).

58. *Vsia Sredniaia Aziia*, pp. 266–68.

59. Zinger, *Evreiskoe naselenie v Sovetskom Soiuze* (Moscow, Leningrad, 1932), p. 14.

60. Schwartz, *The Jews in the Soviet Union*, p. 164.

61. Gitelman, *Jewish Nationality*, p. 387.

62. J. Larine, *Evreii i antisemitizm v SSSR* (Moscow, Leningrad, 1929), p. 302, develops the arguments of those opposed to this location.

63. *Revoliutsiia i natsional'nosti* 10 (1936): 51.

64. Schwartz, *The Jews in the Soviet Union*, pp. 166–67.

65. Quoted by Gitelman, *Jewish Nationality*, p. 431; this phrase was confirmed by A. Ehrlich.

66. Larin, *Evreii i antisemitizm*, p. 153.

67. Regarding the shamans, see *Kratkie soobshcheniia instituta etnografii* 25 (1957): 134 and the research by Robert Hamayon, director of studies at EPHE (5th section), who studies the manifestations of shamanism among the Buryats and neighboring groups; and see N. Onishchuk, *Sovetskoe stroitel'stvo u malkh narodov Severa, 1917–1941*, p. 162.

68. *Zhizn' natsional'nostei*, 10 January 1922 (the general outlines of the policy to follow).

69. Kolarz, *Les colonies russes de l'Extrême-Orient*, p. 103.

70. Ibid., p. 104.

Conclusion

1. V. O. Kliuchevskii, *Kurs russkoi istorii* (Moscow, 1937), vol. 2, p. 423.

2. T. Szamuely, *The Russian Tradition* (London, 1974).

3. C. Black, *The Dynamics of Modernization* (New York, 1966), pp. 6–9.

Bibliography

Rather than repeat the bibliographical information in the notes, this listing will contain only sources, collections, and documents.

Collections and Documents
I. State

Dekrety Sovetskoi vlasti, vols. 1–7 (1917–20) Moscow, 1957–75.

Gromyko, A. A. *Dokumenty Vneshnei politiki SSSR*, vols. 1–7 (1917–1920) Moscow, 1957–62.

Istoriia Sovetskoi Konstitutsii v dokumentakh, 1917–1934. Moscow, 1957.

S'ezdy sovetov soiuza SSR, soiuznikh i avtonomnykh sovetskikh sotsialisticheskikh respublik. Sbornik dokumentov v trekh tomakh, 1917–1936 g, 3 vols. Moscow, 1959–60.

Sbornik deistvuiushchikh dogovorov soglashenii i konventsii zakliuchennyh RSFSR s inostrannami gosudarstvami, vol. 3. Moscow, 1922.

Sobranie uzakonenii i rasporiazhenii rabdochego i krestianskogo pravitel'stva. Petrograd-Moscow, 1917–22.

Gidulianov, P. V. *Otdelenie tserkvi ot gosudarstva v SSSR*: polnyi sbornik dekretov redomstvennykh, rasporiazhenii i opredelenii verkhsuda RSFSR i drugikh sovetskikh socialisticheskikh, USSR, BSSR, ZSFSR, Uzbekskoi i Turkmenskoi, 3d ed. Moscow, 1926, D. 711.

II. Narkomnats

Deiatel'nost'Soveta natsional'nostei i ego prezidiuma. Moscow, 1929.

Denisov, A. *Narodnyi komissariat po delam natsional'nostei, B. S. E.* (1st ed.), vol. 41. Moscow, 1931.

Dimanshtein, S. *Revoliutsiia i natsional'nyi vopros: dokumenty i materialy,* vol. 3. Moscow, 1930 (only vol. 3 exists).

Izvestiia Peterburgskogo Komissariata po delam natsional'nostei. Petrograd, 1920.

Lozovskii, J., and J. Bibin. *Sovetskaia politika za 10 let po natsional'nomu voprosu v RSFSR.* Moscow, 1928 (collection of documents).

Natsional'nyi vopros i sovetskaia Rossiia. Moscow, 1921.

Ochet narodnogo komissariata po delam natsional'nostei za 1921 g. Moscow, 1921.

Politika sovetskoi vlasti po natsional'nym delam za tri goda, 1917–1920. Moscow, 1920.

Spravochnik narodnogo komissariata po delam natsional'nostei. Moscow, 1921.

III. The Party

Istoriia Vsesoiuznoi Kommunisticheskoi Partii Bol'shevikov. Moscow, 1938 (new editions: 1949, 1962, 1970, etc.).

KPSS v rezoliutsiakh i resheniakh s'ezdov, konferentsii i plenumov TsK. Moscow (9th ed. 1983).

Kommunisticheskaia Akademiia, Komissia po izucheniiu natsional'nogo voprosa, *Natsional'naia politika VKP (b) v tsifrakh.* Moscow, 1930.

Sotsial'nyi i natsional'nyi sostav VKP (b): Itogi vsesoiuznoi partiinoi perepisi 1927 goda. Moscow-Leningrad, 1928.

Antropov, P., ed. *Materialy i dokumenty I-go s'ezda Kompartii Turkestana.* Tashkent, 1934

Kommunisticheskaia partiia (b) Gruzii Ochet Tiflisskogo Komiteta mart 1923 goda-mart 1924 goda. Tiflis, 1924.

Musburo RKP (b) v Turkestane. Tashkent, 1922.

Trudy III-go s'ezda Kommunisticheskoi partii Turkestana, vol. 12. Tashkent, 1919.

IV. Censuses

Pervaia vseobshchaia perepis' naseleniia rossiiskoi imperii 1897 g, 89 vols. St. Petersburg, 1905.

Goroda i poseleniia v uezdakh imeiushchie 2000 i bolee zhitelei. St. Petersburg, 1905.

Vsesoiuznaia gorodskaia perepis' 1923 g. Moscow, 1925.

Izvestiia Komissii po izucheniiu plemennogo sostave naseleniia SSSR. Petrograd, 1917–19.

Trudy komissii po izucheniiu plemennogo sostava naseleniia Rossii, 15 vols., 1919–28.

Spisok narodnostei Soiuza Sovetskikh Sotsialisticheskikh Respublik sostavlen pod redaktsii I. I. Zarubiny. Leningrad, 1927.

Turkestan, tsentral'noe statisticheskoe upravlenie-Otdel promyshlennoi statistiki. . . . materialy vserossiiskikh perepisei, 1920 g. Tashkent, 1923.

Turkestan, tsentral'noe statisticheskoe upravleniie, Coefitsent detei Shkol'nogo vozrasta kochevogo i osedlogo naseleniia v Turkestane, 30 vols. Tashkent, 1924.

Vserossiiskaia perepis' chlenov RKP 1922 goda, 1922–1925, vol. 4. 1922.

Vysshee obrazovanie v SSSR: Statisticheskii sbornik. Moscow, 1961.

V. Editions of Works by Lenin and Stalin

Lenin, V. I. *Leninskii sbornik,* 36 vols. Moscow, 1924–59.

Lenin, V. I. *Polnoe sobranie sochinenii* (5th ed., the most complete). Moscow, 1958–65.

Lenin, V. I. *Sochineniia,* 31 vols. (3d ed.). Moscow and Leningrad, 1927–35.

Stalin, J. *Sochineniia*, 13 vols. Moscow, 1946–51.

Stalin, J. *Le Marxisme et la question nationale et coloniale*. Paris, 1949.

VI. Archives

Archives of the French Ministry of Foreign Affairs
  Dossiers Z 617 I
  Dossiers Z 619 II
  Millerand Papers (XX)

Castagne, J. *Archives personelles* (notes taken by J. Castagne in Turkestan; three notebooks of personal papers).

Index

253